ALAN MITCHE

MDF
21
P-51 MUSTANG

THE NORTH AMERICAN AVIATION
P-51 MUSTANG

A COMPREHENSIVE GUIDE

Part 1 Allison Powered

by Malcolm V. Lowe

SAM PUBLICATIONS

Cover illustration by John Fox

MDF 21
The North American Aviation P-51 Mustang
by Malcolm V. Lowe

First produced in 2013 by Media House, under licence from SAM Publications Limited
Media House, 21 Kingsway, Bedford, MK42 9BJ, United Kingdom

ISBN 978-1-906959-02-9

Typeset by SAM Publications, Media House, 21 Kingsway, Bedford, MK42 9BJ, United Kingdom
Series Editor – Andy Evans
Studio Manager – Jonathan Phillips
Printed and bound in the United Kingdom

The MDF Series

- No.1 – De Havilland Mosquito *
- No.2 – Hawker Hurricane *
- No.3 – Supermarine Spitfire (Part 1: Merlin-Powered) *
- No.4 – Avro Lancaster (Inc Manchester & Lincoln)
- No.5 – Supermarine Spitfire (Part 2: Griffon-Powered)
- No.6 – Bristol Beaufighter *
- No.7 – English Electric Lightning
- No.8 – Gloster (& Armstrong-Whitworth) Meteor
- No.9 – Messerschmitt Bf 109 (Part 1 Prototype to E Variants)
- No.10 – Messerschmitt Bf 109 (Part 2 F to K Variants)
- No.11 – British Aerospace Sea Harrier
- No.12 – The F-4 Phantom II (Part 1: USAF)
- No.13 – The F-4 Phantom II (Part 2: US Navy & Marine Corps)
- No.14 – The F-4 Phantom II (Part 3: Overseas Operators)
- No.15 – The Grumman F-14 Tomcat
- No.16 – The Hawker Hunter
- No.17 – The BAe (Hawker Siddeley) RAF Harrier
- No.18 – The Vought F4U Corsair
- No.19 – The General Dynamics F-111 Aardvark
- No.20 – The De Havilland Mosquito (Second Edition)
- * Out of print

Mustang Gallery

For even more images and information on the Allison Powered Mustang, just scan this QR code with your smart phone or tablet to view more exclusive 'on-line' content.

**RAF Mustang Mk.I AM148 RM-G
photographed during the August of 1942**
(Photo: R.L. Ward Collection)

SAM PUBLICATIONS

Contents

Preface

Sleek and purposeful, the Allison-engined Mustang was an excellent low-level performer in roles such as fighter, fighter-bomber and tactical reconnaissance. Despite its outstanding combat record, the type has often been maligned due to the comparatively poor high-altitude performance of its Allison V-1710 engine. This criticism is completely incorrect, and represents a misunderstanding of the originally-intended roles of the Mustang and the somewhat unusual way in which the type was created. In this classic Second World War image, two Allison-engined Mustang Mk.Is of No.2 Squadron, RAF, pose for the camera on a special photo shoot during 1942. The two aircraft are AM112 XV-X in the background and AG550 XV-U nearest to the camera
(Photo: Via Chris Ellis)

There can be few more iconic warplanes from the Second World War era than North American Aviation's wonderful Mustang. Beautifully streamlined, powerful, and very successful in service, the Mustang was at the pinnacle of piston-engined single-seat fighter aircraft design and performance in the latter stages of World War Two. Appropriately named after a very special breed of horse, the Mustang is rightly seen as one of history's great warplanes. Yet to delve a little into the history of this excellent aircraft reveals facts that are often overlooked in the Mustang's story.

Much of the enduring fame of the Mustang derives from the exploits of the Merlin-engined variants in the later part of World War Two, which are rightly regarded as being amongst the best and most successful of the war's front-line combat aircraft. They achieved unrivalled success later in the conflict over both German and Japanese aerial opposition. But before the advent of the Merlin-engined Mustang, a number of front-line Mustang versions went to war powered by the Allison V-1710 inline engine. The Mustang was designed with this engine type from the start, but these early-war models of the Mustang have sometimes been seen as inferior to the later, Merlin-powered Mustangs, because of the Allison engine's comparatively poor performance at higher altitudes.

This made the Allison Mustangs far better performers at lower level and at tree-top height, where they literally excelled. But their exploits in tactical missions, both for the RAF and - later - the US Army Air Force(s), were completely overshadowed by the far more glamorous high level bomber escort work with which the later Merlin Mustangs were supreme. Ground-attack and tactical reconnaissance - the real preserves of the low-level Allison Mustangs - were far less colourful than the high-altitude dog-fighting of the Merlin Mustangs. The Allison-engined Mustangs have always suffered something of an identity crisis because of this - such is the case even to the present day. The historical section of this Book tells the story of the low-level, Allison-powered Mustangs, and shows that there is far more to the history of these essentially tactical-orientated warplanes than many previous publications have given them credit for.

The majority of Allison Mustangs went to war wearing a drab coat of paint, sometimes well-weathered. This was in stark contrast to the often shiny and colourfully-marked Merlin Mustangs that followed them. But this makes the Allison Mustangs no less interesting to model and within the subject area of British and US Allison-engined Mustang service, there was a wealth of varied colour schemes. The modelling section in this book certainly proves this point, and I am indebted to my fellow modellers for their contributions to those pages.

Although this book is not intended to be a 'last word' on the early Mustangs, it is hoped that it will show the Allison Mustang in a positive light, and perhaps help to redress the balance a little in favour of this excellent but sometimes unnecessarily maligned warplane.

In the second volume of this 'Modellers Datafile', the story of the famed Merlin-engined Mustangs will take centre stage.

Malcolm V. Lowe
Poole, Dorset, October 2013.

Glossary of Terms

2nd TAF	Second Tactical Air Force
A	Attack (US)
A&AEE	Aeroplane and Armament Experimental Establishment
AB	Air Base
ACC	Army Co-operation Command
ACG	Air Commando Group
AFB	Air Force Base
AFDU	Air Fighting Development Unit
AI	Airborne Interception (Radar)
AST	Air Service Training
ATS	Air Technical Section
ATSC	Air Technical Service Command
BAC	British Air Commission
BCOF	British Commonwealth Occupation Force
BPC	British Purchasing Commission
BG	Bombardment (or Bomb) Group
BS	Bombardment (or Bomb) Squadron
BuNo	Navy Bureau of Aeronautics Serial Number
BW	Bombardment (or Bomb) Wing
CBI	China-Burma-India (Theatre)
Col.	Colonel
D/F	Direction-Finding
DoD	Department of Defence (US)
ETO	European Theatre of Operations
F	Photographic (US)
FBG	Fighter-Bomber Group
FBS	Fighter-Bomber Squadron
FBW	Fighter-Bomber Wing
FC	Fighter Command
FEAF	Far East Air Force(s)
FG	Fighter Group
FG(P)	Fighter Group (Provisional)
FS	Fighter Squadron
FS(C)	Fighter Squadron (Commando)
FS(P)	Fighter Squadron (Provisional)
FW	Fighter Wing
FY	Fiscal Year
GAC	General Aviation Corporation
GAMC	General Aviation Manufacturing Corporation
GIAP	Guards Fighter Aviation Regiment (Soviet Union)

HVAR	High-Velocity Aerial (or Aircraft) Rocket
IJAAF	Imperial Japanese Army Air Force
ILS	Instrument Landing System
JG	Jagdgeshwader (Fighter Wing) (Germany)
Lt. Col.	Lieutenant Colonel
MAP	Ministry of Aircraft Production (UK)
MoS	Ministry of Supply (UK)
MTO	Mediterranean Theatre of Operations
NAA	North American Aviation, Inc.
NACA	National Advisory Committee for Aeronautics
NG	National Guard
NII VVS	Soviet Air Force Research and Evaluation Institute
OD	(Dark) Olive Drab
OG	Observation Group
OS	Observation Squadron
OTU	Operational Training Unit
P	Pursuit (Fighter) (US)
PG	Photo(graphic) Group
PoW	Prisoner of War
PR	Photographic Reconnaissance
PRG	Photographic Reconnaissance Group
PRS	Photographic Reconnaissance Squadron
RAAF	Royal Australian Air Force
RAF	Royal Air Force
RCAF	Royal Canadian Air Force
RG	Reconnaissance Group
RS	Reconnaissance Squadron
RNZAF	Royal New Zealand Air Force
SAAF	South African Air Force
SAR	Search and Rescue
SWPA	South-West Pacific Area
Tac/R	Tactical Reconnaissance (sometimes written TacR)
TBO	Time Between Overhauls
TRG	Tactical Reconnaissance Group
TRS	Tactical Reconnaissance Squadron
US	United States
USAAC	United States Army Air Corps - to 1941
USAAF	United States Army Air Force(s) - from 1941
USAF	United States Air Force - from 1947
USMC	United States Marine Corps
USN	United States Navy

Introduction

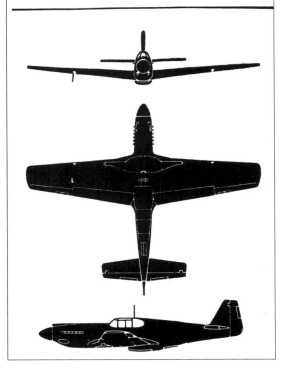

P-51 "MUSTANG"

The Allison-engined Mustang had a very distinctive appearance, as is illustrated in this 1943 recognition silhouette. The creation of the Mustang was completely unconventional, and was born out of Britain's growing need for high-performance fighter aircraft in quantity to face the considerable threat from Nazi Germany *(Photo: USAAF)*

The straightforward but nonetheless striking company symbol of North American Aviation, Inc., the designer and builder of the Mustang *(Photo: NAA)*

The way in which the Mustang was originally created goes a long way to explaining why, in its early production versions, the type was a star performer at low-to medium-level. From the start, it must be remembered that the Mustang, although an American designed and produced warplane, was not under any circumstances created to meet US specifications, or to fulfil a US military requirement. Instead it was born to help answer the increasingly desperate need of Britain for modern fighter aircraft in quantity. It was only much later in the Mustang's story that the type gained any real official interest in the US - the country of its birth. Indeed, there was considerable American opposition to the Mustang in some quarters, which helped to delay the type's acceptance for US military operation and eventual entry into service with the US Army Air Force(s) (USAAF) later in the Second World War.

The creation of the Mustang had many of its roots in events that dated back to the accession to power of Adolph Hitler and the National Socialist (Nazi) party in Germany during early 1933. The Nazi rise to power was followed by an enormous expansion in Germany's armed forces. A significant part of this was the rapid growth in Germany's air force, the Luftwaffe - which had been forbidden in the peace settlements following the end of the First World War. The existence of the new Luftwaffe was publicly acknowledged in March 1935, and was a very unwelcome development for many neighbouring European countries. Indeed, Germany's significant military expansion, coupled with an increasingly aggressive foreign policy that was

pursued by the Nazi leadership, led to a radically new and very problematical situation for the countries of Europe. The response of some - particularly Britain and France - was to foolishly indulge in the appeasement of the Nazi leadership and its aims. In contrast - and fortunately - there were sufficient wise heads in both Britain and France who realised that such a policy had no chance of success, and was in any case absolutely

North American Aviation's facilities at Inglewood (Mines Field) expanded rapidly as the company grew from strength to strength following its move to Southern California. This view is an interesting illustration of early Allison-Mustang production, mixed at this stage with early Harvard manufacture for Britain. NAA's facilities at Inglewood massively expanded in the face of large military orders, with Britain being the most important of the company's initial immediate pre-war and early war customers *(Photo: NAA)*

morally and militarily bankrupt. Reluctantly a policy of rearmament was commenced during the 1930's by a number of European countries, but in most cases this represented little more than a case of catch-up with the high quality rearmament (both in terms of numbers and increasing capability) that was rapidly taking place in Nazi Germany. The Spanish Civil War of 1936 to 1939, which concluded successfully for the Fascist powers in March 1939, illustrated how far German aerial capability had come in such a short space of time, with German pilots and some of the Luftwaffe's new, modern warplanes playing a significant part in the final victory.

A positive response in Britain to the growing Nazi threat saw the Royal Air Force embarking on an 'expansion scheme' that saw a significant influx of more 'modern' combat aircraft to replace the colourful but increasingly outdated biplanes that were in front-line British service well into the 1930's. Britain in fact had several important advantages over many other countries, not least of these being a pool of talented aircraft designers who were not afraid to embrace progress and new concepts in aircraft design and materials. This, coupled with advances that had been made by participation in - and eventual overall success in - the Schneider Trophy races of the 1920's and early 1930's, helped Britain to be amongst the leaders in the field in several key areas of aircraft design and powerplant technology. R.J. Mitchell's beautiful, iconic Supermarine Spitfire, and Sydney Camm's rugged, purposeful Hawker

Hurricane, were the best that the free world had to offer in response to German rearmament, that included the highly important Messerschmitt Bf 109 fighter. Both the Spitfire and the Hurricane were powered by the Rolls-Royce Merlin inline engine, a power plant that was later to have such a significant impact on the story of the Mustang. The problem for Britain was that both the Spitfire and the Hurricane were not necessarily going to be enough by themselves, particularly in terms of numbers, to face the tide of a possible German aerial assault against Britain and her allies. The Hurricane first flew in November 1935, and was well established in RAF front-line service in September 1939 when the Second World War commenced. The Spitfire made its first flight in March 1936, and began to enter front-line squadron service with the RAF in the latter half of 1938. By that time the Luftwaffe's Bf 109 had been in service since 1937, and had proven its worth and considerable potential in combat over Spain from 1937 onwards. Britain, like all other European countries, was becoming acutely aware of her lack of significant numbers of fighter aircraft in depth that were capable of taking on the Bf 109, and the growing array of other high-performance Luftwaffe aircraft - including fast and highly-capable bombers - that would be involved in any general conflict. Nevertheless, even though Britain was faced with the need to catch up particularly in terms of numbers of modern warplanes, she was far better placed than any other allied country in Europe to take

North American Aviation was a very forward-thinking company, which was blessed with some highly capable personnel. The President of NAA and the General Manager of its manufacturing division was the talented businessman and experienced aviation manager James H. 'Dutch' Kindelberger, under whose astute guidance together with the able team that he assembled around him, NAA grew from strength to strength. Kindelberger is seen here seated in the fuselage of an Allison-Mustang (but minus the pilot's seat!), apparently posed on the Mustang production line at Inglewood with a British official (Photo: NAA)

on the Luftwaffe because of the RAF's growing numbers of Spitfires and Hurricanes. No other Western European country could boast anything like either the Spitfire of the Hurricane in their inventories, and several other key allies such as France were struggling to bring modern designs to the fore after years of stagnation in official specifications and long delays in the creation of modern designs. The so-called Munich Agreement of September 1938, which ceded significant parts of one of Britain and France's allies, Czechoslovakia, to Nazi Germany was hoped by Britain and France to end Germany's territorial ambitions. The German take-over of the remainder of Czechoslovakia in March 1939 showed that Munich was simply another debacle, and even Britain's inept and weak government realised that the game was up and the Nazi threat had to be faced up to. The reality, however, was that a large expansion in Britain's armed forces - over and above what was already being achieved - was likely to be a huge strain on the country's increasingly stretched resources. A separate and dynamic source of war material needed to be found, in order to rapidly bridge the numerical and quality gap that existed between much of what the Western allies had in service compared to the growing Nazi war machine.

American Possibilities

The obvious - indeed, the only substantial - potential outside source for production of war material was the United States. A number of European countries, including Britain, therefore established official purchasing organisations to visit the US and work alongside their existing diplomatic cover to place orders with American companies to supply war material as soon as possible. The shopping list for these purchasing agencies did not just include fighter aircraft. In the later 1930's, Britain was well behind in rearmament for just about every military requirement, and combat aircraft of all types, trainers and second-line types, in addition to other war material including armoured fighting vehicles and warships, were significant priorities.

The concept of foreign delegations placing orders with American companies to supply front-line military equipment was, nevertheless, something of a complicated reality. On the one hand, American industry generally welcomed the considerable financial opportunities that these potential orders represented. On the other hand, the US did not officially consider itself involved in what appeared as the 1930s wore on to be an internal European squabble. Much is often written of America's so-called 'isolationism' during that period. In fact America's foreign policy was much more complicated than the often-quoted 'isolationist United States'. President Franklin D. Roosevelt was rather more level-headed than some members of the American Congress, and realised that the US could not stay aloof from the significant problems that were developing in far-away Europe, whether that would be in the long-term interest of the United States or not. In reality the American government tended to turn a blind eye to many of the activities of the foreign delegations that spent an increasing amount of time in the late 1930's negotiating with - and often striking up very good relations with - some areas of American industry. Nevertheless, there were some powerful American individuals - such as Henry Ford - and large companies that were much less than willing to deal with the foreign purchasing organisations.

The facilities that NAA created at Inglewood were amongst the best of any aviation manufacturer in the world at that time. Some of the company's capabilities would nowadays be called 'state-of-the-art'. This included extensive ground-testing of new designs. It has sometimes been claimed that this photograph shows the NA-73X prototype being tested for its structural strength with the addition of many lead weights in the NAA factory. In reality it is actually a non-flying static-test airframe that is being tested to breaking-point in this way. NAA documentation refers to a static-test airframe called the XX-73 additional to the flying NA-73X prototype, and the airframe in this image is presumably that airframe. The photograph was taken in mid-January 1941, and the wing structure failed at five per cent over its intended design load *(Photo: NAA)*

In addition, there were certainly many ordinary people in the United States who were unhappy at America being involved in any way with the developing problems in Europe at that time. It was therefore somewhat fortunate that the British purchasing representatives in particular were able to develop excellent working relationships with several key American armaments companies. It was here that the story of the Mustang began to take shape. A company that British officials developed very good relations with in the later 1930's was a comparatively young organisation named North American Aviation, Inc. (NAA). Sadly no longer in existence (what is left of its heritage is now a part of the large Boeing empire), NAA existed as a major aircraft producer for only just over three decades. Nevertheless, in that time it gave birth to some of aviation's classic aircraft.

The company that eventually grew into the North American Aviation of World War Two could trace its lineage back to 1928. It was originally born largely out of the workings of American corporate big business rather than developments within the US aviation industry itself, because at that time aviation in the US was a comparatively rich business that attracted many money men and investors. Therefore NAA's early history was largely cantered around corporate business affairs, mergers and offshoots designed to make money rather than aeroplanes. Created in December 1928, the original North American Aviation, Inc. was born as little more than a paper organisation. It was not an aircraft manufacturer, but was more or less a holding company for the various aviation concerns within the growing aviation empire of one Clement M. Keys. These included airlines with names such as Eastern Air Transport, Transcontinental and Western Air, and Western Air Express, and aircraft manufacturers such as Berliner-Joyce. For a time, Keys was also associated with several big aviation names including Curtiss and Douglas. The reorganisation of the Berliner-Joyce Aircraft Corporation after it was taken over by Keys' North American in 1930 had created the B/J Aircraft Corporation, with offices at 1775, Broadway, New York, and manufacturing premises at Dundalk in Maryland. However, the financial disasters of the late 1920s and subsequent depression had turned the previously profitable aviation sector in the US into a less than money-making concern - at least for the time being. In 1933 North American Aviation was merged with a separate organisation, the General Aviation Corporation, the latter being the holding company for the aviation interests of the giant General Motors Corporation. The General Aviation Corporation contained within its own organisation the General Aviation Manufacturing Corporation, which was formerly the Fokker Aircraft Corporation of America. Soon the manufacturing parts of each business were consolidated at Dundalk, Maryland, but this arrangement did not last long, however, for in 1934 a major reorganisation took place, in which General Motors relinquished some of its hold on the whole General Aviation organisation, including as it did both airlines and manufacturing capacity, due to a new federal law that required manufacturers to only be manufacturers and not operators or air mail contractors as well. This left the way open for a new North American organisation - at last - to arise as a related but separate entity.

In 1934 the new North American Aviation, Inc. was born, with its offices in the old B/J Aircraft Corporation's premises at 1775, Broadway, New York, and with its own manufacturing division at the previous Dundalk facility of B/J and the General Aviation Manufacturing Corporation - although the General Motors influence was still highly important. Everything went very well from the first for the new organisation. Brought in almost straight away to be the new President of NAA and the

General Manager of its manufacturing division was the talented businessman and experienced aviation manager James H. 'Dutch' Kindelberger, and under his guidance together with the able team that he assembled around him, NAA grew from strength to strength. Kindelberger was an astute businessman with an aviation background that included work with two giants of the US aviation industry, Glenn Martin and Donald Douglas. He had latterly worked as a vice-president for engineering with the Douglas company. Indeed, 'Dutch' Kindelberger is viewed by many as later becoming the father of the Mustang. Backing him up was John Leland 'Lee' Atwood, who became vice-president and chief of engineering for NAA. Amongst the talented team of designers and engineers for the new North American company that Kindelberger assembled, eventually the most important of these was the German-born Edgar Schmued - who was later to have such a major influence on the design of the Mustang.

From the first, the new company intended to design and manufacture its own, new designs as soon as practical. Initially the company built the - for its time - advanced and attractive O-47 single-engined observation monoplane for the US Army Air Corps (USAAC), which owed some of its design to the period immediately before the birth of the new NAA. The first entirely original design of the new North American company was an open-cockpit, tandem two-seat single-engine fixed undercarriage trainer monoplane designated the NA-16, which eventually developed and grew into the hugely successful AT-6 Texan/Harvard series of training aircraft that were so important to Allied pilot training during the Second World War, and which served world-wide in a large number of air arms.

The NA-16 was originally built as a private venture to meet a basic trainer requirement for the US Army Air Corps. The prototype Wright R-975 engined NA-16 prototype, registration X-2080, first flew on 1 April 1935. Its test pilot was Eddie Allen, who later found fame performing flight testing for Boeing, but tragically lost his life in the crash of the second Boeing XB-29 Superfortress bomber prototype on 18 February 1943. NAA was not subsequently the front runner in the USAAC's trainer competition, which was in essence won by a contender from Seversky. The Seversky design duly gained production orders as the BT-8, and was the first aircraft type specifically created as a basic trainer for the USAAC. However, significantly, the considerable influence of General Motors helped to give NAA's NA-16 design enough weight to secure Army Air Corps orders additional to the Seversky model. After some design modifications the initial production derivative of the NA-16, called BT-9 by the Army Air Corps, was first flown by test pilot Paul Balfour on 15 April 1936. The basic design attracted what for their time were significant orders, and North American's production facilities were already being transferred from Dundalk to larger premises in Southern California on the west coast of the US.

Not long after its creation, the NAA began to move its manufacturing premises from the grey skies and limited growth potential of Dundalk to the blue skies and massive growth possibilities of Southern California. The choice of location for NAA was the Los Angeles Municipal Airport, otherwise known to local inhabitants as Mines Field, situated in the Los Angeles suburb of Inglewood. This site in itself is one of the world's famous aviation locations. Selected in June 1928 to be the new Los Angeles Municipal Airport from a shortlist of contenders, the airport grew from small beginnings and limited infrastructure into one of the world's major airports. Re-named as Los Angeles Airport in July 1941 (but still known locally for many years as Mines Field, after the real estate agent who negotiated its sale to the city of Los Angeles in the 1920's), it saw massive growth in the post-World War Two period. Renamed Los Angeles International Airport in 1950, a completely new airport was built on the site in the late 1950's and early 1960's, much of which still remains. It is one of today's largest and most important airports anywhere in the world.

North American Aviation temporarily used a structure known as the Moreland building when the company's manufacturing division relocated from Dundalk to Mines Field in 1935, but soon a purpose-built and state-of-the-art new factory was built there on the south-eastern edge of the airfield on land that was leased from the Los Angeles Department of Airports. This new factory was available for use in early 1936, and construction of NA-16 series trainers soon took precedence. The company successfully negotiated an excellent deal for the lease of the location (the whole site eventually covered some 20 acres), which was available for only $600 each year. At first using the existing facility of the Moreland building, the beautiful new state-of-the-art factory itself opened for production in early 1936, and the North American Aviation entry in 'Jane's' All The World's Aircraft' of 1937 pointed out that the plant covered an area of 172,000 square feet, although this was extended during 1937 to 380,000 square feet and later saw further growth.

For the comparatively new North American company, the move to California from Maryland was an outstanding step forward. The often fine weather in the Los Angeles area allowed for many suitable days of flight testing that were not interrupted by bad weather - although even Southern California is not immune to occasional freak weather, such as the snow falls there in 1944! When large orders were received for later types such as the Mustang, some final assembly work was actually performed outside in the open air in addition to the busy assembly lines within the North American factory complex itself. A well-educated and increasingly well-trained and numerous workforce was also readily at hand in the Los Angeles and Southern California area. It is little wonder that a number of aviation companies made their way to this area when the worst effects of the financial difficulties of the late 1920's and early 1930's and the subsequent economic depression began to subside.

From the earliest days in Southern California, good fortune seemed to favour North American Aviation. The NA-16 design that gained orders subsequent to the Army Air Corps trainer competition proved to be an outstanding success. With various modifications and refinements, the basic layout led to a series of developed models that went on to meet a number of USAAC needs. Eventually the type easily out-sold the Seversky BT-8 which had in essence been officially preferred in the original Army Air Corps basic trainer competition. In addition, US Navy interest in the NA-16's capabilities and potential was a reason for the mating of Pratt & Whitney's excellent R-1340 Wasp radial engine to the basic design, although the original NA-16 design layout envisaged the installation of this engine type in addition to the Wright R-975. The ingredients were then in place that developed into the superb and long-running AT-6/SNJ Texan series of trainers that proved invaluable and served so widely during World War Two. In addition to this domestic success, the leadership of NAA wisely sought out overseas customers. With the required export licenses in place, the basic NA-16 layout that developed into the AT-6/SNJ Texan series was eventually sold in a large variety of versions and configurations to a very wide selection of foreign buyers.

Significant amongst these was Britain and various British Commonwealth countries. As such, the NA-16 series became highly significant in the story of the Mustang in helping to establish important connections between Britain and North American Aviation. One of the first acquisitions of US-manufactured aircraft by British purchasing representatives during the later 1930's was a significant order for NA-16 series aircraft to help Britain's expanding pilot training programme. This was some way before World War Two commenced, and again showed that some personnel in Britain's military establishment were considerably more far-sighted and realistic than many British politicians of the day, in realising the need for rearmament with modern equipment. In the early months of 1938 Britain signed for 200 NA-49, which were the first of substantial numbers of NA-16-derived two-seat trainers that were given the name Harvard in British and British Commonwealth service. The first aircraft, Harvard Mk.I serial number N7000, was passed to the Aeroplane & Armament Experimental Establishment (A&AEE) at Martlesham Heath in Suffolk, England, in late 1938. It was the very first of several thousand Harvard's for British and British Commonwealth employment that included production by North American as well as licence manufacture in Canada by Noorduyn Aviation, Ltd. These aircraft became a vital part of Britain's pilot training system in World War Two, but equally significantly the Harvard was the start of the highly-important relationship between Britain and NAA that directly led to the co-operation out of which the Mustang was derived.

The path that led to the birth of the Mustang was, to say the least, unconventional. Indeed, it was somewhat appropriate that a design that was destined to become such an exceptional combat aircraft should come about in an extraordinary way. Had it not been for Britain's growing need for quality fighter aircraft in large quantities, and the close connections that had grown between NAA and British representatives in the US, then the Mustang might never have been created. The story really commenced when Britain began to search for modern fighter aircraft to buy 'off the shelf' in the United States - although this proved to be more difficult than has often been claimed. The US was undoubtedly a potential major source of fighter aircraft (which were known as 'pursuit' types in the US at that time), but unfortunately fighter aircraft and fighter engine design had considerably lagged behind in the US during the 1930's. There were a number of specific reasons for this. Important amongst them was the increasingly entrenched attitude amongst many senior Army Air Corps officers that fast, well-defended bombers would always get to their targets, obviating the need for anything but the smallest possible fighter force. This mind-set that 'the bomber will always get through' became so well established that officers who argued to the contrary were often sidelined or retired from the service so that their views would not upset the developing status quo of the invincibility of the bomber.

A lack of funding was a further significant factor in the US falling behind in the procurement of what would nowadays call 'state-of-the-art' designs. The Army Air Corps was just that, a component of the US Army, and there was often a considerable difficulty in obtaining money for the development and purchase of new designs – particularly if those types were fighters. The Army was more interested in the Army Air Corps operating close-support types that would work closely with ground forces, and not high-flying fighters. It was not until a very commanding personality took over as the head of the Air Corps that this situation started to change. He was Henry H. 'Hap' Arnold, and his extraordinary influence was to play a vital role in the build-up of the Army Air Corps, its development into the Army Air Force(s) in 1941, and its subsequent vital importance in the air war during the Second World War. Arnold took over as the chief of the Army Air Corps in September 1938, but even at that point it remained a struggle to obtain

funds particularly because the annual US defence budget was even then influenced by the shortages of the economic crisis earlier in the decade.

Similarly, design work on high-performance engines had also slowed in the US during the early 1930's in several key areas. This was most noticeable in the development of inline engines, especially for high-performance fighters. Deficiencies in planning, lack of money, and misplaced research and development work were reasons for this situation, but a further explanation was the general unwillingness within the Army Air Corps to place much emphasis on fighter design and evolution. This was particularly unfortunate because in the 1920's the US had enjoyed a marked advantage over many other countries with several promising inline engine designs. However, this position was lost during the 1930's, and a number of other countries including Britain and Germany, began to develop capable inline engines which had particular application for high-performance fighters. The US instead was a major player in the development of radial engines (which of course had more of an application for bombers and ground-attack aircraft), and in the challenging area of turbo-supercharging (i.e. exhaust-augmented supercharging) for aero engines the Americans literally led the world. Ironically, some attempts 'had been made' during the early 1930's to create a 'modern' high-performance inline engine in the United States, and several manufacturers had either proposed or actually built a number of designs. However, due to a variety of reasons, including changing official requirements and dwindling development funds caused by the difficult economic conditions of the time, only one of these actually reached production status. This was the Allison V-1710, and it was subsequently to have a significant part to play in the Mustang story.

Theoretically a 1,000 hp plus engine with (non-turbo) supercharging, the V-1710 essentially began as a private-venture programme. It received official backing from the Army Air Corps from the mid-1930's onwards, and in developed form it was to power a wide variety of Air Corps and later Army Air Force fighter types. Indeed, it was the only available inline engine of any note in the United States in the late 1930's, at the

time when fighter design in that country was at last starting to gather pace. This was unfortunate in the long run as the V-1710 had a variety of development problems, and although available with supercharging it was eventually installed in several fighter types without the benefit of turbo-supercharging. A significant result of this was that aircraft fitted with this configuration were good at low-to medium-altitude, but were comparatively poor performers at higher altitudes – a factor that was again to have a major part to play in the Mustang's story.

Amongst the aircraft types that employed the Allison V-1710 was the Curtiss P-40. This purposeful-looking but rather sluggish performer was one of the main fighter programmes in the US as the 1930's ended, and the P-40 series in several specific marks and configurations was to play an important role in the Second World War for a number of Allied air forces. The P-40 was developed by the Curtiss Aeroplane Division of the Curtiss-Wright Corporation, which was a famous and long-standing aircraft designer and manufacturer that could trace its roots through the significant personality of Glenn Curtiss right back to the earliest days of aviation in the US. In reality, however, Curtiss was lagging behind in all-metal monoplane fighter design as the 1930's wore on. The company's chief designer, Donovan Berlin, and his design team were undoubtedly talented in their particular field, but in reality the P-40 layout was not particularly aerodynamically refined or advanced. The basic airframe of the P-40 series dated back to that of the famous Curtiss Model 75 series from which it was derived. The original Model 75 had flown in May 1935 and the various subsequent production fighter series (most members of which were referred to as Hawk) were powered by a radial engine, either the Pratt & Whitney R-1830 Twin Wasp or the Wright R-1820 Cyclone. The type had been ordered by the US Army Air Corps as the P-36, having placed well alongside what became the Seversky P-35 in a competition that gave the Army Air Corps its first really modern fighter designs. Importantly for Curtiss, the Model 75 also proved to be an export success, and the type was subject to a particularly significant export order from France. The first of several French contracts was signed in the spring 1938, and was intended to augment French

The fighter that North American Aviation did not wish to build for Britain - or indeed anyone else - was the Curtiss P-40. British purchasing officials in the US would have been happy for the company to have licence-built this aircraft type for Britain in quantity, but fortunately NAA had other ideas, and instead decided to design its own, better fighter. So was born the Mustang. Shown here is a very early production P-40 for Britain, known to the British as a Tomahawk Mk.IIA, serial number AH925. This was a basic Curtiss Model 81 with Allison V-1710 power. The P-40 in several different versions served very widely with the RAF, but the type was certainly outclassed by the Mustang, and NAA did not build any P-40s of any description
(Photo: Malcolm V. Lowe Collection)

One of the great advantages of NAA's relocation to Southern California from Maryland during the mid-1930's was the immediate access to excellent weather. This not only allowed for many days that were available for flight testing unencumbered by bad weather, it also remarkably allowed the company to do some of the final production work on Mustangs in the open air. Evidence of this can be seen in this view of completion work being carried out on virtually-finished Allison-engined P-51A airframes. This mark of Allison-Mustang was the first Mustang type to introduce an internal armament consisting solely of wing-mounted 0.5in machine guns, and also featured an additional small vent window on the left-hand transparent windscreen panel, which was a ready identifier for this mark of Mustang (Photo: NAA)

production of indigenous fighter types - many of which were either increasingly obsolete or were delayed in design and production. Curtiss had, however, seen the growth potential in the P-36 airframe and via a rather tortuous route married the Allison V-1710 inline engine to the Model 75 airframe to create what eventually became - via the XP-37 programme - the famed and very widely-produced P-40 family of fighters.

Making its first flight on 14 October 1938, the updated XP-40 design – known to Curtiss as the 'Model 81' - at once generated considerable domestic and overseas interest. The Curtiss approach to the new aircraft, however, was rather conservative, and drew on so many aspects of the P-36 design that the resulting 'new' P-40 design was a rather dated concept by the time that the first production aircraft were delivered. Power was provided by a supercharged Allison V-1710, but in the event no P-40 production examples were fitted with a turbo-supercharged V-1710. An initial purchase came from the Army Air Corps, which ordered an opening batch of 524 of the Model 81 series as the P-40-CU, P-40B-CU, and P-40C-CU. This was, for its time, a substantial order (in fact it was the largest single military aviation order in the US since World War One), and the new type performed well in a competitive evaluation between several new fighter designs that took place in the late spring of 1939 at Wright Field in Ohio and which also included such types as the new Bell P-39 Airacobra. The Model 81 design also attracted French interest and orders. Significantly for the birth of what became the Mustang, the new P-40 additionally created interest amongst British purchasing representatives. At that time, however, Britain did not place the substantial orders that some published sources have claimed. Instead, it was recognised that due to the large Army Air Corps and French

orders for the Model 81, the existing Curtiss production facilities would be over-stretched for some time to come. Representations were therefore eventually made to Britain's friend, North American Aviation, to see if NAA could augment Curtiss production of the Model 81/P-40 by manufacturing the Curtiss fighter under licence themselves for Britain.

The idea of NAA making someone else's fighter design was certainly greeted warmly by some in the US government and the Air Corps. In any case, the Army Air Corps appears to have drawn up a 'preferred list' of aircraft companies that it felt should be allowed to develop fighter designs. This list included Curtiss but 'did not include' North American Aviation. The Army Air Corps apparently reasoned that NAA was a comparatively new company with no real long-term experience in fighter design, and was therefore unsuitable for instituting its own design studies – but was nonetheless competent enough to become a licence producer of the combat aircraft of other companies.

Licence plans for Curtiss P-40 Construction
The leadership of NAA must have been considerably frustrated by this thought process. Although a comparatively new company, NAA certainly had the capability to introduce new ideas and new approaches to the field of fighter design and technology – and in the event was certainly willing to do so. The exact date that British representatives first made their initial representations to NAA about licence production of the P-40 is not clear. Certainly documents held by Britain's National Archives at Kew outside London, do not suggest a precise date, but it was sometime in the autumn of 1939. At that point the idea was not carried any further, but world events were already

dictating Britain's actions. On 1 September 1939 German forces invaded Poland. On 3 September, following the expiry of a British ultimatum and to honour previous commitments, Britain's government of failed appeasers finally saw the need to stand up to Nazi Germany and reluctantly declared war on Germany. Events in the US at once also took on a more urgent momentum. In early November 1939 President Franklin D. Roosevelt's administration intervened to ensure the enactment of a federal law that allowed foreign countries to purchase war materials in the US, so long as these were then transported away by the purchaser. This was the so-called 'cash and carry' law. It was in effect a revision of the already-existing Neutrality Act, and it effectively repealed - to the dismay of some members of the US Congress - an on-going US arms embargo that had been in existence since the outbreak of war.

Also significantly, the formation of a new British purchasing organisation was announced just three days later, on 7 November 1939. This body was subsequently to have a direct influence on the creation of the Mustang. It was called the British Purchasing Commission (BPC). Contrary to countless published sources, this body did not exist prior to that time. Instead, British aircraft purchases up to then had been handled by specifically-created purchasing missions acting with the authority of Britain's Air Ministry. The establishment of the BPC in November 1939 led to the signing of hundreds of orders by Britain that were rapidly placed with a large number of US companies in the subsequent weeks and months. These orders were principally for much needed war material, including aircraft, but they also involved purchases of armoured fighting vehicles, ships, and weapons and ammunition of all sorts. In addition, orders were placed for many other pieces of equipment including machine tools and other industrial apparatus, and such mundane but important items as binoculars and parachutes.

The BPC existed specifically for purchases in the United States, while a similar body operated in Canada. In fact, the whole British purchasing organisation in North America eventually expanded into a major 'home away from home' for many civil servants and military personnel. So significant was Britain's need for aircraft and aero engines that a British Air Commission was also eventually established to specifically deal with aviation matters, under the director-generalship of Sir Henry Self. Self was a distinguished civil servant who was very familiar with the US aircraft industry. Indeed, he had been involved in the original dealings with North American Aviation over the purchase for Britain of the versions of the NA-16 two-seat trainer design that became the Harvard in British and Commonwealth service.

One of the most pressing requirements for the BPC staff in the winter of 1939-1940 was the provision of fighter aircraft for British service. Also operating in the United States at that time were French purchasing representatives, and in January 1940 a joint Anglo-French Purchasing Board was established in New York. Arthur Purvis became the Chairman of this body, which tried to co-ordinate British and French efforts. The French had already ordered the new Curtiss Model 81 fighter for French air force (Armée de l'Air) service, and British representatives were well aware that Curtiss had full order books for the type. In fact, Curtiss had been very slow to begin series production of the P-40 against the original USAAC and French orders of 1939, and it appeared that any British contracts for the type were likely to be severely delayed. Indeed, Curtiss did not deliver the initial production P-40s to the Army Air Corps until mid-1940, the first production example not having flown until April 1940. The idea of another company being able to manufacture P-40s under licence to bolster Curtiss production therefore looked increasingly attractive. To that end, BPC representatives began to talk once again to North American Aviation about that company possibly licence producing the P-40 at Inglewood.

North American's response was unexpected, and set in motion the train of events that led rapidly to the creation of the Mustang. The whole concept of North American building the P-40 was unattractive to the company and particularly to its management and designers. To begin with, the P-40 was someone else's aircraft. Further, it was not a particularly advanced design by early 1940 standards, as its layout was based on the earlier 1930's aerodynamics and thinking of the Model 75/P-36 design. Although the Army Air Corps, France and Britain had apparently enthusiastically taken to the Curtiss fighter in a very positive, this was rather more a case of the P-40 being available rather than it being a 'must have' due to spectacular performance or capabilities. The early production P-40s could theoretically reach 357 mph (575 km/h), but this was a seemingly rather ambitious total with a full load of fuel and ammunition aboard – and in any case, the low-rated Allison V-1710-33 series engine of 1,040 hp of these early P-40s meant that the aircraft suffered seriously degraded performance above 15,000 ft (4,572 m). Curtiss was also apparently having problems in mass producing the P-40, and if North American became involved in licence-manufacturing the type, it was possible that NAA would have to come to the aid of Curtiss in getting genuine volume production under way.

North American's officials in fact had their own very particular ideas about how to approach the British. The company's designers had kept abreast with fighter developments and progress in Europe, as well as advances in fighter design concepts and aerodynamics. They had the talent, capability and the time available to take a blank piece of paper and draw up their very own new design. This is in a nutshell what subsequently took place. Somewhat fortuitously, both NAA and the BPC had offices in New York which allowed for close liaison between the two sides. NAA's offices were at 1775, Broadway, New York. These premises had long been associated with the grouping from which NAA had emerged as an aircraft producer in its own right, while the British Purchasing Commission's offices were at 15, Broad Street, New York - although Sir Henry Self, as the senior civil servant amongst the British purchasing mission's personnel, later had some rather nice accommodation in the Willard Hotel in Washington, D.C.

NAA duly made initial advances to the British purchasing representatives, to the effect that North American would prefer not to build P-40s, but instead could design its own fighter. The proposed brand new combat aircraft would take into account recent advances in fighter design and aerodynamics, and would include any lessons already learned in the air fighting during the war – including the combat experience of US aircraft such as the Curtiss Model 75, which the French had already flown operationally by that time. The new design would also be an aircraft that could be mass-produced efficiently. In effect, NAA said that it could design and build a better fighter than the P-40. This was quite a claim from a relatively new company that had no real previous fighter design experience. However, the whole idea obviously appealed to the BPC, and from January 1940 onwards the entire concept began to take shape. There appears to have been important communication between the British representatives and the NAA team in New York during that period, with Lee Atwood of NAA providing much of the high-level liaison. Talks also appear to have taken place in England relating to the developing venture. Some of the documents covering aspects of this activity continue to exist in Britain's National Archives at Kew. The scene was set for the birth of the Mustang.

Mustang Genesis

In wartime, military necessity can very often 'get the job done' much quicker than in times of peace. During many conflicts, the time taken to get new weapons into the front-line has been very often foreshortened due to the pressing needs of combat, for it is pointless to spend months if not years developing and testing a new weapon when it is needed straight away. Such was the case with the Mustang. Once fruitful talks had commenced in earnest between representatives of North American Aviation and Britain's BPC in the US, events began to move quickly.

Indeed, by early April 1940 the whole NAA fighter project for Britain was really taking shape, and Lee Atwood prepared a letter of intent contract for the BPC to examine. On 11 April Sir Henry Self wrote in reply to NAA confirming that an initial order by Britain of 400 of the proposed new aircraft was to be made, at a total equipped and armed unit price of $40,000. This was an amazing act of faith by the British in an aircraft that had not by then even flown, but it did show how much the British representatives felt the new aircraft was needed. At that time the new design was referred to as the NA-50B, and the intended power plant was to be the Allison V-1710 as used in the Curtiss P-40.

In reality, however, NAA's thoughts let alone detailed design work were not at that time at an advanced stage. However, a story is often quoted that 'Dutch' Kindelberger telegrammed from New York to the NAA design team in California to rapidly begin detailed work, following a particularly fruitful discussion in New York with BPC representatives (and, apparently, the display of some hastily-drawn sketches - perhaps some of these were made on the back of the proverbial envelope). Certainly, day and night activity did eventually take place at Inglewood to get the new fighter's design on paper. This is claimed to have

happened from 24 April 1940 onwards, with the resulting plans being mailed to New York as soon as possible afterwards. Without doubt a great deal of detailed work had to be undertaken in the shortest possible time by the NAA design team. Of central importance to this process amongst the North American staff were designer Edgar Schmued and aerodynamicist Edward Horkey. The plans that were created by this rapid activity obviously impressed the British, although there were several twists to the tale even at that early time.

NAA's design work on the new fighter was carried out with the knowledge of the Army Air Corps and US procurement agencies. It was at this point that a peculiar love-hate relationship with the new design and with NAA itself appears to have developed amongst some officers in the Army Air Corps. This relationship at more than one point in the future threatened to de-rail the new aircraft's development and service. As related earlier, North American was most definitely not on the prescribed 'list' of companies that the Air Corps considered capable of designing fighter aircraft, and yet here that same company was, in April and May 1940, developing its own fighter design. Worse, this was being accomplished for a foreign power, and not for the Air Corps. There appears to have been several individuals in the Air Corps who developed a dislike for the new aircraft on these grounds. One of the chief opponents is sometimes portrayed as being Col. Oliver Echols, who was the assistant head of the Army Air Corps' Material Command at Wright Field, Ohio, (today's Wright-Patterson AFB, the current home of the National Museum of the USAF, which is still better-known to almost everyone by its long-standing title of 'USAF Museum'). Material Command was charged amongst other tasks with the procurement of new designs and the testing of prototypes. Examining the very close relationships that were developing

Truly a single-seat Harvard lookalike, the very first fighter that North American Aviation produced was the NA-50, seven of which were completed for Peru in 1939. One of them is shown here. The type was derived from the basic NA-16 trainer family layout, and some of the Peruvian machines saw action during a brief conflict in 1941 with neighbouring Ecuador. In Peruvian service they were well-liked, and were nick-named 'Torito'
(Photo: NAA)

between the British and French purchasing representatives and several US aircraft companies, Echols raised the issue in a letter to one of his superiors of the advisability of allowing 'the French and British to go into these plants at this time and enter contract for completely new development. If this is permitted, they can take over the engineering staff of all our manufacturers which will prevent us from obtaining any development whatsoever.' In the same letter, he questioned the 'advisability to permit foreign nations to undertake to design completely new airplanes which are improvements on the models which we now have, and which our manufacturers are trying to sell them'.

Fortunately, the government of President Franklin D. Roosevelt did not share these sentiments. In early May 1940, following the relevant applications by North American Aviation, the required export licences were granted for the new fighter. Indeed, many in the US government saw the obvious and considerable benefits of having foreign orders for US warplanes. At that stage, Britain and France were paying for everything - 'Lend-Lease' was a long way in the future. The substantial funds that were being expended in particular by Britain and France from late 1939 onwards were a great help to the US aircraft industry. Indeed, in a number of instances the huge input of money was allowing new factories to be planned and built. It can be argued that this was the basis from which the US armaments industry grew to its pre-eminent position later in World War Two (and continued post-war) as the so-called 'Arsenal of Democracy' – a position from which it has dominated the aviation world even up to the present day.

Unfortunately, a further twist had by then developed in the creation of North American's new fighter. In an act that has forever after clouded the design origins of the Mustang, NAA purchased from Curtiss in the spring of 1940 a considerable amount of wind-tunnel data. The National Advisory Committee for Aeronautics (NACA - much later, today's NASA) had been working closely with Curtiss to try to help along the rather pedestrian P-40 design, and to assist with the creation of a new Curtiss fighter, the XP-46. The latter was intended as a cleaned-up derivative of the P-40, which would hopefully be a much more aerodynamically advanced and more capable fighter than the rather out-dated P-40 design layout. Like the P-40 and NAA's new fighter design that grew into the Mustang, the XP-46 was to be powered by the Allison V-1710 inline engine.

In particular, Curtiss had been experimenting with the position of the radiator for the XP-46 and its associated intake to provide adequate air flow and ventilation for the engine's liquid-cooling system. A number of locations for the cooling radiator had been tried out, including a placement below and behind the cockpit, for which a 'belly scoop' air intake had been envisaged and tested. In the event, the P-40 did not utilise this position (although the XP-40 prototype was fitted with its main air intake in a number of locations at different times during its development), but the XP-46 most definitely 'did have' a belly inlet. This lower fuselage intake position was also to be one of the characteristics of the NAA design that became the Mustang, and many historians have speculated that the placement of the belly 'scoop' on the Mustang was a direct result of using the Curtiss and NACA wind-tunnel data on the XP-46 that was purchased by North American in April 1940. Lee Atwood was considerably involved in the negotiations with Curtiss on behalf of North American to obtain this material, and it was bought for $56,000. Certainly NAA subsequently made no secret of having obtained the information, and it is possible that the BPC had talked North American into obtaining the data because it felt the company was inexperienced in fighter design and needed the potential helping hand of owning the information. There also appears to have been Army Air Corps insistence that North

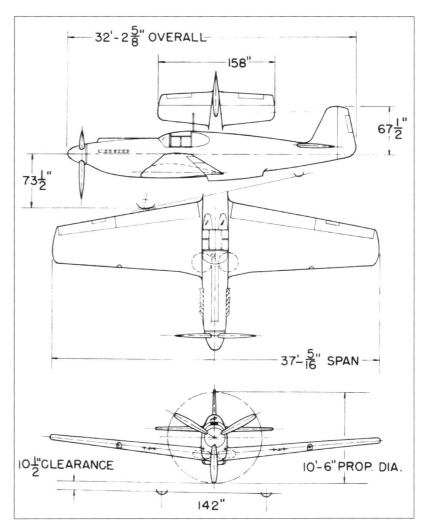

American should have the data at its disposal.

A considerable debate has subsequently existed as to whether the Mustang grew out of this apparent collaboration between NAA and Curtiss. Indeed, some historians have claimed that the Mustang was nothing more than an improved XP-46. Certainly the NACA wind-tunnel data could well have been of help to NAA especially where it related to the placement of the radiator and its associated cooling inlet, but it appears extremely unlikely that the allied data on the XP-46 design itself was of any practical help. The Mustang emerged from NAA's design offices as a far more advanced aircraft compared to the rather ugly and archaic XP-46, and few if any at North American in subsequent statements appear to have considered the Curtiss design to have been of much help to the Mustang's creation. The XP-46 in any case proved to be a poor design when it eventually took to the air in early 1941, and by then Curtiss was looking to continue the development and production of the P-40 series which promised much more than the XP-46 that was supposed to be its superior. Indeed, the XP-46 was eventually quietly abandoned.

Regardless of the debate over the role of the Curtiss XP-46 in the design of what became the Mustang, there is no doubt that the North American design team's work on their new fighter bore fruit in a very significant way. This was despite the company having never before designed a fighter aircraft. The only warplanes of similar role that NAA had at that time created were two specific single-seat fighter derivatives of its already-successful two-seat NA-16 trainer line – and those two fighter derivatives, the NA-50 for Peru; and the NA-50A/P-64 that was originally intended for Siam (Thailand) had only been built in very small numbers.

Dating from the first half of 1940, this very early NAA drawing illustrating a proposed NA-73 layout shows major similarities with the aircraft that was eventually built - and some notable differences. Of particular importance in North American's thinking at this time was the very streamlined cockpit cover, together with the neat installation of the Allison V-1710 inline engine giving as little frontal drag as possible, and the famous under-fuselage air intake for its mid-fuselage radiator. Note also the dimensions, the wing span being of particular significance for the whole Mustang story *(Photo: NAA)*

The experience of NAA in fighter design that predated the Mustang programme was quite limited. The NA-50A seen here was a fighter developed for Siam (Thailand) by NAA from the NA-16 trainer family, and followed after the NA-50 order for Peru. Only six NA-50A were built, with important detail differences compared to the Peruvian machines. All six were embargoed by US authorities due to Thai accommodation with the Japanese in South-east Asia, and they were never delivered. Instead they joined the USAAC under the designation P-64 as improvised fighter trainers. The aircraft illustrated bears its original US civil registration NX25607 on the rudder *(Photo: NAA)*

Detailed Proposals

As already pointed out, in mid-April 1940 British approval was starting to be forthcoming for the new design, based on what had been drawn up and predicted thus far by NAA's designers and engineers. It appears that detailed design work and the creation of working drawings began just subsequent to that time. On 1 May 1940 Lee Atwood wrote a now famous letter to Sir Henry Self. This communication outlined the significant progress that North American had made on their new design up to that time, and actually proposed a construction schedule. It was this letter that also confirmed to the British purchasing representatives that NAA had bought the wind tunnel data from Curtiss previously referred to. Atwood began his letter by saying 'In accordance with our understanding, we are proceeding with the design of a single-seat fighter airplane, our Model NA-73, incorporating an Allison engine and fitted with provisions for equipment and armament [the latter were to be 'Customer Furnished']'. He went on, 'we are prepared to construct and deliver to you 320 of these airplanes before September 30th, 1941'. A detailed breakdown followed of when the aircraft were to be delivered, with the first to be supplied in January 1941. The peak of manufacture would be reached in July 1941, when fifty-three would be delivered. There was also the possibility for more Mustangs to be built, at a rate of fifty per month up to at least the end of 1941, if Britain exercised an option before the end of April 1941 for further aircraft.

The letter made absolutely no mention of the '120 days' schedule that many historians have subsequently claimed was required by Britain, and this alleged demand of 120 days does not appear to have ever been a consideration – instead, the timescales as noted in this letter of Atwood's would seem to have been the basis on which subsequent agreements were reached. It is one of several myths that relate to the Mustang's development story, that Britain required a 120 days schedule, and those who hold fast to this story have clearly not examined in detail the actual correspondence between the British purchasing representatives and NAA personnel from that period.

This highly important letter of Atwood did however actually state that a mock-up had been made of the new fighter design, and that the initial phase of the detail design work had been completed. In addition, the British were offered two alternative configurations of the new fighter. One would have a full armament of eight machine guns (two 0.5-in in the lower cowling and one of these machine guns in each wing, plus two further 0.303-in machine guns in each wing). This arrangement, with armour fitted, was projected to have a maximum speed of 384 mph (618 km/h). Alternatively, a lighter-armed configuration (which NAA called the P-509 layout) was proposed, in which only four guns would be installed, with no armour protection. The planned maximum speed for the fighter in this configuration was projected as 400 mph (644 km/h). These figures were based on a power rating

NAA's early studies on the NA-73 project included the construction of this mock-up. Many of the important features of the eventual Mustang design were included in its construction and were therefore already in place from the earliest days of the programme. The armament layout shown suggests a concept similar to one of the two alternatives offered by NAA to Britain as the project developed in April and May 1940, namely the P-509 layout with fewer guns installed than the eight-gun armament eventually chosen by the British. Of note is the extremely short carburettor air intake housing ahead of the windscreen, which was later much altered *(Photo: NAA)*

from the Allison V-1710 engine of 1,030 hp at 16,000 ft (4,877 m), using 90-octane fuel.

This detailed approach by NAA showed how far the company had progressed as a fighter designer, even with the limited design experience that the company enjoyed in this demanding field of aircraft design and development. Atwood's detailed communication was far more professional and to the point than the projected estimates that had been made several years earlier by the Bell Aircraft Corporation for its XP-39 Airacobra fighter,

which had had very optimistic performance predictions made for it - but these estimates had been made without any military equipment being introduced into the equation. Needless to say, when eventually fitted out with full military equipment, the resulting P-39 production aircraft performed well short of the original estimates made by Bell.

In the event, the British opted for the eight-gun armament proposed by NAA for the new North American fighter (which was consistent with the eight-gun armament philosophy of the

Very elegant, gleaming, and for its day very advanced, there were many superlatives that could be said of the smart new fighter prototype that North American Aviation created in rapid time for Britain during the summer of 1940. Posing for NAA's official photographs at Mines Field not long after its roll-out, the NA-73X was at that time yet to fly, and did not even at that time have its civil registration NX19998 painted on the tail to spoil the overall effect of this beautiful aircraft
(Photo: NAA)

Although NAA had no real experience in fighter design, it is remarkable how effectively the company's designers created such a functional, beautiful, and at the same time successful design layout. Indeed, the whole of the NA-73X's design showed excellent attention to detail and important streamlining to reduce drag and allow optimum performance. An example of this was the engine installation and forward fuselage, where the Allison V-1710 engine was neatly cowled. The installation of the engine was the work of a famous US racing pilot, namely Art Chester. At the time of this picture the NA-73X still had the short carburettor air intake which was later lengthened, and an anti-glare panel painted ahead of the windscreen
(Photo: NAA)

Spitfire and Hurricane fighters then in service in Britain, and the Fairey Fulmar naval fighter which was just entering production). The letter of Atwood additionally included a cost breakdown for the initial 320 aircraft. Each basic airframe would be priced at $33,400, with the engine and related accessories coming to a further $983.95. Additional equipment, excluding the radio and armament, made each aircraft $37,590.45. The overall cost for the first 320 aircraft, including spares, and crating ready for overseas shipment, came to $14,746,964 and 35 cents. Compared to some of the deals that the British purchasing representatives were at that time paying out for, especially where it involved the supply to Britain of utterly useless aircraft such as the Brewster Buffalo alleged fighter, the NAA arrangement was an absolute bargain.

In effect, NAA was in a position to proceed immediately on receipt of a written go-ahead from the British in response to Atwood's significant letter. The company requested a down-payment of ten per cent of the contract amount, and a subsequent payment schedule similar to the previous contracts agreed with the British for the Harvard trainer. NAA was even willing to make modifications required by the purchaser within the contract price, as long as these were requested within three months of the agreement being ratified by the two sides.

This must all have made excellent reading for the British purchasing personnel. They were in effect successfully instigating a new fighter for British service, without there even having been any official British requirement or detailed specification needing to be drawn up. This was completely at variance with the then-existing procedures for military aircraft procurement in Britain. These very formal procedures normally required the identification by the military of a specific need, followed by the translation of this into official requirements and leading to the release of very definite specification information to the British aircraft industry, followed by potentially lengthy design work, construction of prototypes, and a fly-off competition before a winner could be found and initial production contracts could be let. The creation of the Mustang completely circumvented these official procedures. Indeed, the Mustang is one of the few, if not the only, military aircraft for British service that was created in the unique way that the BPC and NAA had pursued in those few heady weeks during the first half of 1940.

Not surprisingly, at NAA's Inglewood project offices, feverish work was undertaken to draw up the new design, and to translate into working drawings the initial somewhat vague but nonetheless advanced concepts with which NAA's staff had originally convinced the British. Much of the detail design work and the creation of production blue-prints took place from early May 1940, with several designers working long shifts to speed the process along – some are claimed to have worked sixteen-hour days. Work continued seven days a week. There were several ideas that were woven into the new design that, when taken together, made the new aircraft into a very special fighter that eventually far out-stripped anything then being built or envisaged in the US. In general terms, the new aircraft was aerodynamically very 'clean'.

The new fighter's fuselage layout in particular showed none of the awkwardness of the Curtiss P-40's rather bulky fuselage cross-section, and the front third in particular included a beautifully-streamlined nose contouring around the Allison V-1710 engine. Whereas the P-40's fuselage had its widest point somewhere near its nose, together with its prominent drag-producing undernose radiator inlet, the Mustang showed none of this unclean contouring. On the contrary, the new North American design included a feature that Curtiss had unsuccessfully toyed with, the so-called 'belly scoop'. This was in fact the lower fuselage inlet for cooling air that would be directed to the aircraft's radiator. NAA's designers totally rejected the cumbersome and drag-producing Curtiss undernose approach, and placed the radiator for the Allison engine's coolant in the mid-fuselage position, below and behind the cockpit. In that position, its air intake was neatly located beneath the fuselage, where it was likely to produce a minimum amount of drag. The positioning of the bulky radiator in that mid-fuselage position meant that it was near to what had in any case to be the fuselage's widest point, the cockpit area, and it therefore did not make the fuselage any wider than it already needed to be. In a further breakthrough, the whole installation was fitted with an outlet slightly further back beneath the fuselage. This allowed the air that had been taken in through the inlet and had passed through the radiator assembly, to be expelled without the need for cumbersome 'cooling gills' which were a feature of the lower nose of the P-40. Instead, the heated air so-produced while passing through the radiator would be expelled out of a variable

The Curtiss XP-46 was the aircraft that some historians have claimed was the prototype for the Mustang. However, as can be seen in this view of the rather ugly XP-46 with its dated 1930's design layout, one would need to be having a nightmare to believe that such an archaic P-40-clone could ever have been the basis of the beautifully elegant and advanced Mustang design. The aircraft shown is believed to be the second of the two XP-46 prototypes, XP-46A 40-3054, which was the first of the two to fly on 15 February 1941. This was several months after the NA-73X took to the air. In the event the XP-46 had poor performance and no development potential, and thankfully for America's war effort it most definitely never entered production (Photo: Malcolm V. Lowe Collection)

outlet in a form of stream that actually created a small amount of rearward-thrust. This process is sometimes called the 'Meredith Effect', after the British scientist Frederick W. Meredith who had discovered the theoretical basis of this concept. It led to a very efficient system of engine cooling for the Mustang that was a major advance compared to the Curtiss P-40, and helped to give the Mustang a very distinctive side view profile.

However, the most significant of the new North American fighter's aerodynamic features regarded its wing. In this area the NAA designers were particularly bold in embracing a developing concept that had no real precedent in its practical employment. The new concept was that of the 'laminar flow' wing. Although the theory of laminar flow aerodynamics was not new, NAA was the first company to effectively put the concept to a successful use on a front-line warplane. Much research had been performed into laminar flow wing shapes by various individuals and by NACA, some of whose personnel eventually worked with NAA's designers to perfect the laminar flow wing for the new North American fighter. The laminar flow wing had a far different cross-section than that of a conventional wing shape. Its thickest point was further back than that of a conventional wing, creating different air flow characteristics over the wing in which the flow of air remained 'attached' to the wing for a greater part of the wing's chord than on a normal wing. This theoretically created less drag by reducing the amount of break-away of boundary air over the rear part of the wing's upper surface. A great deal of work went into getting this right for the Mustang, and the successful use of the laminar flow wing concept for the new fighter was one of the reasons for the type's excellent performance envelope and capability to fly long distances – although the latter was also the result of a considerable and very thoughtful provision for a large quantity of internal fuel.

Initially, however, the laminar flow wing design that was being pioneered for the Mustang did not work well in the wind-tunnel. During initial tests at the California Institute of Technology (Caltech), the wing design that Ed Horkey had been working on appeared to have stall characteristics that would have resulted in the design being discontinued if they could not be put right. However, it was suspected that the problem lay in the wind-tunnel itself, which was possibly not large enough to conduct satisfactory trials on a wooden replica of the new aircraft's wing. Subsequent tests were therefore carried out in a voluminous wind-tunnel at the University of Washington, and these proved that the wing design was more than acceptable. In the event the laminar flow wing proved to be an outstanding design for the Mustang, and the resulting wing cross-section was unique to the Mustang. However, although the laminar flow wing eventually worked well with the Mustang, it did not prove to be a wing design that was much favoured by other manufacturers.

The actual go-ahead for production of the new fighter was finally sealed in late May 1940, when Britain's Ministry of Aircraft Production officially signed for the first batch of 320 of the new NAA fighter. The initial date of the contract was 23 May, although it does not appear to have been formally brought into effect until 29 May. The project at last had its official go-ahead, and it was to be the start of an unrivalled success story. North American wasted no time in cutting metal for the prototype of the new fighter. Indeed, design work was still continuing when the first components were being fabricated. Despite the company's general lack of experience in the construction of high-performance fighters, the manufacture of the first example proceeded with few real hitches, so that the beautiful streamlined new aircraft quickly grew within the NAA facility at Inglewood. On 30 August 1940 it was ready to be rolled out into the California sunshine. This was an incredible achievement, and

one that those involved were justifiably proud of. The first appearance of this aircraft must have been quite a sight for those who were lucky enough to be present when the aircraft was rolled out to make its first appearance in the open air – even though it featured main wheels borrowed from the Harvard production line! To put the event into a wider context, at that time, the Battle of Britain was in deadly progress in the skies over southern England, and the country that had ordered the new aircraft was fighting for its very existence.

Experimental but Successful

The new fighter was company-funded by North American, and as such did not have a military serial number assigned to it. Instead it was allocated the US experimental civil registration NX19998. North American had originally thought of assigning the new aircraft the designation NA-50B, as a follow-on to the NA-50 and NA-50A single-seat fighters that had been developed from the two-seat NA-16 trainer series. However, the new fighter was very much a brand-new design, and as stated earlier it received instead the up-dated company title of NA-73. The prototype therefore received the designation NA-73X, because it was the first experimental machine of the NA-73 design. It was unarmed, but 'gun ports' appear to have been painted onto its wing leading edges at some point in its early life, to mimic the proposed layout of wing guns for the initial British production examples.

The construction of the new fighter had been comparatively smooth, but it was, however, not really yet ready for its first flight. A potentially worrying number of delays subsequently ensued, that centred mainly on the aircraft's power plant. The

Most aircraft are designed by a closely-knit team of designers, engineers, aerodynamicists and other skilled workers, but often one man in particular stands out. In the case of the Mustang, the father of the type was undoubtedly Edgar Schmued, despite later claims by some other NAA employees, although as usual it was a team of talented engineers and designers who were fully involved. In this image, Schmued can be seen either entering or exiting one of his progeny, a P-51 with the US military serial number 41-37322 (Photo: NAA)

Viewed from any angle the NA-73X was a beautiful aircraft. It's streamlined, clean and advanced shape was not only elegant, it also made the aircraft far more advanced than any other pursuit fighter design that was currently being built, or envisaged in the US. This appears to have created a level of animosity towards the aircraft from some personnel in the US military, which was a shame bearing in mind the excellent war record that the Mustang was later to achieve. This official company image was taken in the period before the NA-73X's first flight in October 1940
(Photo: NAA)

engine manufacturer Allison was unfortunately being increasingly overwhelmed as orders for its V-1710 inline engine continued to grow - and it was this engine type that North American needed for its new NA-73X. Mounting demands for Curtiss P-40 production and eventually for the P-39 Airacobra and the P-38 Lightning as well, were causing Allison many problems in gearing up for the type of mass-production that was completely unknown to the company in the past, but which was now needed for the total war that was developing. Programmes such as the P-40 had priority on engine production, and as the NA-73 project was essentially a private-venture concern for an overseas customer, North American could do nothing at all but wait for an Allison engine to be delivered so that it could be installed in the NA-73X. Eventually, in early October, a suitable engine was received, a 1,150 hp V-1710-F3R-series motor, and

work rapidly commenced on installing this power plant, and preparing the NA-73X to make its first flight.

The historic date for the maiden flight of the NA-73X was 26 October 1940. Surprisingly this date is little-known in aviation circles, yet it was on that day that the first flight took place of an aircraft that was to become one of aviation's great warplanes. The NA-73X was at last ready for its initial flight testing, and all it needed was a competent test pilot. In those far-off days, test pilots in the US tended to be celebrities who could command high payments for their services. Several were freelance, and North American needed a pilot from outside the company to fly the NA-73X. NAA of course had no experience in fighter development flying, except for that associated with the limited-production NA-50 and NA-50A adaptations of the two-seat NA-16 two-seat trainer series. Amongst the company's own test

Considerable activity surrounds the NA-73X while it is prepared for a test flight at Mines Field. The pilot in the cockpit is large enough to be the rather well-built Vance Breese, who flew the aircraft during its first four flights and who was a highly competent civil freelance test pilot. In his safe hands the first four flights were accomplished without mishap, but this situation was not to last when other pilots took over flight testing from Breese (Photo: NAA)

Civil-attired ground crew members of the NAA flight test team assist Vance Breese before a test flight in the NA-73X at Mines Field. In the capable hands of Breese the aircraft flew well right from the start, and although there were some minor difficulties to iron out these were not by any means serious, and had more to do with making the design suitable for military operation than with troublesome malfunctions. This again singled out the NA-73X from many other prototypes, because few military aircraft from the Mustang's era flew well right from the start, a notable exception of course being the superlative Spitfire in Britain *(Photo: NAA)*

Some military aircraft have been cancelled for mishaps of less magnitude than this, but fortunately the crash of the NA-73X did not even threaten to de-rail the whole Mustang programme. Paul Balfour's disastrous first flight during November 1940 in the NA-73X at Mines Field resulted in the aircraft finishing upside down in a ploughed field as shown here, in the vicinity of the NAA company premises. Despite being considerably damaged the aircraft was later repaired and flew again, but it was eventually retired from flight testing in the summer of 1941 and might have been donated to a school local to the NAA factories *(Photo: NAA)*

As can be seen in this rather unflattering image of the crashed NA-73X, the aircraft's civil registration was painted beneath the port wing. Bearing in mind the extensive damage that the NA-73X sustained during its crash-landing in November 1940 while being flown by Paul Balfour, it was a testament to NAA's engineers that it was repaired and made flyable again. Note the painted-on gun ports, in the style envisaged for the wing armament of three machine guns in each wing for the RAF's Mk.I production aircraft
(Photo: NAA)

pilots, probably the most senior was Paul Balfour, who had flown the first production derivative of the NA-16, the BT-9. He had also made the maiden flight of a further important new aircraft that NAA was developing, the twin-engine NA-40 design which eventually developed into the famed B-25 Mitchell medium bomber. He was not, however, a fighter pilot accustomed to the new breed of all-metal high-performance monoplane fighters that the NA-73X represented.

The solution for NAA was to hire Vance Breese, an accomplished freelance test pilot who would certainly know his way around the initial test flying an advanced aircraft like the NA-73X. Breese appears to have taken the job in his stride without great ceremony, and in so doing his name has been forever after linked to the Mustang story, although in reality he had little other connection with the type. So it was that Breese took the NA-73X aloft from Mines Field for its maiden flight on the morning of 26 October 1940. This historic flight lasted some twenty minutes, and Breese soon realised that the NA-73X was all that North American had claimed it to be. The aircraft flew well, and certainly seemed to be a sound design. The watching NAA personnel must have been relieved and at the same time satisfied at the result of this initial foray into the skies by the NA-73X. It was certainly a cause for some celebration for the British purchasing personnel, who had now effectively encouraged - without even an official specification - the creation of a new fighter for British service of considerable potential almost completely out of North American's similarly individual approach and initiative.

Test pilot Breese made three further flights in the NA-73X, all of them basically satisfactory. There was basically nothing wrong at all with the NA-73X, which flew well and displayed no real problems. Further and more detailed flight testing thereafter reverted to North American's own personnel. Unfortunately it was at this point that the whole Mustang programme could have come to a sticky end. Taking the NA-73X up on its fifth flight was NAA's Paul Balfour. Vance Breese appears to have had a low opinion of Balfour's abilities, and he was to be proven correct. Indeed there is an oft-quoted story that Breese made a bet that

Balfour would crash the NA-73X on his first outing in the aircraft. Breese was right. Balfour took off in the morning of 20 November 1940, the purpose of the flight being to fly at speed over Mines Field to explore the NA-73X's speed capabilities above set timing positions. Balfour must have been preoccupied with this work because after only around 12 minutes of flying time the NA-73X's Allison engine stopped running, with no fuel reaching the engine. Balfour had omitted to switch to another fuel tank, and the NA-73X immediately reverted to being a glider. Balfour attempted to turn the aircraft towards the active runway but lost height too quickly. The NA-73X touched down into a ploughed field some way short of the runway. With its undercarriage extended, the aircraft at once flipped over onto its back. The shiny new fighter was severely damaged. Balfour eventually scrambled clear of the wreck through a side cockpit window, the rigid turn-over structure and high rear fuselage line behind the cockpit having saved his life.

By that time the NA-73X had only flown some three-hours and twenty minutes. However, during that brief period the aircraft had shown that it was a potentially excellent flyer, and in any case the crash was in no way attributable to the machine itself. Fortunately both North American and more significantly the British had already seen the overwhelming worth of the new design. Plans for the production of the initial 320 aircraft for Britain were already well advanced, and thankfully no one appears to have given a thought to abandoning or scaling-down the project. Indeed, by then the British had already exercised the option for a second production batch of the new fighter, for in September 1940 a further 300 examples had been ordered. These, like the initial 320 aircraft, would be paid for by Britain under the 'cash and carry' arrangements then in force.

The NA-73X was carefully removed from its crash site by crane and it was eventually repaired, and made a number of further flights. Unfortunately a number of writers have claimed that the aircraft was a write-off and was replaced by a second prototype machine. This is completely incorrect, there was only ever one NA-73X. Paul Balfour was not as fortunate as the aircraft itself, however, and his place was taken by Robert

C. Chilton, who assumed the responsibility of chief of the flight testing for the new fighter. Chilton flew the NA-73X after its repair on 3 April 1941, and subsequently flew it twelve more times in addition to at least one other NAA pilot. Louis Wait, another of NAA's test pilots, appears to have similarly flown the aircraft during that period. By that point, however, the whole programme had moved on, and the NA-73X with its original-style under fuselage radiator inlet was no longer representative of the developing design. Sadly this nevertheless important prototype was seemingly eventually scrapped, after ceasing flying on or around 15 July 1941. American historian Michael O'Leary has suggested that it might have been donated to a local school, but what exactly happened to it remains something of a mystery.

Although the NA-73X was without doubt the only flying prototype of what became the Mustang, there was also a static test airframe, sometimes called the XX-73 in company documents, that was tested to destruction during the development phase of the type. However, the next actual aircraft to be built was the first of the 320 production aircraft that had been originally ordered by Britain in May 1940. These initial 320 aircraft were allocated the British military serial numbers AG345 to AG664, and received the company designation NA-73. In the event several of the early production examples in this block were used, mainly by NAA, for test and experimental purposes

relating to the whole Mustang development programme. Nevertheless, it is still a considerable accomplishment for the new aircraft that only one genuine prototype was needed, in stark contrast to many other contemporary designs which were usually only series produced after the construction of a whole selection of prototype and service test examples, together with months of flight testing.

Significantly for the whole programme, it was shortly after the crash of the NA-73X that the aircraft received a new name. In a letter from the British Purchasing Commission to North American dated 9 December 1940, it was officially announced that the name 'Mustang' had been chosen by the British for their new fighter. NAA appears to have accepted this naming without any further discussion, although the name 'Apache' had been favoured by some in the company. The NA-73 and its derivatives forever after became known to the British, Americans, and just about everyone else, as the Mustang. There have been many explanations as to why the name Mustang was chosen for the new fighter, but whatever the reason it proved to be a very appropriate title. The fiery wild horses of the southern parts of the US that already enjoyed the name of Mustang have always been in a class of their own, and the new fighter was to prove of similar stature.

Although apparently re-touched, this image of the NA-73X gives a good idea of the aircraft's undoubted elegance and excellent streamlining. The photograph was probably taken after the NA-73X's unfortunate crash in November 1940, after the aircraft had been made airworthy again (Photo: NAA)

The NA-73X was rolled out bearing no obvious markings, but later in its flight test career it wore pseudo US military markings - even though it was never taken on charge by the US military. In any case the addition of rudder stripes suggests that the picture was taken during the period leading up to the famous crash of this aircraft on 20 November 1940 - or more likely after the aircraft had been repaired following its accident (Photo: NAA)

Britain's Finest

Chapter 2

AG345 was the very first
production Mustang to be
built. It made its first flight in
April 1941. Officially a
Mustang Mk.I, it was later
painted in RAF camouflage of
Dark Green/Dark Earth/Sky,
sprayed with American
DuPont paint equivalents to
the British shades (the Sky
colour has been described by
some observers as a marked
blue-grey shade). In the event
this aircraft was not delivered
to Britain and was instead
retained by NAA for a number
of trials and test work. As can
be seen in this view, it bore
the British serial number
AG345 in small characters on
the rudder, and in larger
characters beneath the port
wing. It has the early-type
short carburettor air intake
ahead of the windscreen
(Photo: NAA)

The first production and initial aircraft for Britain were officially designated as Mustang Mk.I. The very first of these, serial number AG345, made its maiden flight from Mines Field on 23 April 1941 (although a number of subsequent published sources have quoted 16 April). This was somewhat behind the schedule that had been agreed in April and May 1940, in which the first aircraft should have been delivered to Britain in January 1941. As pointed out in earlier in this Book, the armament that the British had chosen for this initial Mustang production version comprised eight machine guns - two Browning 0.5-in in the lower cowling, synchronised and firing through the propeller arc, and one of these machine guns in each wing, plus two further 0.3-in machine guns in each wing, alongside the wing 0.5-in machine guns. Due to the debate that was instituted as to the actual armament that would be fitted in the wings of the British Mustangs, there has been some confusion over the years as to which guns went in which positions in the wings of these very first production aircraft. Interestingly there has additionally been some debate as to whether all of these aircraft were armed with 0.3-in or 0.303-in machine guns in the relevant wing positions. The 0.303-in machine was a British weapon, whereas the 0.3-in was American. Documentation on this point that dates from the time suggests quite strongly that the weapons were 0.3-in, although there has been some suggestion since the war that a number of aircraft were fitted with 0.303-in machine guns following delivery to Britain. This would make sense, particularly if guns needed to be replaced for whatever reason, as the American o.3-in would have been less readily available in the UK compared to the ubiquitous 0.303-in weapon which was standard fit for British made warplanes.

The Mustang Mk.I generally resembled the unarmed NA-73X prototype, but there were also important differences in addition to the provision of armament and its associated sighting and 'plumbing'. One of these changes was the adoption of a revised windscreen layout. In this respect the NA-73X had a smart, one-piece curved windscreen, more akin to a racing aeroplane than a warplane. This was, of course, unsuitable for military operations. The Mustang Mk.I production batch introduced a framed windscreen arrangement with a flat Plexiglas panel ahead of the pilot. The initial Mustang Mk.I production aircraft retained the NA-73X's short carburettor air intake on the top of the cowling, but introduced early in the production run was a lengthened intake that began just behind the propeller arc. This became standard for all subsequent Allison-Mustang production aircraft. There was also some tinkering with the shape of the under fuselage radiator air intake, which as related in the previous Chapter was a major feature of the Allison-engined Mustang design. Although this lower mid-fuselage location proved in practice to work well, it was found that some adjustment was necessary especially with the intake arrangement itself. The original shape as pioneered on the NA-73X prototype was engineered so that the top of the intake was flush with the lower surface of the wing centre section. This design was found during flight testing to be at the mercy of boundary air close to the lower surface of the fuselage. Once identified, this problem was easily and effectively cured by creating a small but nonetheless significant gap between the aircraft's lower surface and a newly created top to the intake itself. A neatly curved shape just behind the intake's front edge allowed the boundary layer air to escape along the sides of the intake and lower fuselage.

Initial Deliveries

The first production Mustang Mk.I, AG345, was retained by NAA for testing and development work and never reached Britain. It was therefore the second production example, AG346 that was the first Mustang to be delivered to the customer. This took place during October 1941, some nine months after the originally-planned delivery schedule of January 1941. Disassembled, AG346 was crated and shipped in the hold of a cargo ship across the North Atlantic. It arrived at Liverpool docks on 24 October 1941, and was subsequently reassembled

The first Mustang off the production line was AG345. Never delivered to the customer and used for trials and testing work by NAA related to the overall Mustang production effort, as can be viewed in this image it carried its British serial number beneath the port wing and had its wing gun ports taped over, or at least covered in some way. The lower forward fuselage machine gun ports are also devoid of armament *(Photo: NAA)*

at Liverpool's Speke airfield. It was the first of many Mustangs that would be so delivered in the forthcoming years. A number of published sources have claimed that AG346 was duly assigned, in November 1941, to the test and evaluation airfield at Boscombe Down in southern England. This Wiltshire airfield had been the home, since the start of World War Two, of the A&AEE – the Aeroplane and Armament Experimental Establishment. Significant evaluation work was carried out there on all aircraft types intended for front-line British military service. However, the A&AEE's own records appear to disprove the assignment of AG346 there at that time, with the first Mustang actually being recorded as delivered to Boscombe Down being AG351. Nevertheless, various official photographs were made of AG346 seemingly at Boscombe Down during that period, and these are interestingly dated November 1941. Whatever the case, the arrival of AG351 or AG346 in November 1941 represented the start of a long connection between the Mustang and the A&AEE that lasted to the end of the war, during which much useful evaluation and service testing was carried out.

Back in Southern California at NAA's Mines Field facilities, production of the Mustang had started comparatively slowly. Nevertheless, it quickly built up to a considerable rate. The Mustang was a well-designed aircraft that was comparatively easy to mass-produce. The NAA factories were also laid out on the most up-to-date principles, with moving assembly procedures and an increasingly skilled and well-paid workforce. Indeed NAA was able to institute a recruitment drive in the Los Angeles and Southern California area for skilled tradesmen specifically for its Mustang production line. All of these positives were in stark contrast to the Curtiss P-40, which NAA had successfully avoided building under licence for the British. The P-40 was not a particularly easy aircraft to manufacture, and NAA's top personnel had felt all along that its cumbersome structures and design would not have suited their own forward-looking production techniques and capabilities. They were completely correct.

The British employed a number of technical representatives

Pictured on a company test flight prior to delivery, this Mustang Mk.I actually wears US national insignia of the early 1940's period. It was painted in RAF camouflage of Dark Green/Dark Earth/Sky, sprayed with American DuPont paint equivalents to the British shades. It must always be remembered that Mustangs painted in the NAA facilities were finished in US paint equivalents to British official colours *(Photo: NAA)*

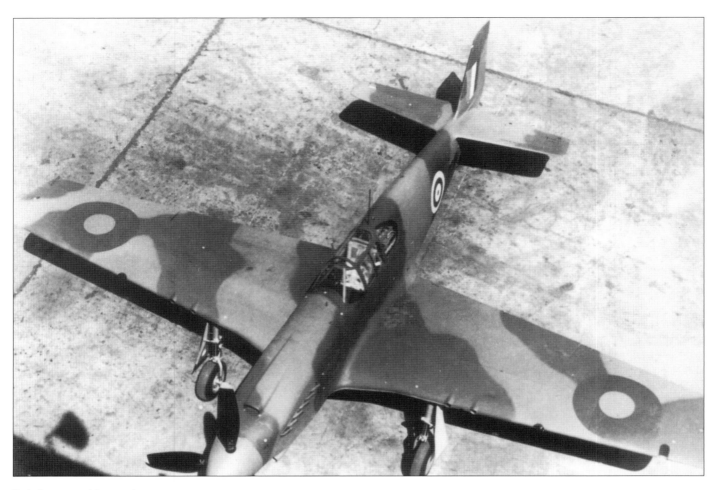

Illustrating some useful details, this virtually plan view image of AG348, the fourth production Mustang Mk.I, shows British national insignia together with the camouflage pattern of Dark Green/Dark Earth uppersurfaces, and the short carburettor air intake on top of the forward fuselage. The soft sprayed edges to the camouflage colours are noteworthy. Often this aircraft has been incorrectly claimed to have been completed for US service as an XP-51 prototype *(Photo: NAA)*

who worked closely with North American on many aspects of the early Mustang production programme. There was always a very positive level of co-operation between the British and NAA, and this relationship existed virtually without cease throughout the war. As previously related, during 1940 the British had set up an overall organisation to oversee the aviation-related North American purchasing effort. Called the British Air Commission, this co-ordinated the work of the British Purchasing Commission and other procurement organisations, and communicated directly with the Ministry of Aircraft Production in London. A letter from the British Air Commission dated 25 June 1941, to the Ministry of Aircraft

Production, stated that the fourth production Mustang for the British order, AG348, would be completed on or around 30 June 1941, and would be representative of the subsequent production standard – although it is interesting to note that contemporary photographs show this aircraft to have initially been fitted with the short carburettor intake above the engine, rather than the longer production-standard intake that began just behind the propeller. Nonetheless, from thence onwards, manufacture of the Mustang against the two initial British orders gathered pace quite quickly.

In fact the whole Mustang programme started to move forward with increasing momentum in a very positive way.

A very historic aircraft, as far as British procurement of the Mustang was concerned. The first production Mustang to be shipped to Britain was this aircraft, Mustang Mk.I AG346. It is seen here prior to dismantling before being crated and transported to Britain by sea. As can be seen, it had the short carburettor air intake on the top of the cowling behind the spinner, which was characteristic of very early production Mustangs *(Photo: NAA)*

Due to this build-up in production, increasing numbers of Mustangs and related spares started to be shipped to Britain late in 1941 and early in 1942, following the initial arrival of AG346. The common procedure was for each finished aircraft to be flight tested upon completion at the NAA factory, before being disassembled and crated in purpose-built wooden packing crates. It is unfortunately unclear from NAA's surviving documentation as to how extensive this initial flight testing for each aircraft was. However, a guide can be judged from the Goodyear Aircraft Company, which built Corsair fighters under the FG designation for British naval operation later in the war – these aircraft were usually flown for a total of two hours, commonly in two separate flights, to check out the basic systems and to ensure that the engine, undercarriage and other primary features functioned correctly. In the case of the Mustang, this flight test work was performed by NAA test pilots, although the British appear to have had at least one acceptance test pilot at Mines Field/Inglewood (the name 'Inglewood' was starting to be more widely used at this time) as a part of the process. Mustangs for the initial British contracts were generally shipped from the east coast of the

United States via the dangerous North Atlantic route, and were usually carried by merchant vessels. These waters were extremely dangerous by mid to late 1941, with German submarines (U-Boats) and long-range anti-shipping aircraft taking a steady toll of the merchant ships that carried a considerable variety of essential goods and war material from North America to Britain. At least twenty of these early Mustangs went to the bottom en route when the ships that they were being transported in were sunk.

It is interesting to note that amongst the documentation from those difficult times that is held in Britain's National Archives at Kew outside London, there is reference to an offer for the Mustangs to be delivered by air. The correspondence is from British purchasing representatives to the Ministry of Aircraft Production in London, and concerned what was described as an offer from 'US Ferrying Command' to fly the aircraft to Britain. Of course this could not have been accomplished non-stop (even though the Mustang's range capabilities were second to none amongst warplanes of that period). Instead, any ferry flights would have needed a stage-by-stage delivery, but would have certainly mirrored what

AG348 was an early Mustang Mk.I that shows off well in this view the wing gun ports, for three machine guns in each wing, of the Mustang Mk.I. This gave the early Mustangs, in addition to the two machine guns mounted in the lower forward fuselage, a considerable punch. Although delivered to Britain, this aircraft was later transferred by Britain to the Soviet Union
(Photo: NAA)

Seen here in late 1941 or early 1942 ostensibly during assignment to the A&AEE Boscombe Down in the south of England, AG346 was the earliest numbered Mustang Mk.I to reach Britain. By the time of this photograph (which is dated November 1941) the aircraft had been refitted with the longer carburettor air intake above the forward fuselage
(Photo: R.L. Ward Collection)

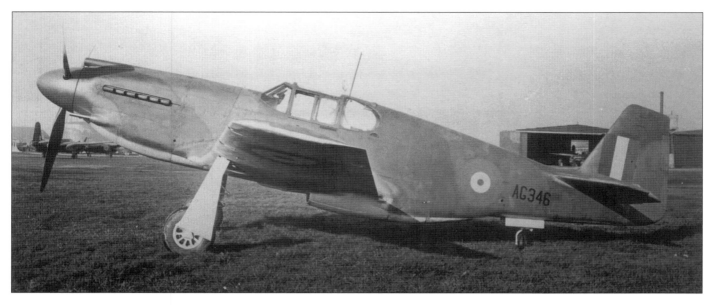

AG346 was the subject of considerable interest at Boscombe Down during its evaluation by the A&AEE. Generally the pilots at Boscombe Down were positive in their appraisal of the type, and up to the late stages of World War Two a number of Mustangs were on the books of the A&AEE for a wide variety of trials and evaluation work
(Photo: R.L. Ward Collection)

happened later in the war when considerable numbers of larger American aircraft of various different types were flown across what developed into the North Atlantic and South Atlantic ferry routes – but usually for subsequent US service. In the event, the British did not take up this kind offer of delivery by air, and the early Mustangs continued to cross the Atlantic to Britain by surface in merchant ships.

Results of the early testing of the Mustang I AG351 at the A&AEE Boscombe Down, and subsequent analysis in Britain of further Mustangs during the early months of 1942, confirmed many of the good points of the new fighter. However, a major vice also showed up. A growing number of RAF pilots flew the type, in addition to Boscombe Down's own test pilots. In addition to the necessary test work that was carried out at Boscombe Down, the Mustang was also introduced to the Air Fighting Development Unit (AFDU) at Duxford in Cambridgeshire. Comparative flights were made alongside Spitfires and eventually against a captured Messerschmitt Bf 109E (although that particular type was by then being superseded by newer and more capable marks of Bf 109). The overall impression was that the Mustang was a fine aircraft to fly, with good flying characteristics and few real bad points in its handling and operation. The eight-gun armament was found to consist of 0.5-in and 0.3-in machine guns, with little vibration when the guns were fired. The cockpit was well laid out, and from a maintenance point of view the Mustang was much easier to look after, with good access particularly for its engine, compared to most other contemporary American

fighters. Fitted with the Allison V-1710-39 (F3R) series engine of 1,150 hp, the Mustang I was clocked in Boscombe Down's tests to be able to attain a maximum speed of 370 mph (595km/h) at 15,000 ft (4,572m). This compared well with the contemporary Spitfire Mk.Vs maximum of slightly over 340 mph (547km/h). Its range on internal fuel was an outstanding 960 miles (1,545km). This gave a potential endurance of approximately four hours, which was roughly double that of the Spitfire Mk.V. Indeed, throughout its service life, one of the Mustang's great strengths was its exemplary range capability. Even these early, quite austere Mustangs were well ahead in terms of range and endurance compared to contemporary Allied single-engine fighters. The Mustang Mk.I had a total internal fuel capacity of 140 gallons (636lt), of which some 130 gallons (591lt) were usable, spread amongst fuselage and wing internal fuel tanks. From the first, North American's designers had provided for plenty of fuel capacity within the Mustang. This was one of the many practical innovations that NAA brought to contemporary fighter design.

However, there was one major problem with the new fighter. This was not a fault of the Mustang's design, but was a significant shortcoming with its power plant. The Allison V-1710 was simply not a good engine for high altitude work – and indeed in the rather austere version that was fitted in these early Mustangs, it was never intended to be anything other than a low-altitude engine. As previously stated, the Mustang Mk.I's top speed was attainable at 15,000ft (4,572m), and although the type had a theoretical service ceiling of 30,000 ft

This excellent front view of AG346 apparently photographed at Boscombe Down, again dated November 1941, illustrates in particular the slightly staggered nature of the three gun ports in the leading edge of each wing. The central of the three appeared from the front to be lower, although it was in fact set slightly back from the leading edge of the wing
(Photo: R.L. Ward Collection)

(9,144m), in reality its performance fell away dramatically the higher that it was flown. It appears to have become quite a handful to fly at heights above 25,000ft (7,620m). Indeed, in practice many RAF pilots found that the type came into its own at or below 9,000 ft (2,743m), and some were able to get the best speeds from the Mustang at around that height. The Spitfire Mk.V actually climbed faster (taking seven minutes to reach 20,000 ft (6,096m) instead of the Mustang's eleven minutes), and was considerably lighter at around 6,900 lb (3,130kg) maximum take-off weight compared to the 8,622lb (3,911kg) of the Mustang Mk.I. As an interesting aside to this latter point, later in the Allison-Mustang's career the type was evaluated by the Russians for potential Soviet service using aircraft supplied from Britain. The Russians concluded - as related later in this book - that the Mustang was a heavy fighter and was not suitable for Soviet military service.

The Allison V-1710, in reality, was a somewhat under-developed engine, and although its turbo-supercharged variants (as used, for example, in the P-38 Lightning) were good enough at high altitude, the versions of this engine that did not have turbo (i.e., exhaust augmented) supercharging were poor performers at higher altitudes. The V-1710-39 series engine that powered the early Mustangs of course did not have a turbo, but was fitted with a simple mechanical single-stage, single-speed supercharger that did little to augment the engine's performance. This shortcoming became very obvious early on, during the British service evaluation of the type. British experience in the air war over North-west Europe had shown that any fighter worth its spurs would be able to take on the best of the German fighters at low, medium, or high altitude as required. The Allison-engined Mustang simply did not fit these performance criteria as a front-line fighter. Fortunately for the RAF, the Supermarine Spitfire was constantly being developed and updated, including its continuing ability to match the best German fighters and to fight at higher altitudes as increasingly more powerful and capable versions of the excellent Rolls-Royce Merlin inline engine were fitted to newer versions of the type.

Such potential shortcomings in the Allison-engined Mustang's performance were therefore not a major problem. In addition, by early 1942 Britain had been saved from the immediate threat of German invasion. It had been this threat, and the potential shortfall in front-line warplanes to meet it that had, in the first place, been a major motivator in the creation of the Mustang. On the contrary, the fight was by early 1942 starting to be taken to the Germans over occupied Europe in an increasingly robust fashion, and there was a growing need for combat aircraft that were capable of operating offensively at lower levels for ground-attack missions that could nevertheless defend themselves if challenged by opposing fighters. In addition, there was starting to be a related and equally significant need for fast, armed reconnaissance, as Britain began to develop her aerial capability and gather intelligence to increasingly act as an offensive rather than a largely defensive force in what was coming to be called the European Theatre of Operations or ETO, namely North-west Europe. It was fortuitous for the Mustang that it arrived on the scene at just the right time to fit perfectly into several of these new and developing roles. At low levels the Mustang was fast, manoeuvrable and was found to be a relatively good gun platform. The initial combat use of the Mustang therefore came to be in the fast, armed reconnaissance and light ground-attack roles, for which the Allison-engined Mustangs were gradually introduced into service. They proved to be fantastic performers in this new combat reality.

Low-Level Genius

The RAF organisation that was charged with the air-ground co-operation that was implied in the attack and tactical reconnaissance roles that the Mustang appeared to be suited was Army Co-operation Command (ACC). Created in December 1940, this organisation aimed to develop a close working relationship between tactical air and ground formations, something that had been disastrously lacking in the abortive British operations in France against the invading Germans in May 1940. In those days the relationship between air and ground forces had been totally and disastrously inadequate, a problem exacerbated by a lack of modern equipment such as radios, often little knowledge of the distribution and strength of enemy forces, and most seriously by a shortage of high performance aircraft. During its early days the Army Co-operation Command operated the Westland Lysander and, increasingly, the Curtiss Tomahawk. The first RAF squadron to fly the Tomahawk was No.26 Squadron, which started to receive the type in February 1941. This unit had flown the Lysander in France during May 1940 and probably welcomed the transition onto higher performance aircraft. Just over two hundred Tomahawks appear to have been assigned to ACC, but the type proved to be inadequate for this developing role and was as quickly as possible removed from operations in North-west Europe as better alternatives came along. Nevertheless the Tomahawk was a quantum leap in performance over the Lysander, and was a useful start in the

Mustang Mk.I AG346 underwent important evaluation at Boscombe Down, in the period before the type entered combat with the RAF. This side view shows the very individual wing section of the Mustang at the wing tip, with its laminar flow characteristics in which the thickest point was much further back than on conventional airfoils
(Photo: R.L. Ward Collection)

Wearing a circular yellow 'P' marking on its fuselage side denoting a prototype or experimental type, Mustang Mk.I AG351 was amongst the earliest Mustangs to reach Britain. It spent some time with the Air Fighting Development Unit (AFDU) undergoing relevant trials
(Photo: Malcolm V. Lowe Collection)

It was during the first half of 1942 and into the summer of that year that the Mustang was gradually assimilated into RAF service. This was a year before the type entered US operations. Early operational RAF Mustangs were re-painted with grey paint replacing the original Dark Earth areas in which early production aircraft were painted delivered. On some Mustangs a distinguishing chord-wise yellow band was painted for a short time on the wing surfaces as seen in this view. The nearest aircraft is Mk.I AL982 (Photo: via Chris Ellis)

embryonic growth of the closer and more effective working together of land and air power, and in the birth of effective tactical reconnaissance.

It was in this operational environment that the stage was thus set for the Mustang to make its operational debut. On 5 December 1941 an early Mustang Mk.I, AG349, was shown off to the Press at Speke airfield, as a shining new example of US equipment for the RAF. Unfortunately it does not appear to have received a glittering amount of publicity, and ironically it was displayed alongside an early Curtiss Kittyhawk (i.e. a later mark of P-40, subsequent to the Tomahawk, and similar to a US P-40 Warhawk) – a type that was already virtually obsolete compared to the sleek new Mustang. The first RAF unit to receive initial examples of the Mustang I was No.26 Squadron. This unit had been the first to transition onto the Tomahawk, and in January 1942 the squadron's first Mustang was received for initial familiarisation. To begin with the squadron was based at RAF Gatwick in the south of England (now the site of one of London's international airports), and No.26 Squadron's roles included the transition of the Mustang into service and a thorough evaluation of the type's operational capabilities. No.41 Operational Training Unit (OTU) at RAF Old Sarum in Wiltshire (formerly the Training Squadron of No.1 School of

Army Co-operation) also began its transition training on the type. Elements of No.26 Squadron moved to RAF Weston Zoyland in Somerset for a thorough shake-down of the Mustang in an operational environment. As 1942 continued a number of further squadrons started to fly the new American fighter. These included No.241 Squadron in February/March 1942, No.2 in March 1942, Nos. 16 and 268 in April 1942, No.239 in May 1942, and No.613 Squadron in June 1942. During the summer of 1942 the first two of three Royal Canadian Air Force (RCAF) squadrons that eventually operated the early Allison-engined Mustangs, Nos.400 and 414 Squadrons, began flying the Mustang. They were joined from January 1943 onwards by No.430 Squadron, RCAF. These RCAF units flew as a part of the RAF but were predominantly manned by Canadian personnel. No.613 'City of Manchester' Squadron, on the other hand, was a Royal Auxiliary Air Force unit that had existed as an army co-operation squadron since its creation in March 1939 and had close links with the city of Manchester. It had formerly flown Hawker Hector biplanes, Lysanders and then Tomahawks (in reality these types overlapped in service, and a dwindling number of Lysanders persisted some way into the Mustang era) before transitioning onto the Mustang Mk.I as its main equipment.

At last in the Front-Line

In the event it was No.26 Squadron, however, that had the privilege of being the first to take the Mustang officially into combat. On 10 May 1942 (interestingly, a number of sources claim that it was 5 May), a low-level armed reconnaissance in the area of Berck on the northern French coast to the south of Boulogne was flown by a single Mustang Mk.I of No.26 Squadron from Gatwick. Its pilot, Flying Officer G.N. Dawson, thus commenced what was to become the Mustang's illustrious combat career. On this first-ever operational Mustang sortie, Dawson 'beat-up' Berck airfield and fired at a goods train before returning safely to Gatwick.

This initial Mustang combat operation had come several months since the Mustang had entered squadron service, but the comparative lethargy with which the Mustang was committed to combat illustrated the fact that at that time there was no immediate need to hurry the aircraft into action.

Rather, the Mustangs and their pilots mixed working-up alongside exercises with army units, and well into the Mustang's combat service these joint air-ground exercises continued to be rotated with actual operational flying. They gave valuable training in the developing use of air and ground assets in a much more combined way that allowed both to work effectively together – a factor that would be very important in the later stages of World War Two following the Allied invasion of Europe in June 1944. One of the most important of these was a major exercise code-named 'Spartan' that took place in East Anglia during March 1943.

In addition, and equally significantly, the Army Co-operation Mustangs similarly gained important and interrelated roles in gathering intelligence and photographic records of occupied Europe. To that end a modification programme had already commenced that saw many Mustangs fitted with a camera behind the pilot's seat, on a mounting

Underlining the fact that the British wanted to show off the Mustang, a well-known set of publicity photographs was made with No.26 Squadron in the summer of 1942, in addition to the large number of photographs that were taken of No.2 Squadron Mustang Mk.Is during that time. Here, Mustang Mk.I AM148 RM-G is seen in a view dated August 1942. This aircraft was from the second batch of production Mustang Mk.I and so was an NA-83 (as opposed to the earlier NA-73 batch), and operated with No.26 Squadron, RAF, the first squadron to receive the Mustang. This unit was also the first to take the type into combat, in May 1942
(Photo: R.L. Ward Collection)

The well-photographed Mustang Mk.I AM148/RM-G of No.26 Squadron in flight during August 1942. By that time the uppersurface colours had changed for Mustangs to Dark Green with a grey shade, either Mixed Grey or Dark Grey or similar (later Ocean Grey was standardised), with Medium Sea Grey undersides. The fuselage band and spinner were painted in Sky. As a further distinguishing feature, the outer wing leading edges were yellow *(Photo: R.L. Ward Collection)*

Amongst the first squadrons to transition on to the Mustang were two Canadian-manned units, Nos.400 and 414 Squadrons, RCAF. Of these, No.400 Squadron was allocated the codes 'SP' which were originally worn on its Lysanders and Tomahawks, before the squadron moved onto the Mustang in the summer of 1942. Shown here is Mustang Mk.I AG528 SP-B *(Photo: via Chris Ellis)*

Although most photographs that were taken on the well-known 1942 air-to-air photo shoot with No.2 Squadron Mustang Mk.Is have become quite familiar, this particular view is rarely published. It appears to show a rather precarious break to starboard by AG550 XV-U, which must have put the Mustang very close to the camera aircraft! *(Photo: Malcolm V. Lowe Collection)*

above and in front of the Mustang's radio equipment, looking backwards and downwards to the left through the rear-vision clear panel behind the main cockpit glazing. Some aircraft had this window partly painted over with just the camera's lens visible. The camera employed for this work was the F.24 type (called the K.24 by the Americans who also manufactured it under licence and used this very useful piece of equipment for their own reconnaissance), which created a five-inch (12.7cm) square negative on a roll of film from which very high-quality and detailed black and white photographs could be made. After some trial and error it was determined that the best pictures came from the Mustang flying a left-hand bank, with the camera 'aimed' using a sighting mark painted on the left-hand wing upper surface which could be aligned with the subject to be photographed. The photographs could be taken at heights up to approximately 9,000 feet (2,743m). Such a procedure allowed good-quality photographs to be taken, and it also gave the aircraft some protection because a banking aircraft was less easy to hit with ground fire than one flying predictably straight and level. Some squadrons preferred their Mustangs to work alone, but others developed tactics for two Mustangs to operate together, with one aircraft delegated to take the photographs while the second acted as a 'Weaver' to defend the first and to look out for enemy air activity.

In essence, although the Mustangs were tasked with armed reconnaissance and light ground-attack roles against enemy targets that presented themselves during individual sorties, they were encouraged not to go looking for a fight with enemy aircraft and so risk the valuable photographs and intelligence that they were gathering. Of course if they were met during their low-level sorties by enemy fighters, the Mustangs were capable of looking after themselves - even against the increasingly widespread and very potent Focke-Wulf Fw 190A fighter of the Luftwaffe - which had not been the case with the previous Lysanders and Tomahawks that the new American fighter was replacing. The worth of the Mustang was soon very apparent, although there were minor problems to iron out as the type began to see widespread service within the RAF's light ground-attack and tactical reconnaissance or Tac/R squadrons. One of these difficulties concerned the Allison V-1710 engines of the Mustangs. These proved to be somewhat unreliable, and although some ran well, others appeared to need considerable attention. Some squadrons had a resident technical expert from Allison assigned to help in the maintenance and operation of the engines. Another problem concerned the famous air scoop intake beneath the fuselage for

the Mustang's radiator and oil cooler. This tended to collect debris while on the ground that was blown into the opening by the rearwards wash from the aircraft's propeller when Mustangs operated from grass or other unprepared surfaces – which they were often called upon to do. It also became apparent that no matter how clever this installation was regarding the cooling of the engine and the extra rearwards thrust that it potentially generated, it helped to make the Mustang a very difficult aircraft to successfully belly-land when required – and emergency landings on water were regarded to be definitely avoided if at all possible.

First Aerial Victory

Following several weeks of comparatively limited but increasingly more widespread combat flying, the real baptism of fire for the RAF's Mustang squadrons came during the unsuccessful Dieppe operation in August 1942. Code-named Operation 'Jubilee', the amphibious landings by a combined Allied force on the French coast at Dieppe on 19 August 1942 were a complete shambles, resulting in considerable loss of life. Although valuable lessons were learned for future operations, this sort of so-called 'reconnaissance in force' was not tried again. The Dieppe operation also saw the first really widespread use by the RAF of the Mustang in strength. Specifically supporting the landings were four Mustang squadrons that had been drawn into a new organisation within ACC, a wing that comprised several squadrons based at the same airfield. No.35 Wing included Nos. 26, 239, 400, and 414 Squadrons and was based at Gatwick. Of course many other Allied air assets were involved in the Dieppe operation, including a considerable number of fighters and medium bombers, but the Mustangs were tasked with reconnaissance of German positions and deployments in and around the Dieppe area, plus the support where practical of the Allied forces on the ground and landing areas. During the ensuing aerial operations, No.35 Wing's Mustangs ran into considerable German anti-aircraft fire from the ground, and a number of combats took place with Luftwaffe fighters. During the course of seventy-two sorties that day no less than nine Mustangs were shot down, including five from No.26 Squadron and one Canadian-operated aircraft – the day's operations marked the real combat debut for No.35 Wing's Canadian squadrons.

However, there was one piece of good news from the day's sometimes quite ferocious aerial fighting. During the Dieppe operation, the Mustang reached a very significant milestone. Flying Officer Hollis Hills, an American volunteer serving with

XV-W of No.2 Squadron shows off all the relevant features of the Mustang Mk.I during the early period of RAF service of the Mustang. The type proved to be well-liked by its pilots, and it represented a huge leap forward over the Lysanders and Tomahawks that it replaced *(Photo: R.L. Ward Collection)*

Want to Buy a Mustang?

The Mustang was originally created by North American Aviation as a private-venture in response to Britain's original needs for increased Curtiss P-40 manufacture. But eventually it became an indispensable combat aircraft for the US military as well as for Britain, and in terms of money it was without doubt one of the most cost-effective warplanes of World War Two. Due to the unique way in which the Mustang was born, neither the British nor later the Americans needed to put the Mustang through an extensive tendering, evaluation, fly-off against competing designs, or major service testing prior to acceptance of the type into service, one of the few modern military aircraft to be so procured. In its production forms the Mustang was similarly cost-effective. During the initial contract negotiations between British purchasing representatives and North American Aviation in 1940, the intended unit price for the initial production Mustangs (which were Mustang Mk.I aircraft for the RAF) was $40,000 (equipped and armed). However, when mass-production against US contracts eventually took place, the price of a new Mustang saw some changes, but the type still remained remarkable value for money. In 1942, when mass production was still comparatively new to the project, a Mustang cost $58,698, but by 1945 this had dropped, for a new Merlin-engined P-51D Mustang including some government furnished equipment to $50,985. This compares with $97,147 for a P-38 Lightning, $83,001 for a P-47 Thunderbolt (1945 production) and $44,892 (1944 figures, prior to production end) for a late-model P-40 Warhawk. Although the Warhawk was cheaper, it was never the overwhelmingly successful aircraft that the Mustang was. Against those comparison figures, and bearing in mind the combat effectiveness of the Mustang, the P-51 was certainly a bargain. At the end of the war, a new lightweight P-51H cost $54,476. A number of Mustangs were 'bought' in war bonds initiatives or by the generosity of individuals or organisations, but the overwhelming majority were paid for by the US government, excepting of course the initial 620 Mustang Mk.I which were directly purchased by Britain.

the RCAF's No.414 Squadron, claimed an Fw 190 in the vicinity of Dieppe to mark the very first enemy aircraft to be shot down by a Mustang. It was certainly not the last. It was indeed appropriate that the first-ever Mustang air-to-air victory was achieved by an American pilot, flying an RAF-operated Mustang - although, to add to the international flavour of the occasion, the pilot and the Mustang concerned were assigned to a Royal Canadian Air Force squadron. Flying Officer Hollis 'Holly' Hills, was born in Baxter, Iowa, in March 1915, and became one of a comparatively small but significant selection of Americans who became members of the RCAF to fight against the Germans prior to the United States' official entry into World War Two. He joined the RCAF in September 1940 for flight training, and in October 1941 he was posted to No.414 'City of Sarnia' or 'Sarnia Imperials' Squadron, RCAF, which had formed at RAF Croydon in August of that year. At the time of Hills' arrival the squadron was flying the Curtiss Tomahawk, and it was not until the summer of 1942 that No.414 began converting to the Mustang Mk.I. The squadron was not completely operational when the Dieppe operation came around on 19 August 1942, but some of the unit's pilots were nevertheless involved from the start.

On the early morning of 19 August, Hills took off with fellow squadron pilot Flt. Lt. 'Freddie' Clarke for an armed reconnaissance in the Dieppe area. They made their second such foray later in the day, by which time the whole Dieppe operation was already going badly wrong. Hills was acting as 'Weaver' for Clarke, the two intending to cover the road from Abbeville to Dieppe and watch for German movements. As the two 414 Squadron pilots headed for the French coast at very low altitude, Hills spotted a flight of four Focke-Wulf Fw 190s higher but on a course that would place them favourably behind the two Mustangs. Hills called a warning several times to Clarke about the Fw 190s but Clarke's radio had failed. Oblivious of the threat, Clarke received fire from the lead Fw 190 which hit his Mustang hard. Hills intervened and tried to cut off the lead Focke-Wulf, but instead he was engaged by the lead Fw 190's wingman. In the ensuing foray Hills successfully manoeuvred behind the second Fw 190 and hit it with at least two bursts from his Mustang's mixed machine gun armament. The Fw 190's engine caught fire and

Many photographs were taken of No.2 Squadron Mustangs while this famous RAF unit worked-up on the Mustang Mk.I during the summer of 1942. By that time the United States was well and truly in the war, and the British were keen to publicize the shiny new fighter from the US for RAF service, virtually limitless supplies of which could be supplied for taking on the Germans in occupied Europe. Here XV-V is seen over a very typical English backdrop *(Photo: R.L. Ward Collection)*

its canopy came off. It crashed into trees somewhere along the Abbeville road leading to Dieppe.

Hills immediately went looking for Clarke, and spotted him heading for Dieppe harbour streaming glycol and being chased by the lead Fw 190. Hills managed to catch the pair and distracted the German pilot by firing at his aircraft enough to cause him to break off his chase of Clarke and instead come after Hills. The two engaged in a low-level game of 'cat and mouse' for several minutes before the German gave up the encounter and headed inland. Clarke had meanwhile succeeded, with considerable airmanship to 'pancake' his Mustang into Dieppe harbour. He is believed to have been at that time the first pilot to have survived a Mustang ditching in water. Saved by an unknown soldier or sailor who swam to the ditched Mustang and pulled him to safety, Clarke was returned to England by ship and later reunited with Hills. He was duly able to confirm Hills' shoot-down of the Fw 190.

In the New Year's Honours List for 1943 'Holly' Hills received a Mentioned in Dispatches for his actions that day. The real unsung hero of the brief but frantic action that brought about the Mustang's first aerial victory was Hills' Mustang. A Mk.I from the initial production batch for the RAF, it had the serial number AG470 and carried the code letters RU-M. Hills himself achieved ace status much later in the war. Intending to join one of the American Eagle Squadrons in Britain but seemingly turned down, he instead during November 1942 became a member of the US Navy. While flying in the Pacific with the US Navy fighter squadron VF-32 equipped with Grumman F6F-3 Hellcats, he scored four further aerial victories. The shoot-down that Hills achieved on that costly day over Dieppe in August 1942 was the very first of the many hundreds that Mustangs would achieve later in the war, and it has often been overshadowed by the exploits and bravado of the US-operated Merlin-engined Mustangs in the later stages of World War Two, but it was nonetheless of great importance to the story of the Mustang.

Flying Officer Hollis Hills achieved the first-ever aerial victory that was made in a Mustang. An American pilot flying with the Royal Canadian Air Force in No.414 Squadron, Hills achieved his aerial victory over a Focke-Wulf Fw 190A near to Dieppe on 19 August 1942. Hills is seen here in the cockpit of a Curtiss Tomahawk of the squadron, prior to or during the unit's transition to the Mustang *(Photo: RCAF)*

Service Excellence

The RAF made good use of the Mustang from the start. In the months that followed the Dieppe operation, the Tac/R ACC Mustangs gradually widened their operations as the true potential of the Mustang became apparent. At the time of Dieppe, some fifteen squadrons were either operational or working-up on the Mustang, and eventually at least twenty-one RAF/RCAF squadrons flew the Allison-engined Mustang (including one Polish-manned, RAF squadron), either as their primary equipment or for a short time while transitioning onto another type.

A Wide Scope of Operations

With the threat of Nazi invasion having been lifted by the time that the Mustang entered RAF service, the scope of Mustang sorties widened out to encompass considerably increased front-line use of an offensive rather than defensive nature. A number of names were given to the specific types of operations that Mustangs came to fly. Amongst the best known, and at the time quite widely publicised, were 'Rhubarbs', which were comparatively small-scale but often effective tactical operations generally flown in bad weather

A posed but nonetheless interesting photograph that illustrates the close links that were forged between Army Co-operation Command Mustangs and the British ground forces with which they were tasked to operate. An RAF Mustang can be seen overflying a Rolls-Royce armoured car during one of the many exercises held in Britain during 1942 and 1943. It is worth noting that this type of armoured car would not have been intended for combat use in Europe by that time *(Photo: via Chris Ellis)*

It is believed that this photograph shows several Mustangs of No.241 Squadron at RAF Bottisham in the late autumn of 1942. Bottisham was later the home base of the Merlin-Mustang-equipped 361st Fighter Group of the US Eighth Army Air Force. However, it is also possible that this image might have been taken at RAF Odiham, when some of No.241 Squadron's Mustangs were transferred to No.168 Squadron at around that time. Visible in this view are AG512/RZ-A, and the apparently freshly-painted 'V' which is believed to have been AM177. No.241 Squadron had been one of the first RAF squadrons to transition onto the Mustang
(via Chris Ellis)

against targets of opportunity. There were in fact many thousands of potential targets in occupied Northern France that were suitable for attack, including German road transport, railways, airfields and the whole range of small-scale German military installations and individual targets that were spread across Normandy and beyond. In this role the early Allison-Mustangs excelled, their eight-gun armament being effective against a wide variety of light targets. There were also 'Circus' operations to escort light bombers or other fighter-bombers; 'Ramrods' which refined the 'Circus' into a specific attack against a designated target; 'Rangers' in which two Mustangs worked together in low altitude attacks against targets of opportunity; 'Lagoon' operations against shipping off the Dutch coast; 'Populars' which were low-altitude photo reconnaissance operations usually in coastal regions; 'Haunch' sorties intended against German aerial efforts with converted Junkers Ju 52/3m minesweepers to detonate Allied-sown magnetic mines; and general fighter 'Sweeps'. Some of these were specifically planned in advance and often aimed at

encouraging the Luftwaffe to engage in battle, as the RAF carried out the long process of chipping away at the enemy's strength and effectiveness over North-west Europe. Mustangs were also tasked on occasion with the very necessary fighter role of trying to combat fast, low-flying Luftwaffe fighter-bombers that were mounting often destructive raids against towns along the south coast of England during 1942 and well into 1943. Much of this latter activity was carried out under the umbrella of the RAF's Fighter Command, because it was somewhat different to that designated to Army Co-operation Command.

Regarding early Allison-Mustang operations, there is an often-repeated but nonetheless interesting story about the long-range capabilities of these Allison-engined RAF aircraft. The first Polish-manned squadron to operate the Allison-Mustang was No.309, which started to convert to the Mustang in June 1942. A pilot from this squadron, Flt Lt J. Lewkowicz, performed a remarkable long-distance flight on 27 September 1942 from the unit's base at RAF Dalcross near Inverness in

This Mustang Mk.I, serial number AM148, was from the second production contract of Mustangs for Britain, comprising 300 aircraft, and as such was an NA-83 as opposed to the initial batch of 320 Mustang Mk.I which had the NAA designation NA-73. The spinner and rear fuselage band were Sky
(Photo: Malcolm V. Lowe Collection)

Three Canadian-manned squadrons eventually flew Allison-Mustangs. Amongst them was No.414 Squadron, one of whose Mustang Mk.Is, AM251 'O', is seen here. This aircraft is from the second batch of Mustangs to be ordered by Britain, and as such was an NA-83. The colour scheme was Dark Green and grey on the uppersurfaces – the grey being a replacement for the Dark Earth in which many early Mustangs were painted in the US. The exact type of grey that was used to replace the Dark Earth has been the subject of considerable debate down the years, with Mixed Grey and Ocean Grey being the main contenders. The undersides were Medium Sea Grey (referred to sometimes as 'Sea Grey Medium'), with the spinner and fuselage band painted in Sky *(Photo: R.L. Ward Collection)*

Scotland, across the North Sea to Norway and back. While over Norway he attacked some enemy positions near Stavanger. The round trip was some 700 miles (1,125 km), which was a proof if any was needed of the exceptional range capabilities of the Mustang. Indeed, on 21 October 1942, an armed reconnaissance was flown by No.268 Squadron to the Dortmund-Ems canal in the northern Ruhr area of Germany – the first time that British-based fighters had been able to perform an effective round-trip into German airspace from British bases in strength. Flights such as these illustrated the exceptional range capabilities of the Mustang, which was a source of growing concern to the Germans, and the type's envelope of operational tasks gradually widened. Indeed, trials were carried out at Boscombe Down and at various weapons ranges in Britain to increase the Mustang's offensive capabilities. One of these installations saw Mk.I AG357 fitted with very cumbersome and drag-producing rocket rails in tests to determine if the Mustang was a suitable platform for such a type of weapon. In reality that particular installation was not used by the Mk.I in combat, neither was an equally burdensome layout tried out on Mk.I AM106 which involved a

40 mm Vickers 'S' gun mounted beneath each wing. A much more bizarre experiment, however, was carried out with Mustang Mk.I AG386. It consisted of the installation of a Maclaren 'drift undercarriage'. This strange concept involved allowing the angle of the aircraft's wheels to be adjustable, depending on the amount of crosswind that was blowing at the airfield that it would be trying to land at - so that even if the aircraft was 'crabbing' at an angle on its approach to compensate for a crosswind, the aircraft's wheels would still be lined up with the runway. Needless to say, this mechanically-complicated and not terribly safe concept never entered production with any aircraft type.

While flying operations the RAF's Allison-engined Mustangs did not score a large number of air-to-air victories and as previously related, combats with enemy aircraft were often not the assigned role of the aircraft. Nevertheless a number of pilots succeeded in achieving aerial victories and during the Allison Mustang period the three Canadian squadrons - according to Canadian sources - scored 24.5 aerial victories. Amongst the most successful pilots were Flt. Lt. Duncan Grant of No.400 Squadron, who achieved three aerial victories

Bearing a circular yellow 'P' marking on its fuselage side denoting a prototype or experimental aircraft, and photographed at the A&AEE Boscombe Down, Mustang Mk.I AM106 was one of some twenty-five Allison-engined Mustangs that at one time or another were at this highly important Wiltshire test establishment in the south of England. AM106 was involved in a number of programmes over several months, having arrived at Boscombe Down in April 1943 primarily for various armaments trials, and was used to clear for operational use at least fourteen underwing stores types or configurations *(Photo: R.L. Ward Collection)*

(although there has been some debate about this score, with some sources only allotting two victories to this pilot), and Flying Officer (later Flt. Lt.) Frank Hanton of the same squadron who also achieved two aerial victories. One of these was the first RAF/RCAF Mustang kill at night, when Hanton shot down a Messerschmitt Bf 110 during August 1943 in the vicinity of Rennes in eastern Brittany while flying a night intruder sortie. Hanton was additionally renowned for his 'train-busting' activities – a favourite target for Allied pilots – and is credited with destroying thirty-five trains. On the other side of the account, the number of ACC Mustangs that were shot down by German fighters was officially put at nineteen, although others that failed to return without any trace could have also fallen in air combat. However, due to their low-level activities, the Mustangs' greatest enemy was light anti-aircraft fire, which the Germans deployed in considerable quantities around key installations such as airfields.

By October 1942 over two hundred Mustangs were operational, and by the end of January 1943, according to British historian Roger A. Freeman, no less than 691 Mustangs had been delivered against British orders. This total included deliveries against the 320 originally ordered in May 1940, plus the additional 300 ordered in September 1940. This second batch began with Mustang Mk.I serial number AL958 (a listing of the RAF's Mustang serial numbers is included in the Appendices at the end of this Book), but there were some minor differences in equipment layout and configuration between these aircraft and the original 320 Mustang I production, including alterations in armour plating and rudder trim provision, leading to a different NAA designation of NA-83 (as opposed to NA-73 for the original 320 Mustang Mk.Is). Any potential slight differences necessitated a thorough examination by the A&AEE at Boscombe Down, and to that end AL997 was tested there from July 1942. In that same month trials were carried out at Boscombe Down on another of the NA-83 Mk.I aircraft, AL973, to try to resolve a problem that had been experienced on operational aircraft that related to high oil temperatures. Eventually a new type of oil cooler was successfully tried out.

New Versions of Allison-Mustangs for the RAF

The total just referred to of 691 Mustangs that had been received from NAA production by the end of January 1943 included not only the original Mk.I Mustangs, but also introduced a fresh Mustang version. This was the Mk.IA, and this new Mustang model represented a number of brand new developments for the Mustang line. The fact that further Allison-Mustangs were ordered by Britain showed how well-received the original Mustangs had been, and this new development continued the close relationship between Britain's purchasing representatives and the North American company. The way in which these newly-ordered aircraft was paid for was also new. The original 620 Mk.I Mustangs had been bought by Britain with hard currency. That was the way in which all the original purchases made by the BPC had been carried through, but by late 1940 a considerable amount of concern was being raised by the British government and by the British purchasing representatives in the US. Basically the problem was that Britain was running out of money. There had been so many purchases made of US war material and plant that Britain's dollar and gold reserves were starting to dwindle away. Added to this problem was the British taking-over of the purchases made by France before that country's defeat in June 1940. Britain was simply getting into a position where she could no longer afford to buy any further war material. This problem was certainly no secret to the American government, which in essence could itself not afford to see Britain run out of money and therefore lose the means to defend herself.

Fortunately Britain had a considerable and continuing ally in the form of President Roosevelt himself. He had successfully steered the US in November 1939 towards the 'cash and carry' agreement that had so helped Britain at that time. Now he was to engineer with his close allies in the US Congress a further act of magnanimity that saved Britain's dwindling means to pay for any further war material. In March 1941, still a long time before the US became a genuine combatant in World War Two; legislation was hastily enacted to allow Britain to – effectively – receive further war material for free. Known forever after as Lend-Lease (although many contemporary documents called it 'Lease-Lend'), the legislation allowed the

Special underwing pylons were fitted to Mustang Mk.I AM106 for the various armaments trials that were carried out at the A&AEE Boscombe Down using this aircraft. The pylons were non-standard. One of the trials included the installation of a 40 mm Vickers 'S' gun beneath each wing, the installation proving to be a success but was not taken up for operational Mustangs. In this view AM106 is carrying a podded container beneath each wing, resembling a fuel tank *(Photo: R.L. Ward Collection)*

Only one A-36A Invader actually reached the RAF in Britain, although others were 'borrowed' from the Americans for RAF service elsewhere. The solitary A-36A in Britain was EW998, which was examined at Boscombe Down from March 1943 onwards. It is seen here in flight, showing off to advantage the wing air brakes of this unique mark of Mustang, and the distinctive location of the pitot on the right-hand wing leading edge near to the tip. This aircraft was painted very smartly in full RAF camouflage and markings, with Dark Green and Ocean Grey uppersurfaces, and Medium Sea Grey beneath *(Photo: R.L. Ward Collection)*

President to sell, lease, lend, or transfer title of any defence materials that he considered vital to a particular friendly country's defence and whose own defence was considered (presumably in the end by the President himself) to be vital to that of the US. Payment under this rather loose arrangement was not really detailed, and could be settled in whatever satisfactory means could be found at some unspecified date in the future. This development was very welcome news to Britain, although for many in the US it represented a significant step towards that country becoming embroiled in the war. It was also correctly seen as a totally unexpected, apparent extension of the President's own powers. The relevant Lend-Lease Bill was introduced to the US Congress in January 1941, and became law two months later. Thereafter, all Mustangs for Britain were supplied under the terms of the Lend-Lease regulations – in effect they were subsequently ordered by the US authorities and their procurement agencies as if they were for US military service, but were actually ordered for - and then allotted to - Britain.

The first Mustangs that were supplied under Lend-Lease were known to the British as the Mustang Mk.IA. These aircraft were significantly different from the previous 620 Mk.I aircraft in that they were armed with four 20mm cannons, two being installed in each wing. The eight machine gun armament of the original Mustangs was thus dispensed with, and the considerable punch of the 20mm cannons of the Mustang IA was subsequently to prove equally of destructive capability against ground targets. Altogether 150 Mustang Mk.IA were ordered. However, the new Mustang Mk.IA version was still in its early stages of tooling-up and manufacture when a very significant event took place that was to change the course of the Second World War. On 7 December

1941 the Japanese struck against the US Pacific fleet and installations in and around Pearl Harbour in Hawaii, and followed this with attacks on other targets in the Pacific and South-east Asia. Suddenly the US herself was at war. All the isolationist sentiments in the US and unwillingness by some to become embroiled in the war as it had previously existed were swept away in an instant. Now the US needed real, capable warplanes, for its own armed services, and the Mustang's story was to be irrevocably shaped by these major and largely unexpected developments.

As far as the Mustang Mk.IA production's production was concerned, a proportion of the intended batch for Britain was taken over in the months after Pearl Harbour for use by the US Army Air Force. Some forward-looking members of the USAAF had been interested spectators of the Mustang's early service with the RAF thus far, and the Tac/R role that the RAF's aircraft grew into was one that the USAAF could certainly find useful. In the event, fifty-five of the intended 150 Mustang IA batch were requisitioned for USAAF employment, plus two others that were retained by NAA. Many of the fifty-five were delegated for conversion to carry camera equipment in a similar fashion to the RAF's aircraft. The initial designation that they were given in US military service was P-51 or F-6A (a full explanation of the early USAAF use of the Allison-engined Mustang can be found in the following chapters, to explain more fully these American designations). Due to their differing armament the Mk.IA Mustangs received the new NAA designation NA-91, and the first was assigned the British serial number FD418. However, as US procurement from NAA of the Mustang belatedly crawled into place, Britain was delegated fifty examples of a slightly different Mustang model to compensate for the loss of

The only A-36A Invader that actually reached the RAF in Britain, EW998, is the subject of this photograph at Boscombe Down, showing amongst other A-36A features the relocation of the pitot installation to a prominent fitment unique to this variant on the starboard wing leading edge. It was powered by an Allison V-1710-87 (-F21R). In theory the A-36A could be cleared to carry a bomb of up to 1,000 lb beneath each wing, but the normal operational load was a 500 lb bomb under each side *(Photo: R.L. Ward Collection)*

some of the Mk.IA production. These fifty odd Mustangs were designated Mustang Mk.II, and their serial numbers began with FR890. They were equivalent to a new Mustang version for US military service that was known as the P-51A.

This model was significant in being the first Mustang to introduce an internal armament that comprised solely of wing-mounted 0.5-in machine guns – the combination that was highly significant for later, Merlin-powered Mustang versions. The P-51A was intended to be powered by a slightly different model of the Allison V-1710, the V-1710-81, which gave 1,200 hp as opposed to the 1,150 hp of the earlier versions. These aircraft were also fitted as standard with underwing pylons, the NAA production lines having incorporated this necessary addition as the selection of potential Mustang ordnance was widened, and the ability to carry external fuel tanks to further extend the type's already excellent range characteristics was incorporated. Thus, by the latter stages of the Allison-engined Mustang's operations with the RAF, the type in its Mk.II form was able to carry 500 lb (227 kg) bombs (one beneath each wing) or external fuel tanks on specially-stressed underwing pylons. It was a credit to NAA that the company always kept closely abreast of developments with the RAF's combat employment of the Allison-engined Mustang - and the

introduction of the potential use in particular of external fuel tanks by the Mustang was to have a very significant impact on the type's story in the ensuing years. One member of the Mk.II batch, FR901, was fitted in Britain with curious experimental underwing fuel tanks which were not adopted as standard because the provision of underwing pylons on the Mk.II allowed for the carriage of what were becoming standard external fuel tanks or 'drop tanks'. The fifty Mk.II Mustangs were the final Allison-engined Mustang production model for Britain, and they – like the Mk.IA – were integrated into several of the RAF's operational Mustang squadrons, notably some of the units that flew the Allison-Mustang late in its RAF career such as Nos.2 and 268 Squadrons.

Maturing Service with the RAF

During 1943 the RAF's Mustang force began to undergo a number of important changes. One of the last RAF squadrons to receive Mustangs did so in May 1943, this being No.14 Squadron in the Middle East - although the Mustang's service with that particular squadron was brief and it was not the main equipment of the unit. A somewhat unusual organisation that started to fly the Allison-Mustang during the first half of 1943 was No.516 Squadron at RAF Dundonald in Scotland.

Nice in-flight view of the only A-36A Invader that actually reached the RAF in Britain, EW998. The aircraft underwent evaluation at Boscombe Down (home of the A&AEE) in the south of England but the type was not adopted for RAF service – although a small number of Invaders were 'borrowed' from the USAAF for brief RAF service elsewhere in Europe. While with the A&AEE, EW998 might have been allocated the local designation Mustang Mk.I (Dive Bomber), because the title 'A-36A' was of course purely an American designation
(Photo: R.L. Ward Collection)

A number of A-36A Invaders were 'borrowed' by the RAF from US forces when required. This well-known example, HK944 coded 'C', wearing US Dark Olive Drab and Neutral Grey colours but with full British national insignia, was photographed at Foggia in Italy in November 1943, having been used by No.1437 (Strategic Reconnaissance) Flight. By the time of this photo it had probably passed to No.260 Squadron, RAF *(Photo: Howard Levy via R.L. Ward)*

The exact location of this photograph of an RAF-operated A-36A that had been 'borrowed' from the USAAF remains the subject of some debate. It is often claimed to have been taken in Libya during 1943, and therefore possibly at Sorman West landing ground. It is believed to have had the US serial number 42-84016 or possibly 42-83906, and carried the individual identification letter 'D'. In July 1943 it was one of six A-36A that were assigned to the RAF's No.1437 (Strategic Reconnaissance) Flight
(Photo: D.H. Newton via R.L. Ward)

This unit was tasked with army ground/air and co-operation training, including the use of aircraft to provide realistic low-level attacks against commando and assault troops undergoing training, and it flew a number of Allison-engined Mustangs in addition to other types.

An important organisation which had several Allison-Mustangs on its books was the Air Fighting Development Unit (AFDU) at RAF Duxford in Cambridgeshire. This unit performed relevant trials and testing on front-line types and the Allison-Mustang was of great interest to many of its pilots, the majority of whom were experienced combat veterans. Not content with just examining in friendly skies the Mustang and

its undoubted merits, however, several of the unit's pilots took the fight to the enemy with Allison-Mustangs of the AFDU. They included a well-known fighter ace from combat over Malta, Squadron Leader James Maclachlan, who joined the AFDU in the summer of 1943. On 29 June of that year, Maclachlan in company with Flt. Lt. Geoffrey Page flew an offensive intruder patrol over France. In the ensuing combat the two pilots shot down six Luftwaffe aircraft. This made Page's total aerial victories exceed five claims, making him the first RAF pilot to become an 'ace' at the controls of a Mustang.

As the newer Mk.II Allison-engined Mustangs started to make good some of the attrition losses of the original Mk.I

In this posed photograph, a Canadian pilot from a squadron of No.35 or No.39 (Reconnaissance) Wing waits while the F.24 camera is manhandled in the area behind the pilot's seat of his Allison-Mustang where it was fitted. The sizeable (and in this location, rather cumbersome) F.24 was a high-quality photographic instrument that created large, detailed negatives allowing clear black and white prints that were ideal for photo-interpretation. Allison-engined Mustangs were ideal for the low- to medium-level photographic Tac/R role, in which they excelled – with some soldiering on in service well into 1945
(Photo: R.L. Ward Collection)

Mustangs, the overall organisation of the RAF Mustang squadrons in England underwent some major changes. On 1 June 1943 the Army Co-operation Command was disbanded. Henceforth, RAF assets were increasingly developed for what was hoped would be a forthcoming successful invasion of Continental Europe. The RAF's Mustang squadrons were thereafter largely split between Nos.83 and 84 Groups. The former included the RCAF's No.39 (Reconnaissance) Wing with No.400 Squadron at RAF Redhill in Surrey and Nos.414 and 430 at Gatwick. No. 231 Squadron, RAF, was the fourth squadron in the Wing, and flew from Redhill. However, a number of the RAF's squadrons were starting to relinquish the Mustang altogether, and moving onto other types. No.613 Squadron, for example, began converting to the twin-engined de Havilland Mosquito FB.Mk.VI in October 1943.

The RAF's Mustang assets thereafter largely came under the newly-formed 2nd Tactical Air Force, and a general run-down

of the Allison-engined Mustangs commenced. This was partly due to the end of the production of this particular variant of the Mustang. NAA's manufacture of the Allison-engined Mustang ceased during 1943, leaving the RAF potentially short of the kind of long-range low-level coverage that the Allison-engined Mustang had by then successfully made its own. With no new aircraft being made, the numbers available to front-line squadrons was bound to dwindle. It was therefore with considerable regret within the RAF that the process of converting some of the Mustang squadrons to other types commenced, so that by the time of D-Day in June 1944 the Allison-engined Mustang was only flown by a handful of squadrons. These included the RCAF's Nos.414 and 430 Squadrons, plus the RAF's No.168 Squadron, within the RCAF's No.39 (Reconnaissance) Wing based at RAF Odiham in Hampshire which also included the Spitfire PR.Mk.XI-equipped No.400 Squadron (previously an Allison-Mustang

operator), and which provided coverage in particular for the British Second Army. The Canadian First Army was supported in part by No.35 (Reconnaissance) Wing at Gatwick, which included the Mustang-equipped Nos.2 and 268 Squadrons. These various units had around one hundred Allison Mustangs available. Following D-Day, the units of 2nd TAF moved across to the Continent to follow the advancing front lines, resulting in many squadrons flying from austere advanced landing grounds or damaged former Luftwaffe airfields that taxed the capabilities and durability of pilots, ground crews and aircraft.

Thereafter the numbers of front-line Allison-engined Mustangs dwindled. By the end of hostilities in Europe, only one 2nd TAF unit, No.268 Squadron, had successfully continued operating the type right up to the end (although it had spent a period after D-Day also flying Hawker Typhoons, before fully converting back on to Allison-engined Mustangs before the end of the year). On 1 January 1945 the squadron was based at Gilze Rijen in Holland, and was caught up in the major New Year's Day Luftwaffe attack on Allied airfields on the Continent. This major operation, known to the Germans as 'Bodenplatte', was intended to be a knock-out blow to Allied air assets on the Continent, but it totally failed in its objective.

The Allied air response to the 'Bodenplatte' attacks was largely successful, and although the Luftwaffe did achieve a considerable amount of damage at some forward airfields, the Allies were easily able to make up the losses. Amongst the Allied air assets that became unwittingly involved as 'Bodenplatte' took place were the Allison-Mustangs of No.268 squadron. One of its pilots, Flt. Lt. A. Mercer, claimed a twin-engined Junkers Ju 88 which crashed near Utrecht (subsequent examination of fragmentary Luftwaffe records suggests that the German aircraft may have been a Ju-188, possibly shared with Flt. Lt. J.B. Lyke of the same squadron.). This is generally believed to be amongst the last, if not the last, recorded air-to-air kill by an Allison-engined Mustang in World War Two. By the end of the war the squadron was in the process of re-equipping with a dedicated reconnaissance version of the Spitfire Mk.XIV, but continued to have the Allison-Mustang on strength until August 1945. By that time No.268 had become part of the Allied occupying force in Germany and was eventually based at Celle where it was re-numbered. In addition, No.26 Squadron also had several Allison-Mustangs on strength at the end of the war in Europe. This unit had been the first squadron of any kind to take the Mustang into

combat, in May 1942, but had subsequently converted onto Spitfires. Much later it had taken Allison-Mustangs back on charge from the autumn/winter of 1944 onwards for reconnaissance over the Low Countries in the Allied effort to locate V2 rocket launch sites. The squadron also had a naval artillery co-operation role. Many of the remaining Allison-engined Mustangs of these two squadrons were very war-weary by the end of the war, and were amongst the oldest and longest-lived aircraft within the RAF's front-line inventory at that time. Nevertheless, in total the Allison-engined Mustang had proven to be a great success at low-level for the British and Commonwealth squadrons that had flown it over North-west Europe and the type had certainly played a very important role in the RAF's operations from 1942 onwards.

The success of the RAF-operated Allison-engined Mustangs in North-west Europe was not quite the whole story of the British use of these early Mustangs. In another theatre of the war, Allison-engined Mustangs also operated – albeit in very small numbers - with British forces. This was in the Mediterranean and Southern Europe, where some Allison-engined examples served briefly with British units. This often forgotten employment of the Mustang centred on No.1437 (Strategic Reconnaissance) Flight, which flew 'borrowed' former US-operated Mustangs. Most if not all of these Mustangs were actually A-36A Invaders, the dive-bomber version of the Mustang that is described in the following chapters. Six A-36As were taken on charge in early July 1943 for the use of No.1437 Flight, which was based at a landing ground called Sorman West near the town of Sorman in Libya. The unit had actually flown its first missions in the Western Desert in October 1941, and had operated Martin Baltimore twin-engined light bombers primarily for reconnaissance prior to re-equipping with the A-36A. The need for intelligence in support of the coming Allied invasion of Sicily dictated that the Invaders were put into action as soon as possible, and to this end several of

the aircraft temporarily deployed to RAF Luqa on the island of Malta from where the first reconnaissance sorties were flown on 12 July. The A-36As were found to be very useful for the reconnaissance tasks that they undertook, often watching for enemy troop movements as the battle for Sicily took place. Usually missions comprised two aircraft, one as lead and the other as 'Weaver' to cover the leader.

The fluid nature of the ground operations resulted in the Flight moving to a landing ground named Francesco on Sicily itself near to the town of Lentini from the end of July 1943 onwards. Most missions were flown at low level, but as the end neared in Sicily enemy anti-aircraft defences increased in the north-east of the island, and some missions were therefore flown at higher levels, with a rapid dive and pull-out to obtain the required information. In early September some elements of the unit moved to a landing ground called Milazzo East, but by that time two A-36As had been lost on operations (both pilots survived) and most of the remaining aircraft were in a poor state of repair. Nevertheless No.1437 Flight later moved to southern Italy, and eventually on 6 October was able to move in to Foggia Main airfield, one of the complex of airfields in the Foggia area. Several days later, with no hope of obtaining replacement A-36As, the flight disbanded. At least one of the surviving Invaders appears to have ended up with the locally-based No.260 Squadron, a predominantly Curtiss Kittyhawk unit that later flew Merlin-engined Mustangs as well. Another RAF squadron that operated a small number of US Allison-engined Mustangs was No.225 Squadron, which used at least one P-51/F-6A reconnaissance Mustang (and possibly more) that was 'borrowed' from US forces. A Mediterranean-based bomber unit, No.14 Squadron, which operated Martin Marauders as its main equipment in Algeria, also flew early Allison-engined Mustangs briefly in May 1943. These were used for tactical reconnaissance operations, but only remained with the unit for a short time.

Without doubt, Allison-engined Mustangs served the RAF very well, and some continued to fly right to the end of World War Two. Illustrated at Eindhoven in Holland, this battered No.39 (Reconnaissance) Wing Mustang was damaged during the 1 January 1945 Luftwaffe attack on Allied airfields (Operation 'Bodenplatte'). At that time several 2nd TAF squadrons still included Allison-engined Mustangs as a part of their equipment, although only one, No.268 Squadron, was actually flying Allison-Mustangs as the war ended. These Mustangs saw some combat on 1 January during the 'Bodenplatte' attacks. One German aircraft fell to the guns of No.268 Squadron aircraft. Flt. Lt. A. Mercer claimed what is now believed to have been a Ju 188, possibly shared with Flt. Lt. J.B. Lyke of the same squadron. This is generally regarded as the last recorded air-to-air kill by an Allison-engined Mustang during the Second World War
(Photo: M. Robinson via R.L. Ward)

America Takes an Interest

The two XP-51 aircraft were assigned the USAAC (later USAAF) serial numbers 41-038 and 41-039 (sometimes simply written as 41-38 and 41-39), and both were eventually evaluated at Wright Field in Ohio. This photograph shows the starboard side of what is believed to be the first of the two XP-51s, in this NAA company image. The aircraft wears full early-war style US national insignia and a predominantly 'natural metal' finish, with a matt Dark Olive Drab anti-glare panel ahead of the cockpit (Photo: NAA)

There can be no doubt that the Allison-engined Mustang, although limited in its effectiveness mainly in low and medium level operations, was nevertheless a very capable warplane if employed within the confines of its performance envelope. It certainly turned out to be a worthwhile combat aircraft in RAF service. Although completely overshadowed by the exploits later in the war of Merlin-powered Mustangs, the US Army Air Force also successfully operated Allison-engined Mustangs, in an aspect of the Mustang's service life that is often overlooked and sometimes completely forgotten. Under the designation P-51, the Mustang was to become famous in US employment, almost exclusively due to the Merlin-powered P-51 versions in American service, but the very first P-51 Mustangs that flew in combat with the USAAF were Allison-engined. These early P-51s served in a number of useful roles from 1943 onwards. By that period of the war, the RAF's Allison-Mustangs had already more than proved their worth.

No Initial US Requirement

From the outset, the Mustang had been created in 1940 by NAA specifically for British use. There was absolutely no requirement whatsoever at that time for the type in US service. Instead, during that time a number of fighter designs were being developed for US Army Air Corps use, and the Mustang was most definitely not amongst these. They instead included the radical, mid-engined Bell P-39 Airacobra, which first flew in April 1939 (and not 1938 as claimed in some published sources). Powered by an Allison V-1710 initially with, but afterwards without a turbo-supercharger, the P-39 promised much on paper and in early tests. However, many of its dashing performance qualities were lost when military equipment was added during the type's development. Lacking a turbo-supercharger, the P-39 was a practical if unspectacular performer at low level, but was definitely not for high-level combat. Although P-39s were a useful tool in the early part of America's fight in the Pacific against the Japanese after the Pearl

The two XP-51 aircraft for the USAAF were in fact the fourth and tenth Mustangs that were completed, and not the fourth and tenth Mustang Mk.I aircraft numbered in sequence for the RAF. One of the two XP-51s is seen here, resplendent in early World War Two USAAF markings; the then-Army Air Corps had little real interest in the NA-73 project at the time of its creation in 1940, regarding the NA-73 as export business only for North American Aviation. However, as a condition of the granting of export licences for the type, two examples were required to be supplied for examination in the US at Wright Field, where the service evaluation of new types was carried out (Photo: USAAF)

Harbour attack of December 1941, the type was hardly distinguished - although it certainly proved very valuable to the Soviet Union, which operated Airacobra's in large quantities. The RAF very briefly flew the type in combat, and found it completely unsuitable for operations in North-west Europe.

Additional to the Airacobra, the US also had the Curtiss P-40 as an up and coming fighter type in 1940. However, as mentioned elsewhere in this Book, the P-40 series was most definitely not the most significant or distinguished American fighter of World War Two. It did, however, provide useful service at various times and was a workhorse that was available in significant numbers in several theatres of the war. The Mustang on the other hand was definitely a far better combat aircraft than the P-39 and P-40, but in US service Mustangs were later to be partnered by two very significant American fighters, the Lockheed P-38 Lightning and the Republic P-47 Thunderbolt. The radial-engined Thunderbolt was in a class of its own, having first been conceived as a point interceptor but later growing into a bulky, heavy fighter and fighter-bomber that excelled in ground-attack operations but also flew as a bomber escort – a role for which it lacked range until specifically re-modelled for long-range operations. The twin-engined P-38 Lightning was a very significant fighter project from the start, and was much encouraged in the late 1930's and early 1940's by the then US Army Air Corps. The first Lightning flew in January 1939, and the type evolved into a long-range fighter that proved to be a success particularly in the Pacific theatre later in World War Two. The P-38 was powered by a pair of turbo-supercharged Allison V-1710 engines, which proved the capability of the Allison engine when specifically configured for higher-altitude work with the significant addition of turbo-supercharging.

It is important to note that all of these fighter types – the P-38, P-39, P-40, and the P-47 – received considerable patronage, interest and support from the US military during their creation and development. This was in total contrast to the Mustang, for which there was no official interest insofar as the type was officially regarded as being only intended for British operation - and production of the Mustang was expected by the US authorities including the USAAC to end when the British orders had been fulfilled. Indeed, important animosity developed amongst some officers in the Army Air Corps against the type.

North American Aviation had after all not been regarded by the pre-war Air Corps as being capable of designing its own fighters, yet the company had nevertheless gone ahead contrary to this opinion and started its own fighter design in 1940 that led to the Mustang. The Mustang in any case was a 'foreign' project, which was seen by some officers as having no potential home within the US military. Significantly, however, some personnel in the Air Corps took a close interest in events that were taking place in Europe as World War Two continued into 1940, and lessons were learned as to the nature of the air war and particularly regarding the relative successes or failures of specific warplanes and tactics. Nevertheless, it was certainly not by original intention that the Mustang came to be such an important combat aircraft for US operations.

The Earliest US Delivery

However, in spite of all this, the Mustang did feature in US procurement plans from its early production time, albeit in the smallest of numbers. As a part of the agreement for the Mustang to be released for export sales, under an existing release for foreign sales arrangement, the US government took sufficient interest in the programme that two examples from the first Allison-engined Mustang production batch for Britain were officially ordered for US testing. A purchase order for two Mustangs (Authority for Purchase No.165265) was issued on 24 July 1940, with a formal contract being approved on 20 September of that year by the US Assistant Secretary of War. However, the exact identity of the two aircraft involved has very regularly been misidentified in the years after the war. The US requirement appears to have called for the two aircraft to be taken from the Mustang production line and supplied to the major US Army Air Corps prototype testing and evaluation establishment at Wright Field in Ohio. In a statement that has clouded the issue of the story of these very first US Mustangs for many years, the US requested the fourth and tenth production examples from the first batch of 320 Mustang Mk.I destined for Britain to be supplied for US testing and evaluation. That would have apparently meant that the fourth aircraft (British serial number AG348), and the tenth aircraft (AG354) would have turned over to the US authorities. Many writers have subsequently stated that this was indeed what happened.

It is believed that this image shows the second XP-51, 41-039, during evaluation or testing in the US, possibly with NACA at the time of this photograph. Both XP-51s were typical Mustang Mk.Is – they had after all been taken directly from the Mustang Mk.I production line at NAA – and had the same armament (not apparently fitted in this view). Externally, however, their paint job was obviously very different to the British aircraft. Note in particular the lack of yellow tips to the propeller blades *(Photo: USAAF)*

The fourth production Mustang Mk.I destined for Britain was AG348. It is this aircraft that is often, incorrectly, claimed to have been turned over to the USAAF as the first of two XP-51 airframes. In reality, AG348 was transported to England, and became one of ten Mustang Mk.I that were later transferred from Britain to the Soviet Union – a photograph of this same aircraft in Russian markings appears later in this book (Photo: NAA)

A number of Mustangs were delegated to NACA over the years for various trials and development work. This is one of the two XP-51 Mustangs, possibly 41-038, having received a coat of camouflage paint (Dark Olive Drab uppersurfaces and Neutral Grey below). The six wing gun ports have been sealed and the lower nose gun port is empty – the two XP-51s were the only US Mustangs to have this armament arrangement, which was identical to the Mustang Mk.I for Britain – both XP-51s, it must be remembered, were actually Mustang Mk.Is. Particularly evident is the long carburettor air intake above the nose, and a special recording device below the right-hand wing-tip for measuring yaw, which was a fitting peculiar to the aircraft's NACA work. 41-038 was tested by NACA between March and May 1942, but the other XP-51, 41-039, also spent time with NACA (Photo: NASA via Srecko Bradic)

However, there is no doubt that this 'did not' take place in the case of AG348. Instead, this aircraft was definitely intended for shipment to Britain – and was then assigned by Britain as one of the Mustang Mk.Is that were supplied by Britain to the Soviet Union. Apparently arriving in the Soviet Union in May 1942, AG348 was evaluated by the Soviet air force's aviation research centre NII VVS. There is more detail about the Russian connections with the Mustang in the section on other Mustang operators later in this Book, and there are photographs in existence of this aircraft in Russian markings but clearly wearing the British serial number AG348. The tenth production Mustang for Britain, AG354, is also recorded in Russian documentation as having been supplied by Britain to the Soviet Union, and therefore this aircraft too does not appear to have been built for the Army Air Corps. Therefore, unless there were two Mustang Mk.I that were painted as AG348, and two painted as AG354, it is not true that the fourth and tenth production aircraft for Britain were supplied to the US Army Air Corps – instead they ended up in the Soviet Union. The reality appears to be that it was the fourth and tenth Mustangs that were 'produced' and/or 'completed', and not the fourth and tenth that received British serial numbers and actually found their way into US service.

In June 1941 the US Army Air Force was brought into existence as the successor to the US Army Air Corps, and the Mustang was one of the new breed of high-performance warplanes that was just coming to the fore at that time. The two Mustangs that were received by the new Army Air Force were designated XP-51, 'X' being for 'experimental prototype' and 'P' being for 'Pursuit' or simply 'Fighter' (the more appropriate 'F' prefix was at that time reserved – for some strange reason – for 'Photographic' and referred only to reconnaissance aircraft). The two XP-51s were assigned the USAAC serial numbers 41-038 and 41-039 (sometimes

referred to officially as 41-38 and 41-39), meaning that they were procured under US government Fiscal Year (FY) 1941 budgeting, and were the 38th and 39th aircraft procured under the FY 1941 funding programme. It must be remembered, however – and this cannot be stressed too much - that these two aircraft were actually Mustang Mk.Is in all but name and paint job. They were taken directly from the Mustang Mk.I production line at NAA, and had all the recognition features and armament stations of the Mustang Mk.I.

The first of the two XP-51s, 41-038, made its maiden flight on 20 May 1941, with Robert Chilton at the controls. It was delivered to Wright Field on 24 August of that year. This was some six months late – as pointed out previously in this book, the construction by NAA of the initial Mustangs was carried out well behind schedule, with deliveries to Britain of the Mustang Mk.I not keeping up with the timescale that had been agreed upon between NAA and the British in the spring of 1940. In the event the second XP-51 in fact was even more delayed, and was finally delivered to Wright Field on 16 December 1941 (at least, that is the officially recognised delivery date). It should have been handed over in March 1941. By the time of its delivery the US was well and truly involved in World War II, following the Japanese attack several days earlier on Pearl Harbour and other targets in the Pacific. Interestingly, it has often been claimed by a number of writers that the two new XP-51s were simply pushed into a hangar at Wright Field after their delivery and forgotten about. This was not the case. In reality the evaluation of the aircraft was delayed and protracted, and this was due to several factors. One of the underlying causes of the relative inactivity of the two aircraft was unserviceability. There were problems with bad weather at Wright Field which appear to have had a bearing on the test schedules of the new aircraft, causing problems with the undercarriage retracting mechanism and radiator intake

LMAL 34304

mechanism due to cold weather. Aileron and flap bracket bolts also caused difficulties, a problem which NAA appears to have encountered with other Mustangs during manufacture. A setback with engine backfiring also seems to have taken place which took some time to rectify. The two XP-51 were powered by the Allison V-1710-39 (or –P3R, according to the eventual Wright Field report on the XP-51), giving 1,150 hp take-off power. They were armed like the Mustang Mk.I, with three machine guns in each wing in the same layout to the British machines, and similarly with two 0.5-in machine guns in the lower nose. Some equipment was different to the British machines, however, where US-standard kit rather than that specified by the British was installed. For example, fully automatic gun charging equipment developed by the Bendix Corporation was eventually fitted and tested in the second aircraft, but the first XP-51 was not originally fitted with gun charging equipment.

There was, however, another less rational reason for the delays in the testing of the two XP-51s, and that lay in the priority that was given to the evaluation of other types at Wright Field. With the benefit of hindsight, it is amazing to think that the Mustang at that time was of no official interest to the Army Air Force, and so was not given any kind of priority. This was in spite of the aircraft being clearly superior to the rather pedestrian Curtiss P-40, and definitely far better than the hopeless XP-46 and XP-60 projects that Curtiss was pursuing in order to wring some kind of modernity out of the tired P-40 layout. There were seemingly many in the USAAF who were simply not interested in looking into the potential of the new North American fighter, and one of the chief opponents appears to have been Oliver Echols, who eventually became a Brigadier General and rose to the leadership of the Material Command at Wright Field. Without doubt, in comparison, much of the evaluation and testing that was carried out at Wright Field on other types during the war years was excellent work of the finest quality, and so it seems doubly unfortunate that the Mustang was not given the same priority as other programmes.

Positive Report

Eventually, the Wright Field report on the two XP-51s (Report No. 4801) was released, dated 15 July 1942. It was compiled by Captain W.G. Logan, and approved by Col. F.L. Carroll, who was the chief of the Experimental Engineering Section of the Material Command. This was almost a year since the first XP-51 had been delivered to Wright Field, and by that time the RAF already had the Mustang Mk.I very successfully in front-line service. The report nevertheless gave some interesting insights into the XP-51 layout's performance and capabilities. Official performance flight tests were conducted between 8 October and 22 December 1941, and the maximum speed that Wright Field was able to gain from the XP-51 testing was 382 mph (615

km/h) at 13,000 ft (3,962 m), with a design gross weight of 7,934 lb (3,599 kg). At a cruising speed of 325.5 mph (524 km/h) the XP-51 flew for 780 miles (1,255 km). The type had a design altitude of 15,000 ft (4,572 m), but could reach an absolute ceiling of 31,900 ft (9,723 m) – which must have been a rather uncomfortable experience for both aircraft and pilot. (remember that the Mustang would not have been an effective fighting machine at that height, or indeed anything near to it). The Allison V-1710-39 had a supercharger 'blower' ratio of 8.8 to 1, but could only attain a maximum of 1,150 hp as the supercharger was of the simplest single-stage form. Incredibly, some writers still cling to the notion that the Allison engine had no supercharging whatsoever, which is nonsense – although it did not of course have 'turbo' (i.e. exhaust-driven) supercharging when fitted to the Mustang.

Without doubt, those reading the final Wright Field report must surely have been impressed by the XP-51's capabilities. However, despite this, the road to getting the type into US service was a long and complicated experience. In fact, the initial breakthrough for the Mustang as far as US service was concerned, came about when the Lend-Lease legislation of March 1941 resulted in military procurement for Britain being subsequently made through US government agencies. Whereas the initial Mustangs for Britain (the Mustang Mk.I production) had been paid for with real money, from the Mustang Mk.IA onwards the examples of this type that were intended for Britain were ordered and paid for by the US on behalf of the customer. Therefore the batch of 150 Mustang Mk.IA that was ordered by the US authorities was the first to be procured under these contingencies, and they were allocated US as well as British serial numbers. The order was made on 7 July 1941, and the serial numbers allocated were FD418 to FD567 (British) and 41-37320 to 41-37469 (American). This order was a welcome boost to the Mustang's production requirement, but because manufacture of the original batches of Mustang Mk.I for Britain was running behind schedule, the Mustang Mk.IA order was not fulfilled when the United States was plunged into World War II with the Japanese attacks of 7 December 1941. The events of those momentous times changed a great deal for the USAAF. Overnight there was a sudden need for high-performance warplanes of any and every kind, and in as large quantities as possible. Even then, however, the entrenched lack of enthusiasm for the Mustang particularly at the Material Command continued virtually unabated. Fortunately there was sufficient need in the AAF for aircraft of the calibre of the Mustang, to start to erode this incomprehensible situation, and a significant proportion of the Mustang Mk.IA order was requisitioned by the US authorities for USAAF use. Just who made this requisition has sadly not been recorded, but their actions at last began the process of the Mustang becoming an Army Air Force combat aircraft for front-line service.

The second XP-51, 41-039, is seen here during assignment to Wright Field. It carries the Wright Field 'arrow head' identifier on the fuselage side, and presents a scene of pre-war smartness in its 'natural metal' finish – even though the US was fully involved in the Second World War by the time of this photograph. The final Wright Field report on the Mustang was favourable, and despite official and personal opposition to the type in some quarters, sudden wartime necessity called for modern warplanes for the USAAF – and truly one of the best available was the Mustang
(Photo: USAAF)

Early US Operations

One of the very first American Mustangs. This aircraft was the second Mustang in the production batch designated P-51 (Mustang Mk.IA) and was assigned the US serial number 41-37321. It was repossessed from the RAF Mustang Mk.IA order and received full US markings and insignia, with Dark Olive Drab uppersurfaces and Neutral Grey below. The serial number on the fuselage side was yellow. It was armed with the standard Mustang Mk.IA armament of four 20mm cannons, two in each wing
(Photo: NAA)

The dire need that the US found itself in for modern combat aircraft during the days and weeks that followed the Pearl Harbour attack in December 1941 in some ways mimicked the similar situation that Britain found herself in when the Second World War started in September 1939. To that end, any modern warplanes that might be of use were suddenly of interest to the USAAF. As explained in the previous chapter, that came to include the export aircraft that NAA was up to that time making solely for Britain, the already well-established Mustang.

In total, fifty-seven of the intended Mustang Mk.IA production batch for the RAF was repossessed for US employment. Of these, two were retained by NAA for other work including trials and development studies (and also possibly as a 'run-around' and familiarisation aircraft for NAA's flight test staff), but the fifty-five remaining aircraft were the first to see action with the Army Air Force. These aircraft had the NAA company designation of NA-91, which was the same title allocated to the batch of British Mustang Mk.IAs – which makes

sense, because they were repossessed from the Mustang Mk.IA production, and were essentially the same aircraft – right down to the same armament of four 20mm cannons, two being installed in each wing.

British experience in the air war over North-west Europe up to that time had created sufficient interest within the AAF to encourage the use of these aircraft for US service in ways similar to the RAF's own established employment of the Allison-engined Mustang. To that end, these first-ever operational US Mustangs were fitted with cameras, and prepared for combat as fast, low-level reconnaissance and light ground-attack aircraft. The cameras fitted were US K.24 units, similar to the F.24 cameras installed in the RAF's Mustangs, and the installation was similar – behind the pilot, looking out obliquely through the left-hand window behind the main cockpit glazing. The first installation was trialled by NAA, but the remaining fifty-four aircraft were modified at AAF depots. They featured the same armament as the

In-flight view of P-51 serial number 41-37324. The distinctive nose shape of the Allison-Mustangs is very evident in this view, with contours that were strikingly different to those of the Merlin-powered Mustangs that came along later in the war. A peculiarity of these early US Mustangs was the placement of the aircraft's serial number on the rear fuselage, rather than across the vertical tail, with the latter location becoming the norm for most USAAF aircraft at that time *(Photo: USAAF)*

Unfortunately the wartime censor appears to have painted out the serial number of this P-51 from the rear fuselage behind the fuselage star national insignia. This view does however show the layout of the P-51, the first of the American Mustangs to see action, and illustrates this version's armament of two 20mm cannons in each wing. These P-51s were basically identical to the Mustang Mk.IA of the RAF, except for a new paint job and various detail equipment changes, because they were taken from the Mustang Mk.IA production line as repossessed aircraft - and were allocated to the USAAF in the aftermath of Pearl Harbour *(Photo: USAAF)*

Mustang Mk.IA, namely two 20mm cannons in each wing, with no nose guns. The designation P-51 was allocated, with no prefix, making these the first true production P-51 Mustangs. However, they also appear to have been designated P-51-1-NA and P-51-2-NA to signify that they were of a converted configuration (i.e. with the camera installation added), but in line with their new reconnaissance role the designation F-6A was additionally drawn-up. However, in service they appear to have been more straightforwardly

known simply with the P-51 title. At first there was a desire within the AAF to name them Apache, and this name is often quoted for many of the early American Mustangs – indeed the name 'Apache' appears to have been favoured by some for the whole Mustang line back in 1940, before the name Mustang was bestowed by the British. Indeed, the British appellation of Mustang seems to have gained almost universal acceptance amongst the Americans using them once the type started to be an operational US warplane.

Posed but nevertheless interesting photograph of a USAAF P-51 undergoing maintenance work. The P-51 version was the first Mustang mark for the USAAF, and comprised Mustang Mk.IAs originally intended for Britain which were repossessed for use by the Americans. Note the early-war US star national insignia beneath both wings of this aircraft *(Photo: NAA)*

Mustangs for US Service At Last

As what eventually became the first of many Mustangs for US service, the first production example of the P-51 batch initially flew on 29 May 1942, with NAA test pilot Louis Wait at the controls. The aircraft had the US serial number of 41-37320. Even then, however, it was some time before these first combat-capable American Mustangs actually saw front-line service. In the mid and latter stages of 1942 the USAAF began to expand its reconnaissance assets, as well as its related training organisation. Drawing on lessons gained from Britain's experience with the RAF-operated Tac/R Mustangs, the AAF training facility at Colorado Springs began teaching relevant tactics along the lines of the evolving British model, and the tactical reconnaissance school at Key Field, Mississippi, commenced the indoctrination of pilots destined to fly the P-51 in combat. The Key Field facility operated a variety of aircraft types, and due to their relatively small numbers the P-51/F-6A were always in short supply at bases in the Continental US.

During early 1943, thirty-five of the reconnaissance-configured F-6A Mustangs were shipped from the US via England to North Africa. Having arrived there, the aircraft were prepared for operations and were assigned to elements of the 68th Observation Group which was assigned to the Twelfth Army Air Force. This unit has a true claim to being called the 'Pioneer Mustang Group' of the USAAF, a title that was later declared as their own in England by the Merlin-Mustang 354th

Fighter Group during the latter part of 1943. The 68th OG was made up of several Observation Squadrons, most of which were equipped with an odd assortment of aircraft types. Supermarine Spitfires, Douglas Havocs and other types such as Airacobra's were sometimes to be found in reconnaissance units in these comparatively early days of USAAF wartime operations. Into this strange mixture the first Allison-engined Mustangs of the Army Air Force arrived. Within the 68h OG, two of the assigned squadrons were the 111th and the 154th Observation Squadrons. Both of these were National Guard units that had been called to active duty and sent overseas. Both were to play a central role in introducing the Mustang into front-line service for the USAAF.

The 154th was from the Arkansas National Guard, and had flown the North American O-47 before the US entry into World War Two. Prior to its historic but largely unsung introduction of the Mustang into combat during April 1943, the squadron operated P-39 Airacobra's in North Africa, becoming operational on that type in early 1943. The 154th started to receive a trickle of P-51/F-6A Mustangs in the spring of 1943 and training and familiarisation on this new type was commenced. Truly nomadic, both the 154th and 111th underwent many location changes during this time, as dictated by the often moving front lines in North Africa and constantly changing situation on the ground. In early April the 154th Observation Squadron moved to Sbeitla in Tunisia, and it was from here on 9 April 1943 that the

Interesting three-quarters rear view of an early P-51 (repossessed Mustang Mk.IA), possibly 41-37324. Beneath the mid-fuselage, the unique early Allison-Mustang features of the opening radiator air intake and outlet can be clearly seen, with both open in this view. The blue and white star national insignia is positioned above the port wing only (Photo: NAA)

Fast low-level armed tactical reconnaissance was a chief role of Allison-engined Mustangs, as pioneered by the RAF. To that end many early Allison-Mustangs were fitted with an oblique-mounted camera behind the pilot. This applied to US as well as British-operated Allison-engined Mustangs, the RAF calling this role Tac/R or tactical reconnaissance. The Americans similarly used some early Mustangs in USAAF service for this role, and a number of experiments were carried out in the US to determine the best type of mounting for the camera. This close-up photograph shows an experimental bulged Plexiglas rear cockpit window fitting that was tried out at Wright Field on a P-51/F-6A (repossessed from the British Mustang Mk.IA order), serial number 41-37320. Also very prominent in this image is the open lower mid-fuselage radiator air intake and outlet of this particular early mark of Mustang. The bulged window fitting was not widely adopted, but an arrangement similar to this was installed on some operational aircraft (Photo: USAAF)

first-ever US Mustang operation was flown, by one of the squadron's assigned P-51s. American records suggest that the pilot was Lt Alfred Schwab. The mission was an armed reconnaissance in and around the area of the Axis-held Kairouan airstrip. This momentous but little-heralded event took place almost one year 'after' the RAF had initially flown its Mustangs in combat.

In the weeks that followed this first sortie by a US-operated Mustang, these first US Mustangs from the 154th OS began to spread their wings. Many armed reconnaissance missions were flown, much of this work being similar to the experience of the RAF-operated Mustangs that had already been in combat for some time before them. Bearing in mind the considerable amount of time that it had taken the Americans to get their Mustangs into combat, combined with the opposition to the Mustang that existed in some parts of the USAAF, it was therefore somewhat ironic and definitely appropriate that the Mustang was taken to war for the very first time in American service by reservists and 'weekend flyers' - who were, no doubt, in comparison to their regular service comrades, very glad to get their hands on such a potent and modern warplane.

Sadly the first combat loss for the 154th occurred on 23 April 1943, when a P-51/F-6A was shot down by American anti-aircraft gunners in what would nowadays be called a 'friendly fire' incident. It was the first of many occasions for the Americans in which a Mustang was mistaken for a Messerschmitt Bf 109. The 154th OS flew the P-51/F-6A in combat for a comparatively short time, until around the second week of May 1943, after which the squadron was withdrawn from operations and later performed a training role followed by weather reconnaissance missions much later in the war predominantly with P-38 Lightning's.

The majority of the US-operated Mustang armed tactical reconnaissance missions in the Mediterranean theatre, following the withdrawal of the 154th, were subsequently performed by the 111th OS. This squadron was a Texas National Guard unit which, prior to its pioneering Mustang days had been equipped, amongst other types, with the North American O-47. It flew the Douglas A-20 and some P-39 Airacobra's in North Africa prior to transitioning onto Mustang combat operations in the summer of 1943. Appropriately nicknamed the 'Snoopers', this squadron was re-designated as the 111th Reconnaissance Squadron

Excellent side view of an early P-51 (repossessed Mustang Mk.IA), with the US serial number 41-37324. It was customary on USAAF aircraft to paint this military serial number prominently somewhere on the airframe, and in the case of Allison-Mustangs it was usually on the rear fuselage. The style of presentation was to omit the first digit of the Fiscal Year (here 1941) and the dash, giving in the case of this aircraft the displayed number '137324'. The wing-mounted 20mm cannons with their attendant prominent fairings that protruded from the wing leading edge are clearly seen in this image (Photo: NAA)

One of the repossessed Mustang Mk.IAs which thus became a P-51 for American use was involved in a somewhat bizarre experiment in camouflage finishes during the mid-war period. At that time some strange concepts were being devised for the camouflaging of combat aircraft. Painted black and white on its horizontal surfaces and underneath in a strange 'dazzle' scheme, sometimes referred to as 'confusion camouflage', but with the uppersurfaces remaining in standard Dark Olive Drab, the P-51 gave a strange but striking appearance. Needless to say the application was not used in combat. In this image, work is progressing on the painting of the aircraft, while two officers discuss the finer points of the experiment using a scale model of the Mustang for reference. At least one other Mustang was employed in 'confusion camouflage' tests using a different scheme (Photo: USAAF)

The uppersurfaces of the strange 'dazzle' painted P-51 remained in standard Dark Olive Drab, with the then-current circular US star national insignia on the port upper wing surface. This unusual camouflage finish, needless to say, was not standardized for combat *(Photo: USAAF)*

It was in April and May 1943 that the 154th Observation Squadron operated the P-51/F-6A in North Africa, and so introduced the Mustang into combat for the whole of the USAAF. US records suggest that one of the aircraft involved at that time was P-51/F-6A serial number 41-37322, named 'Mah Sweet Eva Lea' (the latter word is sometimes spelled 'Lee' in published sources). The Mustang prominently wore the 'Stars and Stripes' on its vertical tail, as an added recognition feature – this marking was carried by many of the early US fighter and reconnaissance aircraft in North Africa in the initial phases of US involvement there *(Photo: USAAF)*

(Fighter) in May 1943, and thence as the 111th Tactical Reconnaissance Squadron in November 1943. Throughout that time the unit flew the P-51/F-6A, its missions including the whole range of tactical reconnaissance and light-attack operations that the RAF's Tac/R Mustangs were successfully already flying and continuing at that time to fly in North-west Europe. The 111th, however, remained in the Mediterranean and Southern Europe throughout its time with the Allison-Mustang.

With its 20mm cannon wing armament prominently visible, P-51 (Mustang Mk.IA equivalent) 'Betty Jean' of the 111th Tactical Reconnaissance Squadron rests between missions during the long and hard-fought Italian campaign. Also featured in other photographs in this chapter, this particular aircraft displays in this image a revised tail marking with a letter code, without the 'Stars and Stripes' that was originally painted on the vertical tail of many US aircraft following their arrival at the time of the North African campaign onwards. The influx of US aircraft into North Africa from 1942 caused many headaches of aircraft recognition amongst the Allies, and so any additional recognition markings were welcomed
(Photo: R.L. Ward Collection)

Beginning its service at first in North Africa, the 111th commenced operations during the early part of July in earnest (it appears from the squadron's history that the first sorties were flown on 7 July) from Bou Ficha and Korba, Tunisia, after a period mainly spent performing training. However, the squadron soon moved to Sicily in the period around 14 July 1943, as the Allies gradually worked their way into Italy with the initial landings in Sicily following the Axis surrender in North Africa. In September 1943 the 111th moved to Italy proper, keeping up closely with the Allied ground offensives and performing various tasks including spotting for naval and field artillery. In fact the 111th was the only US tactical reconnaissance squadron in the Southern Europe area, giving the unit much work to do – which was a good showing for a squadron that had originated in the Texas National Guard. The P-51/F-6A's armament of four 20mm cannons proved to be very useful for air-to-ground work in addition to the primary function of reconnaissance. However, as the Allison Mustangs became increasingly tired and war weary, the 111th gradually re-equipped during the spring and summer of 1944 with later marks of Mustang. During that time the 111th was assigned directly to XII Tactical Air Command due to the disbandment of the 68th TRG in June 1944. The final Allison Mustangs appear to have been withdrawn (on paper at least) by the squadron in July 1944.

The role of the 68th Observation/Tactical Reconnaissance Group role in pioneering the Mustang in combat with the USAAF is nowadays largely forgotten, as indeed is the contribution specifically made to the Mustang story by its 111th and 154th Observation Squadrons, but these units were the true pioneers of US Mustang operations.

On the evidence of this photograph, it appears to have taken approximately eight men to manhandle a Mustang on the ground. The aircraft in the picture is 'Betty Jean', a 20mm cannon-armed P-51 (Mustang Mk.IA equivalent), operated by the 111th Tactical Reconnaissance Squadron and seen here at a temporary airstrip in April 1944 during the period of heavy fighting after the US landings at Anzio in Italy. Serial number 41-37367, this aircraft shows the worn appearance of the standard Dark Olive Drab upper and Neutral Grey lower finish of many of the Allison-engined Mustangs as they fought a long and often forgotten war. *(Photo: US Army)*

The often-photographed 20mm cannon-armed P-51 41-37367 'Betty Jean' of the 111th Tactical Reconnaissance Squadron is aided in this image to its revetment by two men, one sitting on its tail and the other on the right-hand wing, to give directions to the pilot. Without this kind of help, taxiing a Mustang, especially in austere conditions such as those seen here, was not easy for the pilot. The primitive conditions during the Anzio landings in Italy, which began in January 1944 and which is where this photograph was taken in April 1944, are representative of the sometimes very difficult conditions in which many Mustangs operated – especially those tasked with tactical missions in support of local army units *(Photo: US Army)*

Successful US Service

The A-36A final assembly line at NAA's Inglewood (Mines Field) facility, with the fuselage and wing assemblies successfully mated, and the many subsequent tasks under way to connect everything up, both hydraulic and electrical, and to install additional equipment and fittings. In this view the retractable lattice-style airbrake that was installed on each wing's upper surface of this dive-bomber derivative of the Mustang can be seen – there was also one of these dive brakes under each wing. The fact that these aircraft were Allison-powered is illustrated by the carburettor air intake above the nose. All Allison-engined Mustangs were built at Inglewood *(Photo: NAA)*

The P-51/F-6A had been taken on by the USAAF very much as a requisitioned type from a foreign procurement, by repossessing some of the intended Mustang Mk IA production originally destined for Britain. However, in 1942 – at last - the Army Air Force actually ordered its own Mustangs. But, in yet another irony in the Mustang's story, it was not as a fighter that the type was initially bought by the US military. In a bizarre twist, particularly bearing in mind the Mustang's later success as a fighter, the first purchase of the Mustang for the USAAF was as a dive-bomber.

A number of explanations have been advanced over the years to rationalize this extraordinary turn of events. Certainly the US military was well aware of developments in the air war over Europe during the first years of World War Two. The Luftwaffe's initial successes with the Junkers Ju 87 'Stuka' dive-bomber had apparently justified this type of military action. Using a dive to aim a bomb on a specific target was definitely a potentially much

more accurate way of delivering the ordnance compared to bombing from a horizontal attitude. Unfortunately for the advocates of this type of aerial warfare, the dive-bomber tended to make a good target if fired at by alert and well-trained anti-aircraft gunners, particularly if several aircraft dived over the same target one after another, allowing the gunners time to refine their aim. The Ju 87 had also proven itself to be a poor adversary if met by opposing well-armed high-performance fighters, as proved to be the case during the Battle of France and thereafter particularly during the Battle of Britain. Dive-bombing is additionally by its nature a highly dangerous means of attack, needing a very physically fit crew and the capability to correctly judge the pull-out to prevent the aircraft from slamming into the ground. Nevertheless the USAAF encouraged North American Aviation to develop a dive-bomber version of the Mustang, utilising the type's already good dive performance. Writing in his book 'Mustang: A Documentary History', the late

Jeffery Ethell pointed out that due to the opposition to the Mustang in some offices within the AAF, and following the spending of the amount of money available for fighters in the FY 1941 and FY 1942 budgets, the only obvious way to get the Mustang into production for the USAAF was to dress it up as a fighter-bomber. That way it could be procured under the funding for bomber and attack aircraft!

The Mustang Becomes a Dive-Bomber

It is obvious that there was strange logic or behind-the-scenes machinations to get the Mustang into production, that were pursued by the comparatively small number of friends that the type had at that time within the upper echelons of the US military. Nevertheless, the Mustang actually emerged as a capable if generally unheralded dive-bomber. Development work at NAA began in the late spring of 1942, following official go-ahead on 16 April (contract no. AC-27396), and the resulting dive-bomber derivative of the Mustang was a very different beast to the basic P-51/Mustang Mk IA configuration. NAA later claimed to have spent 40,000 man hours of work developing the A-36 from the basic P-51 layout. The armament was completely revised, with the nose-mounted 0.5-in machine guns retained, but the wing gun layout was altered to two 0.5-in machine guns in each wing. Indeed, the whole wing structure was altered and strengthened, with provision for a pylon beneath each wing just outboard of the main undercarriage stressed to carry a 500 lb (227 kg) bomb. To aid in the dive-bombing mission, a retractable lattice-style airbrake was installed on each wing's upper and lower surface, to help bring the new type's velocity in the dive to an acceptable margin – this being a speed of some 300 mph (483 km/h). Many other alterations were also introduced to the basic Mustang layout, including the installation of a 1,325 hp

Allison V-1710-87 engine. The underwing pitot installation of earlier Mustangs was changed to a prominent fitment unique to this variant on the right-hand wing leading edge, near to the tip. Perhaps most noticeably, there was a complete change to the underfuselage air intake. On the basic P-51 and RAF Mustang layout up to that time, this lower mid-fuselage intake had a moveable portion. On the new dive-bomber, the intake was of a revised design that was fixed.

Allocated the designation A-36 ('A' meaning 'Attack'), the type entered production in the late summer of 1942. Altogether, 500 were ordered, and assigned the US serial numbers 42-83663 to 42-84162 (a listing of the US military serial numbers that were allocated to Mustangs is included in the Appendices at the end of this Book). They were built as A-36A-1-NA, and because they were of a revised configuration the new NAA company designation of NA-97 was allocated. The first aircraft flew on 21 September 1942, with Robert Chilton at the controls, and the type must have had few if any problems, because the first deliveries are recorded as having been made the following month. Indeed, there does not appear to have been any need for a prototype or development airframe. However, it was some time before the A-36A saw combat.

Initial deliveries of production A-36As were made in October 1942 for training in the continental US, and two combat Groups – the 27th and 86th Bombardment Groups - were intended for A-36 deployment. A number of US-based training squadrons subsequently received A-36As for transition and dive-bombing training. These included several of the units in the numerical sequence 632nd to 638th Bombardment Squadrons (Dive), which were mainly concentrated in the south of the US, with Drew Field in Florida being one of the training bases associated with several of these little-known training squadrons. A number

An A-36A Invader is run up, probably following delivery to the USAAF (note what appears to be an incomplete B-26 Marauder in the right-hand background). The A-36A was easily distinguished from all other marks of Allison-engined Mustang, not only by its wing dive brakes (which are not visible in this view), but also the twin landing light installation in the leading edge of the left-hand wing, and the relocated pitot fitment near to the right-hand wingtip, the latter moved from its usual underwing position due to the dive brakes. In the background to the left of the picture is another A-36A, serial number 42-83771. The A-36A was armed with six 0.5-in machine guns – two in each wing and two in the lower nose *(Photo: USAAF)*

Manufacture of the A-36A Invader kick-started the whole production effort of the Mustang for US service, although the extraordinary thinking in some offices of the Army Air Force saw the Mustang as being best suited as a close support aircraft and definitely not as a fighter. Photographed here is A-36A Invader serial number 42-83671. Evident from this angle is the twin-light fitment in the leading edge of the left-hand wing, and the two 0.5-in machine guns in the lower nose, although the gun ports for the wing 0.5-in machine guns have been sealed, underlining the fact that this is a US-based trainer or trials aircraft (Photo: R.L. Ward Collection)

of these instructional squadrons were a part of the 407th BG (Dive), which became the 407th Fighter-Bomber Group in August 1943 when there was a general reclassification of AAF dive-bomber units as fighter-bomber units. Training also appears to have taken place at Key Field, Mississippi. Most pilots were positively impressed with the A-36's speed and manoeuvrability, but dive-bombing training was an exacting and dangerous proposition. There were a number of fatal accidents that were mainly attributable to inexperience with this type of tactics, although some A-36s found the stresses involved to be too great and – sadly – broke up in flight.

Dive-Bomber Mustangs in Action

Of the operational units that were intended to fly the A-36A in combat, the 27th BG (Light) had previously flown the Douglas A-24 (the AAF's land-based variant of the US Navy's SBD Dauntless carrier-borne dive-bomber), and elements of the Group were in the Philippines during the Japanese invasion in early 1942. After the loss of the Philippines the unit was subsequently deployed back to the US where it flew Douglas A-20 Havoc twin-engined light bombers before starting to convert onto the A-36. This transition continued after the Group moved to North Africa, its advanced echelon relocating there in late 1942 and January 1943. It became a constituent part of the Twelfth Army Air Force, and gained operational status on the A-36A at Ras el Ma, French Morocco, in April 1943. The constituent squadrons of the 27th were the 16th, 17th, and 91st Bombardment Squadrons (Light). Initial operations were flown

by the Group's aircraft on 6 June 1943 against Axis forces on the heavily-defended Italian island of Pantelleria, 62 miles (100 km) south-west of the south-western extremity of Sicily, and 43 miles (70 km) east of the North African coast. At that time the 16th and 91st BS (L) were based at Ras el Ma, but the 17th was deploying to the airstrip at Korba – again illustrating the rather nomadic lives that existed for combat units in the North African theatre. These first operations were actually armed reconnaissance flights over Pantelleria, and unfortunately one aircraft in the first wave of eleven A-36As over the island was shot down by anti-aircraft fire. Dive-bombing operations commenced the following day. The ultimately successful aerial bombardment of Pantelleria by the A-36As together with other Allied aerial assets and its take-over by Allied forces (Operation 'Corkscrew') also aided the Allied takeover of the similarly strategically-important islands of Lampedusa and Linosa, which represented a very successful start to operations for the A-36A. The Group was subsequently fully involved in the Allied invasion of Sicily (Operation 'Husky'), which began on the night of 9-10 July 1943 and was completed on 17 August with complete Allied victory – aided in large part by the successful operations of Allied air assets.

During that month there was a major reshuffling of US air assets which included a considerable amount of renaming and some renumbering of flying units. This included the 27th and its component squadrons. The 'Light' category was withdrawn, and the 27th was renamed the 27th Fighter-Bomber Group. Its component squadrons were renamed as Fighter-Bomber

A-36A serial number 42-83671, prominently bears the number '71' or the letter/number combination '7I', and was probably photographed somewhere in the Continental US. Each mark of the Allison-engined Mustang had its own peculiarities, the A-36A for example having a specific form of radio mast on the 'razorback' spine behind the cockpit as seen in this photograph
(Photo: R.L. Ward Collection)

Squadrons, and were renumbered as follows – the 16th became the 522nd; the 17th was altered to 523rd; and the 91st was renumbered 524th. The 27th subsequently continued its dive-bombing operations, and ultimately took part in the invasion of mainland Italy. This included cover for the landings at Salerno, and it was during those operations that the Mustang really started to gain its laurels. On 10 September the Group participated in frantic Allied efforts to defend the fragile bridgehead that had been established at Salerno, which was coming under fierce attack from German forces. During the course of these operations, in which several pilots flew a number of sorties during the day, the 27th was instrumental in preventing three German armoured divisions from reaching the increasingly pressured Allied forces in the bridgehead. For these actions the 27th was subsequently awarded a Distinguished Unit Citation. It was the first, but certainly not the last, occasion that a Mustang unit received this highest US military award for a combat unit

By then, the 27th had been joined by the second A-36A unit to see combat in the North African and Mediterranean theatres with the Twelfth AAF. This was the 86th Bombardment Group (Dive), which had started to move to North Africa from the US in the spring of 1943 – and was therefore the second, and final, A-36A unit to move to the Mediterranean theatre. The initial base used by the 86th was La Senia in Algeria, and the Group's flying units consisted of the 309th, 310th, and 312th Bombardment Squadrons (Dive). The unit's A-36As first entered combat in July 1943, and during the following month the Group's squadrons were renumbered and redesignated in the same fashion to those of the 27th BG (Light). The 309th became the 525th Fighter-Bomber Squadron; the 310th was altered to 526th Fighter-Bomber Squadron; and the 312th was renumbered 527th Fighter-Bomber Squadron. The 86th itself became the 86th Fighter-Bomber Group. The unit's A-36As had by then already mounted dive-bombing and ground-attack missions against Axis forces during the Sicily campaign, the headquarters of the Group moving to Gela on Sicily in July 1943. Like the 27th,

the 86th was afterwards fully committed to combat during the Allied landings on mainland Italy, and the subsequent often slow and difficult advances. The unit's headquarters moved up to Sele in Italy in mid- to late September. In similar fashion to the 27th, the 86th was involved in attacking a wide range of tactical targets. These included rail lines, trains, supply dumps, troop concentrations, gun emplacements, armour and transport columns, shipping, bridges, and strongpoints. A diving A-36A with its airbrakes deployed was said to make an unnerving noise not unlike that of the Luftwaffe's Ju 87 'Stuka'. Tactics were evolved during the time that the 27th and 86th operated the type. For dive-bombing missions, each aircraft would often carry a 500 lb (227 kg) bomb on each wing pylon. There were often twelve aircraft involved in specific missions, usually broken into flights of four. Attacks would be mounted from around 8,000 ft (2,438 m) to 10,000 ft (3,048 m), with individual aircraft 'peeling off' from the formation to drop vertically or near vertically on the target. Unfortunately this tended - not surprisingly - to alert the target's defences, so that by the time the fourth or so aircraft was hurtling down towards the same spot from the same starting point, the anti-aircraft fire would often be coming upwards accurately. Attrition in combat was therefore relatively high, although losses were similarly encountered during strafing attacks at low level. Against heavily-defended targets, diving attacks would normally be initiated from lower altitudes, with pull-out of the dive achieved at near ground-level. Some missions were however flown as horizontal conventional fighter-bombers at higher altitudes, which was somewhat safer. Sometimes as many as three or four sorties could be flown by pilots each day, with some flights being as short as fifteen-minutes, others lasting up to three and a half hours.

As an important aside, it is interesting to note that although the A-36A was almost universally known as a 'Mustang', the name 'Invader' was sometimes used for the type. Invader was an appropriate title, as the A-36As were involved in several invasions during their period of operational service, and it is a name that some historians appropriately use to describe the

Two of North American Aviation's greatest products fly side-by-side over California, in a photograph dated March 1943. The Mustang is actually an A-36A Invader, serial number 42-83861, in the standard Dark Olive Drab and Neutral Grey colour scheme adopted for US combat aircraft in the early war years. Beside it is an AT-6 Texan in natural metal and silver finish. Both aircraft were possibly assigned to a training unit, or were awaiting delivery
(Photo: NAA)

Pictured at Hergla, Tunisia in a photograph dated 13 June 1943, this A-36A reveals its type by showing off its upper left wing dive brake against the yellow wing stripe. The dark blue and white star national insignia have a yellow surround. Two Twelfth Air Force units flew the A-36A in combat in the MTO, the 27th Fighter-Bomber Group and the 86th Fighter-Bomber Group, and the type was generally successful if little publicised in the fighter-bomber and dive-bomber roles. As far as is known, this aircraft was assigned to the 27th FBG, or at least what became the 27th FBG in July 1943, and had the serial number 42-84057 or '058' (and not 42-80457 as sometimes claimed)
(Photo Howard Levy via R.L. Ward)

type. In more recent times, the name 'Apache' has been specifically ascribed to the A-36A. This is a strange development, because the name 'Apache' was originally going to apply to the whole Mustang line, until Britain renamed it as the Mustang during 1940. The name Mustang stuck for all versions of this aircraft type, and the title 'Apache' was dropped – yet for some reason has in recent times become associated specifically with the dive-bombers of the Mustang line.

In similar fashion to their tactical reconnaissance colleagues, the A-36A pilots did not have the mission of countering the Luftwaffe high on their agenda. However, whereas the reconnaissance pilots were usually actively discouraged from taking on enemy fighters unless it was to defend themselves and the vital intelligence that they were gathering, the A-36A pilots were able to 'mix it' more often and sometimes with considerable success. The A-36A, like all Allison-engined Mustangs, was capable of looking after itself so long as the combat took place at low or relatively low level, and several AAF pilots scored comparatively well on the type. The 27th FBG achieved at least 45 confirmed aerial victories (according to official USAF summaries created after the end of the war), with the 522nd FBS claiming 26. Amongst this squadron's pilots, Lt Michael T. Russo was unique in achieving ace status on the A-36A. He had originally joined the 27th BG (Light) in June 1943, and was

assigned to the 16th BS (Light). This squadron became the 522nd FBS on 23 August 1943, and Russo achieved his first aerial victory on 13 September over a Focke-Wulf Fw 190 off the Italian coast near Salerno. He subsequently brought down a Fieseler Fi 167 'Storch' liaison aircraft on 24 October, and a Junkers Ju 52/3m transport over an airfield near Avezzano on 8 December. On 30 December he shot down two Messerschmitt Bf 109s to become an ace. He was therefore one of only a very small number of pilots to score five aerial victories in an Allison-engined Mustang – a unique achievement in itself, but all the more remarkable that he was flying the dive-bomber variant of the type, and he was the only A-36A ace.

Despite their undoubted prowess, the comparatively high loss rate of the A-36As had the unfortunate result that the Invader was running out of combat effectiveness by early 1944. Replacements were not available due to the cessation by NAA of Allison-engined Mustang production during 1943, and the type consequently began to be withdrawn from service. The 27th FBG was the first to trade in its A-36As, and for a short time had to revert to flying the P-40 Warhawk. This took place in the opening weeks of 1944, with the unit's last Invaders out of service in February (the final A-36A mission was flown on the 21st), but the unit converted onto the much more capable Republic P-47 Thunderbolt to continue its fighter-bomber work within a few

Photographed performing training duties in Florida in 1943, this P-51A bears the fuselage code 'E25' which is believed to signify attachment to the training airfield at Eglin Army Air Field. Although they were comparatively small in numbers, the P-51A Mustangs performed valuable service and this P-51A shows off some of the distinguishing features of the type, including two 0.5-in machine guns in each wing, a lack of armament in the lower nose, and a single landing light installation in the leading edge of the left-hand wing. As with many Allison-engined Mustangs, its Dark Olive Drab upper surface colour appears to be very worn *(Photo: R.L. Ward Collection)*

months. The 27th's surplus A-36As were transferred to the 86th FBG to fly alongside its existing Invaders, but that Group too began to transition off the A-36A in the summer of 1944, eventually moving onto the P-47 Thunderbolt for fighter-bomber missions while also flying some P-40 Warhawk's. The final A-36A mission by the 86th took place on 15 July 1944. Around 14 A-36As did, however, find a completely new home. They had been transferred to the 111th TRS, to supplement that unit's P-51/F-6A Mustangs described in the previous Chapter of this Book, although July 1944 also marked the end of that unit's Allison-Mustang operations altogether.

The A-36A was flown by one further USAAF unit in combat, but this one was based a very long way from the heat of North Africa and the rain and mud of Italy. The unit concerned was the 311th FBG in the CBI (China-Burma-India) theatre. Comprising the 528th, 529th, and 530th Fighter-Bomber Squadrons, the former was equipped with the A-36A when the 311th commenced operations from northern India in late 1943. These squadrons were previously known as Bombardment Squadrons (Dive), but were redesignated as Fighter-Bomber Squadrons on 30 September 1943. Assigned to the Tenth Army Air Force, the Group operated in support of Allied forces in the north of Burma. Originally stationed at Nawadih, India, in September 1943, having moved to India via Australia in July-August 1943, the 311th's headquarters moved on to Dinjan in the same country from October 1943 and later to Burma in July 1944 as the Allies started to make headway against Japanese forces. Primarily equipped with the A-36A was the 528th FBS, based for a time at Sookerating in Assam, in the north-east of India, although in reality a number of the dive-bombers were held throughout the 311th FBG.

As was the case with many of the Allison-engined Mustang units, the 311th's squadrons lived a rather nomadic existence and often operated from comparatively primitive airstrips. The 311th flew its first combat mission with the A-36A on 16 October 1943, but three of the eight aircraft committed were lost. In reality, however, the A-36A had proved itself by the time that the 311th's squadrons entered combat to be a capable and

sometimes very effective dive-bomber – and some had been flown for training by the 311th prior to leaving the US. The A-36A was definitely a much better and more successful aircraft in the operational role of dive-bomber than the other main types of dive-bomber that the AAF operated at that time – the Douglas A-24, and the Vultee A-31 and A-35 Vengeance. Approximately 300 of the 500 A-36As that were built found their way to an operational command, and 84 enemy aircraft were claimed shot down by A-36A pilots. One example of the A-36A was officially passed to Britain (serial number EW998, ex-42-83685, which was trialled at Boscombe Down during 1943), but in the field a number of examples were used by the RAF on occasion as operational demands dictated the 'borrowing' of some US-operated Mustangs, as explained earlier in this book. Eventually most surviving A-36As were passed to training units, some were used as 'hacks' in the communications role, while others were simply scrapped – having been worn out by their operational exploits.

By mid-1943 - at last - the US Mustang had had a comparatively good official report written about it in the United States – in contrast to the negative reporting that it had originally received from some of the officers at the Materiel Command at Wright Field. In late 1942 the Materiel Command had finally allowed the Army Air Forces Proving Ground Command at Eglin Field, Florida, to test the A-36A (actually three aircraft were eventually assigned) and assess its suitability for combat. Eglin should have had a Mustang to test long before that time, but vacillation and seemingly deliberate obstruction from Wright Field had resulted in constant delays. The subsequent report, signed by Capt M.A. McKenzie, a Project Officer at Eglin, was dated 15 April 1943 and was little short of a glowing testament to the Mustang. In fact the report's writers were not particularly impressed with the A-36A as a dive-bomber (and actually recommended that the type's wing dive brakes should be eliminated), but were highly impressed with the type's flying characteristics, stability, well balanced controls, and good stall characteristics. The Eglin test pilots who flew the three aircraft discovered a maximum speed for the type of 324

The P-51A was the first version of the Mustang line that was a true fighter. It was armed simply with two 0.5-in machine guns in each wing. The P-51A illustrated here was probably assigned to a US-based training unit, but other P-51As from the relatively limited P-51A production run found their way to some very far-flung battlegrounds *(Photo: USAAF)*

mph (521 km/h) at the engine's optimum altitude of 5,000 ft (1,524 m). Unfortunately one of the three test aircraft was destroyed while diving when it broke up, and speeds of some 450 mph (724 km/h) were encountered even with the wing dive brakes open. However, the Eglin test pilots realised that when the A-36A was unencumbered with bombs, it was potentially an excellent low-level fighter. This confirmed the views of many of the British and Commonwealth pilots who were already at that time flying Mustangs in combat over North-west Europe. The scene was set for the Mustang to be regarded as a fighter for AAF service.

The Mustang Becomes a Fighter

The production of Allison-engined Mustangs by North American Aviation ceased in the summer of 1943. This accounts for the growing shortage of A-36As for operation in Italy, as recounted earlier in this chapter. Nevertheless, before manufacture ended, one further Allison-engined Mustang version was produced. This variant, the P-51A, was – at last - a fighter version for US service. The growing realisation by many in the upper echelons of the Army Air Force that the Mustang was a worthwhile combat aircraft, coupled with increasingly glowing reports from the pilots who were flying the type in combat, at last started to result in the Mustang having more friends than enemies within the US military. It began to be apparent to many that the Mustang was a better aircraft than existing Army fighters such as the Curtiss P-40 Warhawk and Bell P-39 Airacobra, and was potentially as good – if not better –

than the more advanced (compared to the P-39 and P-40) Lockheed P-38 Lightning and Republic P-47 Thunderbolt. Indeed, in a scathing letter dated 31 August 1942 to the chief of the Materiel Command at Wright Field (Echols), Major Gen Muir S. Fairchild (the director of military requirements at the HQ of the USAAF in Washington, D.C.) showed his surprise at the apparent vacillation in the procurement of the Mustang, and stated that "The P-51 airplane appears to be the most promising fighter in existence. Its production and increased performance are of paramount importance". During the summer of 1942 the FY 1943 funding year began. This included a fresh and expanded budget for new fighters to be purchased, and as soon as possible the Allison-engined Mustang was added to the fighter procurement. This took place on 23 June 1942 (Contract No.AC-30479, with the NAA designation NA-99). Again, just who was able to get the Mustang onto the list for purchase is not known – there certainly appears to have been little or no encouragement directed from Wright Field towards the military purchasing offices in Washington - and even now there is some confusion as to the exact intention of this purchase. It has been speculated that the total P-51A procurement was planned to be 1,200 aircraft, but several writers have subsequently argued that the total of 1,200 included the 500 A-36As already mentioned. In the event only 310 P-51As were in fact funded. However, this was a good start, and the new model included several further refinements to the basic Mustang layout.

Power for the P-51A was provided by an Allison V-1710-81 engine of 1,200 hp. Significantly, there was provision for the

Side view of P-51A-1-NA serial number 43-6008, showing all the relevant features of the P-51A layout, albeit with the addition of underwing three-tube 'bazooka' type rocket launchers. Each tube carried a single 4.5-in unguided rocket, and although many writers have claimed that these weapons were widely used and highly effective, the story is not so straightforward. Unwieldy, drag-producing and inaccurate, they were additionally bad for the Mustang's centre of gravity and trimming. It was also impossible to effectively dog-fight with these cumbersome appliances installed. 'Zero-length' rocket rails were made available by NAA for factory installation much later in the Mustang production, and they proved to be far more successful *(Photo: NAA)*

carriage of underwing bombs or long-range fuel tanks. Although as previously related the Allison-engined Mustang already had a fine endurance and range on its internal fuel, the ability to carry a 75 US gallon 'drop tank' beneath each wing added significantly to an already good capability. It was the beginning of the transformation of the Mustang into a long-range escort fighter, although as yet the metamorphosis was by no means complete. The P-51A dispensed with the two synchronised machine guns in the lower nose of other Allison Mustangs, and simply mounted two 0.5-in machine guns in each wing. A small but significant distinguishing point of these new Allison-engined Mustangs was the addition of a vent window in the left-hand transparent windscreen panel. The first P-51A flew on 3 February 1943, with Robert Chilton at the controls. Of the production run of 310 machines, 50 were supplied to the RAF under Lend-Lease as Mustang Mk IIs to offset the requisition of the 57 earlier Mustang Mk IAs intended for the RAF that instead were used by the Americans as the P-51/F-6A. The USAAF serials for the complete P-51A production run of 310 examples were 43-6003 to 43-6312, in three major production blocks – all were built by NAA at Inglewood, as indeed was every Allison-engined Mustang.

With such a short production run, the Army Air Force employed its comparatively small number of P-51As very sparingly, but in the second half of 1943 they started to reach combat units. The first to take the P-51A into action was the 311th Fighter-Bomber Group. As previously explained, the 311th deployed to India to become a part of the Tenth Army Air Force in September 1943. In addition to its 528th and 529th Fighter-Bomber Squadrons, which flew a variety of tactical missions including light-attack and reconnaissance with the former in particular being associated with the A-36A, the 311th also comprised the 530th FBS. Despite its name, this unit from the first was principally a fighter squadron, and although it apparently had some A-36As assigned at the start, it was primarily equipped with the P-51A. The unit's initial base was at

Dinjan, comparatively near the border between northern Burma and India, but the 530th forward-deployed to Kurmitola and the famous Allied air base at Cox's Bazaar (sometimes spelled Cox's Bazar) for its initial long-range forays into action. On 25 November 1943, the 530th flew its first major combat mission. The occasion was an escort for North American B-25 Mitchell medium bombers which were tasked with a raid on the Japanese air base at Mingaladon in Burma. The Mustangs were fitted with 75 US gallon external fuel tanks beneath their wings for this mission. The Japanese met the raid in force and a number of major air battles ensued, during which two Mustangs were shot down. The Japanese were flying the highly-capable single-engined Nakajima Ki-43 Hayabusa 'Oscar', and the twin-engined Kawasaki Ki-45 Toryu 'Nick' heavy fighter. The 530th achieved its first victory that day, when Lt James England claimed a 'Nick'.

Two days later the squadron flew escort, together with P-38 Lightnings of the 459th FS, for Allied raids in and around the Burmese capital Rangoon. The bomber force comprised B-24 Liberators of the 308th Bombardment Group, and B-25 Mitchells. The P-51As of the 530th struggled to provide cover for the Liberators, and came up against the battle-hardened 'Oscar'-equipped 64th Sentai of the Imperial Japanese Army Air Force (IJAAF), which they had first encountered two days earlier. Two Mustangs were shot down, as were two Lightnings and a Liberator. However, the 530th also gained victories, with James England shooting down an 'Oscar', and Lt Robert Mulhollem downing two 'Oscars' and claiming a third as a probable. Years after the war it became increasingly likely that the 'probable' claim was particularly significant because it concerned an ace pilot of the 64th, Lt. Yohei Hinoki, who succeeded in limping back to base badly injured. Hinoki subsequently had a leg amputated, and was only able to return to combat within weeks of the end of the war, thus depriving the Japanese of one of their most gifted fighter pilots for much of the rest of the conflict.

Increasingly in combat, the Mustangs again flew escort for Allied bombers for strikes in and around Rangoon on 1

Well-known but nonetheless interesting photograph of two P-51A Mustangs of the 1st Air Commando Group over rugged Burmese terrain in 1944. The nearest aircraft coded '13' was named 'Mrs. Virginia', but the Mustang in the background coded '1' was allocated to the commander of the 1st Air Commando Group, the colourful Col Philip Cochran. Both aircraft wear the five diagonal white stripes around their rear fuselages over their worn Dark Olive Drab and Neutral Grey colour scheme that signified the Air Commandos in that area. Cochran's aircraft was serial number 43-6199, a P-51A-10-NA *(Photo: USAAF)*

December 1943, once more with mixed results as one Mustang was lost but one claim was also made. Shortly after this, the 530th's aircraft had to act as defending fighters when the Japanese attempted to strike at the Allies' forward airfields. The Mustangs claimed two Mitsubishi Ki-21 'Sally' twin-engined bombers and an escorting 'Oscar' fighter without loss to themselves. The Mustangs subsequently deployed back to their base near Dinjan, but were again called upon to defend rather than attack on 27 March 1944. On that day a major Japanese air raid on the complex of Allied airfields in the Ledo, north-eastern India area, took place. Several pilots from the 530th were in the thick of the action, and James England claimed two 'Oscar' fighters plus a Nakajima Ki-49 Donryu 'Helen' twin-engined bomber to become an ace. The 311th FBG subsequently increasingly went onto the offensive as the Allies slowly began to regain the initiative against the Japanese. The Group's A-36As and P-51As were involved in many attacks that harassed the Japanese aerial power in central Burma. On 30 May 1944 the 530th was redesignated as the 530th Fighter Squadron. Earlier that month the squadron had participated in three significant attacks on the major Japanese air base at Meiktila, on the 11th, 12th and 14th, when a number of Japanese aircraft were destroyed in the air and on the ground – the P-51A's range capabilities being a significant factor in these operations. Robert Mulhollem shot down a Nakajima Ki-44 Shoki 'Tojo' on the 12 May mission to become the squadron's second Allison-engined Mustang ace. Several of the unit's Mustang pilots also scored a growing number of ground victories. However, the 311th (which had been redesignated as a Fighter Group in late May 1944) moved to Burma in July 1944, from where it flew some support missions for Merrill's Marauders, the American special operations force that harried the Japanese on and behind the front lines. During August 1944 the 311th was transferred to the US Fourteenth Army Air Force in China, taking up residence at Pungchacheng in China. At that time increasing numbers of Merlin-engined Mustangs were arriving that would eventually completely replace the veteran and increasingly tired Allison-engined Mustangs of the 311th. By then James England had become the top-ranking Allison-Mustang ace with eight confirmed aerial victories, having scored his eighth (a 'Tojo') on 14 May 1944 in the action over Meiktila airfield.

Increasing Combat Activities

It is a little-known fact that in the Chinese theatre, the Allison-engined Mustang had by that point already seen considerable combat. This had commenced at virtually the same time as the 311th FBG had taken the P-51A into combat over Burma. The USAAF Group that flew the Allison-Mustang in action over China was the 23rd Fighter Group, which was the successor and rightful heir to the legendary American Volunteer Group or 'Flying Tigers' of the early war years. The 23rd FG had been activated in China in July 1942 (although it had existed, at least on paper, before that time), and from the first contained a number of the experienced pilots who had flown with the Flying Tigers. In its early months of existence the unit flew Curtiss P-40 Warhawks, but began to transition onto the P-51A Mustang during the early winter of 1943. On 4 November 1943 Col David L. 'Tex' Hill became the new commanding officer of the 23rd FG, just as the P-51A started to re-equip the 76th Fighter Squadron of the 23rd FG. The squadron was based at that time at Hengyang in China, with a forward detachment at Suichwan, but later in the month the unit moved to Kweilin where the 23rd was headquartered. From there, it flew its first mission on 25 November 1943. This operation was specially planned by Hill, and took into account the Mustang's excellent long-range capabilities. Photo-reconnaissance by a Lockheed Lightning the previous day had shown considerable Japanese air assets at Shinchiku airfield on Formosa (today's Taiwan). This base had previously been well out of the range of the 23rd's P-40 Warhawks, resulting in unescorted attacks having to be made by AAF bombers. However, on 25 November a raid was flown by B-25 Mitchells escorted by eight 76th FS P-51As and eight Lockheed P-38G Lightnings of the 449th FS. The operation was a major success. The attacking force flew at low level and achieved complete surprise. The Lightnings directly escorted the medium bombers, allowing the Mustangs to strafe the airfield and shoot up any Japanese aircraft that took off. In the subsequent attack the Lightnings and Mustangs created havoc amongst the Japanese air assets, claiming 14 Japanese shot down and over double that number destroyed on the ground, while the Mitchells successfully bombed the airfield's installations. Hill himself shot down an 'Oscar', and none of the attacking US aircraft were lost.

Gradually, the Mustang supplanted the P-40 Warhawk as the main US fighter in China during the first half of 1944, but re-equipment was very slow. The CBI theatre was comparatively low on the list of priorities of the USAAF, and deliveries of the later Merlin-engined Mustangs for other commands were of greater priority. Nevertheless several pilots achieved aerial victories in the P-51A, and the type proved to be effective in ground-attack operations as well. The 76th FS made good use of its limited number of P-51As, although set-piece operations like the 25 November 1943 strike were not the normal type of mission flown. Victories were somewhat piecemeal. On 12 February the commanding officer of the 76th, Captain John Stewart, succeeded in shooting down an 'Oscar' that had tried to escape from him at low altitude. The Mustang easily out-ran and out-manoeuvred the Japanese fighter which in previous times had been a major thorn in the side of Allied pilots flying the Curtiss P-40. The 23rd FG eventually re-equipped with a variety of Merlin-engined Mustang models, but for the US pilots who flew the type and were able to compare it to the P-40, it was very clear which was the better fighter. For the first time the AAF had a combat aircraft in the Mustang that was capable of holding its own, and very often bettering, the Japanese fighters that had

given the P-40 such a hard time in the months before the Allison-Mustangs started to arrive at unit level in China in November 1943.

Again little-known, a further unit in the CBI flew the Allison-Mustang against the Japanese. This was the 1st Air Commando Group. Very much a pioneer of the type of combined forces operations and close air support that often characterise military action today, the Air Commandos were set up within the USAAF to support ground forces in specific areas and to provide comprehensive aerial capability for specific ground operations. To this end the 1st ACG featured fighter, bomber, transport, and glider assets within its organisation, and it was with the former that the P-51A gained a measure of success in the first half of 1944. Operating primarily in north-eastern India and northern Burma, the 1st ACG used its P-51As mainly in support of ground forces, which specifically included Wingate's Chindits behind the enemy lines in Burma. The 1st ACG was activated in India on 29 March 1944, and was initially based at Hailakandi in India although in practice its air elements were stationed wherever required. Prior to that time a provisional unit designation, the

Excellent detail view of the cockpit area of a P-51A. Many relevant details are visible, including the cumbersome cockpit opening panels, the additional small vent window on the left-hand transparent windscreen panel that was unique to the P-51A, and the area behind the pilot where the radio was installed on fighter Mustangs, but was occupied by an oblique-mounted camera on Mustangs configured for reconnaissance. The 'quarterlight' D-shaped window that normally covered that space has been removed in this photograph. The P-51A was the first true production fighter Mustang that was made specifically for the USAAF, previous Mustangs finding their way into the US inventory being repossessions from British orders or specifically made as dive-bombers (Photo: NAA)

Believed to have been photographed at Karachi, India, this line-up comprises P-51A Mustangs of the 1st Air Commando Group. The aircraft were awaiting redeployment to a forward base nearer to the fighting in Burma. The Air Commandos were by their nature nomadic, and often operated from austere airstrips while performing their tasks of close-support of ground units, some of which were operating behind enemy lines *(Photo: USAAF)*

5318th, had covered the early days of this unit – the air commando personnel were famous for their disdain of red tape and so the official paperwork took some time to catch up with them! The Group operated a comparatively small number of P-51As (although approximately thirty appear to have been delegated to the unit on its creation) that were distinctively adorned with five diagonal white stripes around their rear fuselages. The commanding officer of the Group was initially the colourful Col Philip Cochran, but aerial victories were in very short supply for the Mustangs of the unit – fighting the Japanese in the air definitely not being a priority. However, a notable victory was scored by a 1st ACG Allison Mustang pilot, this being an 'Oscar' over Imphal, India, on 17 April 1944 by Lt Col Grant Mahony. This shoot-down made Mahony an ace, his four previous victories having been achieved in the dark days of the Philippines and Java campaigns in late 1941 and early 1942, his first being on 8 December 1941 in a P-40 while with the 3rd Pursuit Squadron on Luzon in the Philippines. In the 1st ACG, the Allison-Mustang was replaced later in 1944 by P-47 Thunderbolts. However, for its initial air operations (that included the P-51As) between March and May 1944, the 1st ACG was awarded a Distinguished Unit Citation.

Reconnaissance Assets

In every sense a world away from the P-51A operations in the China-Burma-India theatre, a comparatively small number of P-51As also operated in North-west Europe. Amongst the 260 P-51As that were assigned to the USAAF (excluding the fifty that were diverted to Britain as Mustang Mk IIs from the total 310 production run), thirty-five were converted to reconnaissance standard. This involved the addition of a K.24 camera behind the pilot, in an installation similar to that in the original reconnaissance derivative of the P-51, the F-6A. The reconnaissance version of the P-51A was designated F-6B (and not F-6A, as incorrectly claimed in many published sources), and it retained the normal armament of the P-51A. It is possible that some examples were fitted with a second K.24 camera,

mounted vertically in the fuselage behind the openable radiator air outlet. Approximately two dozen of these aircraft were shipped to Europe, where they were assigned to what is believed to be the only reconnaissance unit that flew the type operationally. This was the 107th Tactical Reconnaissance Squadron of the 67th Tactical Reconnaissance Group, US Ninth Army Air Force. In similar fashion to the 111th and 154th Observation Squadrons that flew the P-51/F-6A in North Africa and the Mediterranean, the 107th was a National Guard squadron (actually a component of the Michigan National Guard) that had been called to active duty on 15 October 1940. Shipped to Britain in August/September 1942, it had taken some time for the AAF to organise its reconnaissance assets in England and get them into combat. However, the F-6B contingent started to arrive in October 1943, and this gave a considerable capability to the 107th, which was designated as a Tactical Reconnaissance Squadron in November 1943. Previously based at RAF Membury and then, from December 1943 at RAF Middle Wallop in the south of England, the unit began from late 1943 an increasingly wide-ranging reconnaissance of Northern France from the end of the year onwards. This included photo-reconnaissance and visual reconnaissance, as well as weather reconnaissance and bomb damage assessment. In the face of increasingly intense anti-aircraft defences, the squadron flew many tactical reconnaissance missions along the coast of Northern France in preparation for the Allied invasion in June 1944. This was extremely hazardous work, and was carried out in conjunction with other Allied reconnaissance assets including USAAF F-5 Lightnings (reconnaissance versions of the P-38 Lightning twin-engined fighter), but the Mustangs' speed and endurance made them particularly valuable. As was the case with the RAF's Tac/R Mustangs, tangling with the Luftwaffe was discouraged except when deemed necessary, so as to ensure that the valuable reconnaissance data could be returned home safely and not put in jeopardy due to unnecessary aerial combat. In common with other tactical assets of the Ninth

Army Air Force, the 107th moved across to Northern France after D-Day, initially being based briefly at A-4 (Deux Jumeaux) airstrip from late June onwards. By then the increasingly tired F-6Bs were being supplemented by reconnaissance versions of the Merlin-powered Mustang, but some examples soldiered on for a considerable time after the Invasion had taken place.

Production of the Allison-engined Mustang was ended with the completion of the last P-51A in the summer of 1943. Unfortunately the exact number of Allison-Mustangs that were built has been the source of continuing confusion in many published sources, but the total is not hard to work out. There was the one initial NA-73X prototype, which was followed by 320 and then 300 Mustang Mk Is for the RAF (of which at least one was retained by NAA). There were two XP-51s, which might have been additional to the Mustang Mk I production, or could simply have been taken from the Mustang Mk I production lines. There were then 150 Mustang Mk IAs (of which 55 went to the USAAF as P-51/F-6As, and two were retained by NAA). There were 500 A-36A Invaders (of which one was officially handed over to the British, but others were 'borrowed' by the British as necessary), and 310 P-51As (of which fifty were supplied to the RAF as Mustang Mk IIs, and thirty-five became F-6Bs). Total Allison-Mustang manufacture, including the prototypes (and assuming that the two XP-51s were additional airframes within the Mustang Mk I production), therefore was 1,583 – or 1,581 if indeed the two XP-51s were simply Mustang Mk I airframes repossessed, which seems the most likely. Of these, at least 763 were supplied to Britain, and 816 went to the USAAF, with at least four being used by NAA.

Although totally overshadowed by the exploits of the Merlin-engined Mustang, the Allison-Mustang played a very valuable role in World War Two. Its achievements are nowadays largely overlooked, especially when compared to its illustrious Merlin-engined development. True, it had its shortcomings, particularly at altitude, but it was nonetheless a competent combat aircraft that was far superior to many other Allied fighter types of the earlier war period. Nevertheless, the stage was already being set, by the time that Allison-engined Mustang production was at an end, for the appearance of the legendary Merlin-engined Mustang to make its entry.

A P-51A of the 311th Fighter-Bomber Group's 530th Fighter-Bomber Squadron is worked on prior to another mission. This unit was the first to take the P-51A to war in a major fashion at unit strength. The aircraft carries a 75 US gallon 'drop tank' beneath each wing, probably signifying that it was being readied to embark on a long-range bomber escort mission. In the CBI theatre the P-51A was often called on to perform this type of mission, but as a bomber escort fighter the Allison-engined Mustang was not at all suitable, lacking the high-altitude performance needed to effectively cover heavy bombers. The photograph was possibly taken at Kurmitola or Cox's Bazaar (Bazar), which were forward bases used by the 311th FBG during its long-range escort missions from November 1943 onwards
(Photo: M.V. Lowe Collection)

Future Developments

Originally an Allison-engined Mustang Mk I before being converted, AM208 was one of the five prototype/development Mustangs that were employed as flying test-beds for the Merlin installation into the Mustang airframe by Rolls-Royce in Britain. This aircraft was the second Merlin-powered Mustang Mk X to fly, making its first flight under Merlin 65 power on 13 November 1942. This view of the aircraft in flight clearly shows the highly modified nose contours of the Merlin installation, including the very prominent 'chin' air intake and the lack of an intake of any kind above the nose *(Photo: Malcolm V. Lowe Collection)*

Without doubt, the Allison-engined Mustang proved to be, during its service deployments, a very competent warplane. For many, however, it was clear from the start that the type had a major limitation regarding potential high-altitude performance. For the RAF, this was not a serious problem. Consigned to low-level operations where their speed, range and agility were of greatest importance, the low-level Tac/R Allison-Mustangs did an excellent job for the RAF from 1942 onwards – with some continuing on operations right through to the end of World War Two. High-altitude combat for the RAF could be performed by the Supermarine Spitfire, and so the need to develop the Mustang any further into a high-altitude performer was not of paramount significance – at least not to begin with. Nonetheless, the RAF was rightly always keen to improve performance, and many in the RAF came to recognize that the capable warplane that the Mustang was, could nonetheless be developed further into an excellent all-round performer if the need arose, with the addition of more power and a high-altitude rated engine. As 1942 drew on, the need for ever-more capable fighters to counter continuing Luftwaffe developments made the development of a better-performing Mustang an increasingly attractive idea.

For the USAAF, however, the Allison-Mustang's high-altitude shortcomings were of a more immediate matter for consideration. With the onset of heavy bomber operations over North-west Europe in 1942, and their wider application in 1943, the USAAF found itself with the problem of not having a high-altitude fighter to provide cover for the high-flying B-17 and B-24 heavy bombers of the Eighth Army Air Force. Having neglected the development of high-performance, long-range fighters, the USAAF had nothing with which to escort its increasingly vulnerable bombers on their increasingly far-flung daylight raids over Occupied Europe. The Americans simply did not have an escort fighter worth the name – particularly one with any kind of long-range, high-altitude capabilities. This became more of an issue when the Germans made considerable efforts to improve and deepen their air defences over Germany against the USAAF's heavy bombers, leading to increasingly heavy losses to Luftwaffe fighters.

Thankfully for the increasingly hard-pressed B-17 Flying Fortress and B-24 Liberator bomber crews of the Eighth Air Force as 1943 progressed, salvation was potentially at hand. Even so, it was not immediately obvious where the knight in shining armour was going to come from. Experience with the Allison-engined Mustang as a bomber escort, as explained in the previous Chapter, showed that the P-51A was not ideal in that particular role, lacking the high-altitude performance to stay with heavy bombers like the B-24 Liberator – although as a low-level escort for tactical bombers such as the B-25 Mitchell the type was far better, drawing in particular on its long-range capabilities, manoeuvrability and stability as a gun platform. Long before the 311th Fighter-Bomber Group was taking the P-51A into action as a bomber escort in late 1943, however, moves were already in place to transform the Mustang into the superlative, long-range high-altitude fighter and bomber escort for which it will be forever renowned.

Britain Takes the Lead

On 30 April 1942, a British test pilot named Ronald Harker visited the RAF's Air Fighting Development Unit (AFDU) at Duxford airfield in Cambridgeshire. Harker was a service-liaison company test pilot for the famous British engine designer and manufacturer Rolls-Royce. It was his brief to fly examples of the aircraft then in RAF service or set to become operational (whether they were Rolls-Rolls powered or not), as well as any available captured enemy aircraft. His visit to Duxford on that day was specifically to fly the Mustang Mk I, which was on the verge of becoming fully operational with the RAF's No.26 Squadron. Harker flew Mustang Mk I AG422, and his impressions of that half-hour long flight, and the action that followed them, were to help change the course of World War Two. Harker was an engine-orientated test pilot, it was not his brief to look at the Mustang from the point of view of an all guns blazing battle with a Luftwaffe Focke-Wulf Fw 190. Instead he examined the Mustang from an evaluation viewpoint of its engine performance, and how it could be improved if required. He was highly impressed by the Mustang, for which the performance claims that had been made for it by its manufacturer appeared to be justified. He found that the Mustang was 35 mph (56 km/h) faster than the then pre-eminent Spitfire Mk V, and felt that it should prove to be a formidable low- and medium-altitude fighter. Previously three examples of the Curtiss P-40 Tomahawk had become available to the Rolls-Royce experimental flight test establishment at Hucknall airfield in Nottinghamshire, and these had been viewed as less than impressive by the Rolls-Royce test pilots and engineers. In comparison Harker found the Mustang to be a fine performer at low to medium levels, but without doubt he was the first person to recognize, from a practical, hands-on perspective, that the Mustang would benefit from the installation of an effective, powerful, high-altitude rated engine. Rolls-Royce, his employer, had such an engine then in continuing development. This was the 60-series derivative of the already famous and highly successful Rolls-Royce Merlin inline engine. Developed from the Merlin engines that had powered Supermarine Spitfires and Hawker Hurricanes during the early war years and most notably during the Battle of Britain, the 60-series Merlins were aimed specifically at giving the Spitfire an improved high-altitude

and all-round performance, particularly to counter the Luftwaffe's excellent Focke-Wulf Fw 190 single-engined fighter. They included improved supercharging, using a two-stage, two-speed supercharger with automatic control – a feature that Allison was unable to successfully develop for the V-1710 that powered the early Mustangs until late in the war.

Harker wrote a very important report about his experiences of flying AG422, which was dated 1 May 1942. It was addressed to his superiors and colleagues at Rolls-Royce, including senior managers at the company's main offices at Derby. One of those who the report was destined for was Ernest Hives (later Lord Hives of Duffield), the influential General Works Manager and member of the board of directors of Rolls-Royce. In the days that followed there was considerable activity at Rolls-Royce, and much communication between the company and the Ministry of Supply and other government bodies, as the momentum began with a view to Rolls-Royce obtaining one or more examples of the Mustang to re-engine with a Merlin power plant. This was actually not as easy as it might have at first seemed. The 60-series Merlin had already been successfully tested, and every new series example was seemingly going to be needed for installation in the new production mark of Spitfire, the Mk IX. It was in any case somewhat irregular for a company to want to set about a significant re-engining programme all by itself, particularly when the service for which any production spin-off would be destined, the RAF, was at first rather lukewarm on the whole idea.

Nevertheless, the concept of fitting the excellent new high-altitude 60-series Merlin engine into the already proven Mustang airframe seemed to be a very attractive idea, and this is exactly what happened in the ensuing months. All the early initiative to re-engine the Mustang with the Merlin engine came from Britain. The conversion work was performed mainly by Rolls-Royce, but with input from the RAF, NAA, and US representatives in Britain. Fortunately, the Mustang's creator and manufacturer, North American Aviation, turned out to be an enthusiastic bystander in the whole process, and appeared to be untroubled by others taking its already winning product and turning it into a changed and developed aircraft type.

In the event, both Britain and the US commenced their own

In the US, one of the two Merlin-powered XP-51B prototypes shows off its new nose contours following conversion to Merlin power. At first called 'XP-78', the two prototypes were former Mustang Mk IA aircraft originally destined for Britain that had previously been taken over by the US as P-51 Mustangs and were armed with 20mm cannons. Evident in this view is the 'stepped' appearance of the lower fuselage just back from the nose, which was eventually done away with in the need to streamline as much as possible the new Packard V-1650-3 (Merlin) installation, and the evolving shape of the main lower fuselage radiator air intake. The intercooler radiator was located differently compared to the Rolls-Royce conversions; hence the much smoother lower nose contours of the NAA-converted machines compared to the Rolls-Royce work. This aircraft bears the NAA company symbol on its vertical tail, a marking not often seen on Mustangs of any version (Photo: NAA)

conversion programmes to re-engine the Allison-Mustang with the Merlin engine, and this development work led directly to the creation of the superb, world-beating Merlin-Mustang. The story of the birth and subsequent superlative combat record of the Merlin-powered Mustang will be told in detail in the next part of this 'Modellers Datafile' on the Mustang. It is sufficient to record here that all the airframe and test-flying development work that eventually took place, both in Britain and later in the US, to create the Merlin-Mustang, was performed using Allison-Mustangs suitably converted.

Conversions to Merlin Power

In Britain, five Mustang Mk Is that were originally Allison-engined, were specifically employed by Rolls-Royce as test aircraft for the installation of the Merlin engine. They were AL963, AL975, AM121, AM203, and AM208; they have often been called Mustang Mk X aircraft. A further Allison-Mustang, AG518, was evaluated during this programme but was not converted. AM121 was later passed to the Americans. The first of these to be converted to Merlin power, AL975/G, first flew under Merlin power on 13 October 1942, piloted by Rolls-Royce's chief test pilot at Hucknall airfield, Capt R.T. Shepherd. AL975 had a 'G' prefix added to its serial number, to signify that it had to be guarded at all times when on the ground if away from its usual factory location or base – it was a very important aircraft.

In the US, it was NAA that performed the conversion work, for the installation of the American, Packard-built V-1650 Merlin engine to replace the Allison V-1710 power plant. Two Mustangs were chosen by NAA for the prototype conversion into Merlin power, and they were the two aircraft that the company had retained from the batch of 150 Mustang Mk IA that were originally destined for the RAF, when that batch was broken up following the US entry into World War Two and fifty-five examples were transferred as P-51s to the USAAF. The aircraft in that production batch received US as well as

RAF serial numbers, because they were ordered for Britain under the then-new 'Lend-Lease' arrangements. The two NAA aircraft were 41-37352 and 41-37421. Both were armed with two 20mm cannons in each wing, as was the case with the other aircraft in that production batch. Under the USAAF's procurement policies, a new designation was sanctioned for the two aircraft for when they were converted to Merlin power, as they were effectively going to be of a 'new' pursuit type. Thus they were initially designated XP-78, and that nomenclature was employed in a considerable amount of documentation that related to them at the time. However, in the end the established type designation P-51 continued to be used for the planned new Mustang version with Merlin power, and so the two aircraft adopted the intended P-51B designation that was eventually given by the USAAF to the initial NAA production model of the Merlin Mustang. The two prototype aircraft were thus eventually simply designated as XP-51B, with the 'X' standing for 'experimental prototype'. They received the company designation NA-101. Conversion work was comparatively slow, and it was not until 30 November 1942 that NAA was able to get one of its converted airframes airborne, when Robert Chilton took 41-37352 into the air for its maiden flight from Mines Field (Inglewood) under V-1650-3 power. It was a significant milestone along the road that led to the introduction and subsequent large-scale production of the Merlin-Mustang.

A large amount of work needed to be carried out by NAA to create the production-standard Merlin-powered Mustang layout. NAA later stated that the whole job took up 223,000 man hours to get the configuration right. What is probably the first prototype XP-51B aircraft displays in this photograph one of the stages in the whole process, with an interim lower fuselage radiator intake, although the photograph appears to have been 'retouched' to hide or enhance some details. This aircraft was a former Mustang Mk IA, but interestingly in this image the wing 20mm cannons are not present, having been presumably removed during the conversion process. The general configuration seen in this photograph eventually led on to the first of the production marks of Merlin-Mustang, the P-51B. *(Photo: NAA)*

Other Operators

As recounted elsewhere in this book, the principal operators of the Allison-engined Mustang were Britain's RAF (remembering once more that the Mustang was originally designed for British service) and the American USAAF. A number of the RAF Allison Mustang squadrons were actually Canadian and Polish-manned. Indeed, the Canadians had a long and very successful association with the Mustang, that eventually lasted into the 1950's – although latterly with Merlin Mustangs. As explained earlier in this book, the Canadians operated important numbers of Mustangs during World War Two in Europe (both Allison-engined and Merlin-powered), with three Canadian-manned squadrons eventually flying Allison Mustangs - including one that was amongst the first to operate the Mustang in front-line service. This wartime use was alongside the RAF as a part of the overall British and Commonwealth war effort employing aircraft that were effectively RAF machines 'loaned' for Canadian operations. Post-war, the Royal Canadian Air Force (RCAF) flew the Mustang in Canada itself, which will be further explained in the second part of this 'Modellers Datafile' on the Mustang.

Other than RAF and USAAF service, the Allison Mustang was only operated by a small number of additional countries. With production ending during World War Two, the type was fully committed to the Allied war effort, and few survived the war to become available for export – a fact that was in complete contrast to the Merlin-engined Mustang, which went on to have a very illustrious career after World War Two had finished. Nevertheless Allison Mustangs did turn up in a number of mainly unexpected places, both after the war and actually during it.

Soviet Union

It is nowadays often overlooked that the Soviet Union was supplied with significant numbers of US warplanes during World War Two, following the attack on the Soviet Union by Germany in June 1941, in addition to considerable quantities of other war materials. Good use was made by the Soviets of many of these supplies, in what the Russians call the Great Patriotic War against the Germans. Even somewhat less than first-rate fighters such as the Bell P-39 Airacobra and Curtiss P-40 Warhawk proved to be useful in Soviet service. Such was the willingness of the Western Allies to assist the Russians after June 1941 that all kinds of munitions were earmarked for transportation to the Soviet Union. It is a little-known fact that the Mustang became caught up in this major effort to help the Soviet forces. Despite the Mustang having been created specially for British service, even in the early days of Allison-engined Mustang production for Britain there was a growing desire on the part of some British officials (and presumably some politicians also) to divert to the Soviets a quantity of the much-needed Mustang production intended for Britain. Indeed, the initial batch of 320 Mustangs ordered by Britain in May 1940 and the subsequent batch of 300 examples plus the first Lend-Lease Mustangs became the focus of intended diversions to the Soviet Union rather than delivery to Britain.

In August 1941 Britain established the basis for assistance to the Soviets that was formally covered in an agreement of June 1942. Similarly, in November 1941 the Lend-Lease arrangements that the US had created with regard to Britain were extended to include the Soviet Union as well. Correspondence that involved

The Soviet Union received approximately ten Mustangs from Great Britain, beginning in the first half of 1942. These aircraft were assigned for test purposes after delivery and are believed not to have seen widespread active service, although a small number are believed to have undergone combat evaluation. Amongst them was Mustang Mk.I AG348, which was the fourth production aircraft for Britain, and is the aircraft that some historians have claimed was handed over to the USAAF as the first of the two XP-51 Mustangs. As can be seen from this poor-quality but rare image, this was not the case, because the aircraft's serial number can be clearly seen together with the Soviet stars applied where British insignia were painted out by the **Russians** *(Photo: Malcolm V. Lowe Collection)*

British purchasing representatives in the US dated 4 November 1941 speculated that thirty to forty Mustangs would be shipped to Russia direct from the US in December 1941, with further quantities to follow later. Subsequent correspondence on 12 December 1941 hypothesized that of those initial Mustang batches, enough examples would be retained for British service to allow for four UK-based squadrons, with the remaining aircraft supplied to Russia! Fortunately wiser heads appear to have prevailed somewhere at higher levels and in the event these shipments were not made. However, it is certain that a number of Mustangs were supplied to the Soviet Union, possibly up to ten Allison-engined Mk.I examples from amongst the early production Made particularly for Britain.

Subsequent to the end of the Cold War, Russian archives have been much more accessible to historians and researchers than in previous times. According to Russian sources that have come to light during the past twenty years or so, at least four of the Mustangs that found their way to the Soviet Union can be identified. They were AG348, AG352, AG353, and AG354. It is interesting to note that the first of these, AG348, was the fourth production aircraft intended for Britain, and it is this aircraft that some historians have claimed was handed over to the USAAF as the first of the two XP-51 Mustangs! Clearly this was not the case, and there is sufficient photographic evidence of AG348 wearing RAF camouflage but with its RAF roundels (and fin flash) painted out and Soviet red stars over-painted to completely disprove this theory. As far as is possible to verify, these four identified Mustangs appear to have been shipped to the Soviet Union from Britain in May 1942.

At least AG348 was examined at the Soviet air force's research and evaluation institute (NII VVS). Tantalizingly, it is possible that

up to three were subsequently tried out in combat by the Soviet air force's 5 GIAP (5th Guards Fighter Aviation Regiment) of the 3rd Soviet Air Army in the Kalinin area during the autumn of 1942. One of the pilots believed to have flown the type was the regiment's commander, V.A. Zajtsev, who was an accomplished fighter pilot with at least thirty-four aerial victories by the end of the Great Patriotic War and was eventually a double holder of the Hero of the Soviet Union decoration. The results of these evaluations, however, were negative. The Soviets appear to have concluded that the Mustang was a heavy fighter that was not suited to front-line operations. This is exactly what some American opponents of the Mustang within the USAAF similarly thought of the Mustang at that time. Without doubt, no major deliveries in terms of quantity were made to the Soviet Union of Mustangs following that time.

However, in addition to these limited deliveries of early British Mustangs, the Soviet Union also came to 'own' a further number of Mustangs much later in the war. These were all Merlin-engined Mustangs, and were aircraft that were left behind when the USAAF employed several air bases in the Ukraine for 'frantic' shuttle missions. Again, more will be said about these in the second part of this 'Modellers Datafile' on the Mustang.

Naval Mustangs

The Mustang was not designed with nautical connections in mind, and was every inch a land-based combat aircraft. No Mustangs ever served in a combat capacity at sea on board aircraft carriers. This did not stop a number of Mustangs from having naval connections, however. Most significantly, at least two Mustangs were evaluated by the US Navy to assess the type's possible suitability for aircraft carrier operation, and for this reason a small number of Mustangs developed naval associations during and just after World War Two. The connection began in earnest during (it is believed) May 1943, when the US Navy employed an Allison-engined Mustang for examination, to test the suitability of the type for naval operations, possibly even aboard aircraft carriers. This subject still has some mystery surrounding it, but the Mustang concerned appears to have been an aircraft from the batch of Mustang Mk.IA fighters intended for Britain, fifty-five of which were eventually retained for US service. It was therefore from the first Lend-Lease batch, and so had a US serial number (41-37426) in addition to a British serial number (FD524). It was apparently assigned the naval serial number BuNo 57987. Just how extensively it was evaluated or used in other capacities while with the US Navy is not clear. In a further

Gerry Beck's Mustang N8082U 'Precious Metal' which crashed in July 2007. *(Photo: MA Smith Collection)*

twist to the tale, historian M.J. Hardy suggested a number of years ago that the US Navy subsequently fully evaluated a Merlin-engined P-51B against a fully-fledged naval fighter, namely the Vought F4U Corsair.

The trials are claimed to have taken place in early 1944 against an F4U-1 and an F4U-1A, with the Mustang proving to be slightly superior to the naval types at higher altitudes in terms of speed and climb, with the Corsairs proving superior in most respects at lower altitudes and also having better control at slow speeds including on landing. Interestingly, precise details and the exact text of these findings are now elusive. Although details of the US Navy's associations with the Allison Mustang remain rather sketchy, what is certain is that the US Navy definitely evaluated a Merlin Mustang in late 1944. The aircraft concerned was a P-51D-5-NA, serial number 44-14017, and more details of this aircraft's naval connections will be included in the following volume of this 'Modellers Datafile' on the Mustang.

Latin America

Comparatively large numbers of Merlin Mustangs were supplied by the US under various assistance programmes to 'friendly' rulers and dictators in Latin and South America following the end of World War Two. At that time there was a large number of Merlin-powered Mustangs available, despite the mass scrapping of warplanes after the end of the war. However, few Allison Mustangs had survived into the post-war period, and a comparative shortage of spares and know-how precluded the emergence of the Allison Mustang as a viable aircraft due to this for supply to client countries. Nevertheless, at least one state, the Dominican Republic, did have a brief flirtation with the Allison Mustang. Unfortunately details are still scarce of this involvement, and indeed some of the Dominican Republic's long association with the Mustang remains open to debate, especially the connection in later years with Cavalier Mustangs.

What is certain is that the Dominican Republic was a major user of US hardware in the post-war period, resulting in a considerable expansion of the country's armed forces. This build-up of weaponry was a product of the desire of the Dominican Republic's dictator, Rafael Trujillo, to defend his repressive régime at any costs. The first Mustangs were obtained by the Dominicans in - it appears - the summer of 1948, comprising a bizarre assortment of Merlin-powered and Allison-engined types. This was unique in itself, the Dominican Republic therefore being one of the very few – if not the only – front-line operator of the Allison-engined Mustang outside of British/British Commonwealth and US service. It appears that some of these initial Mustangs were surplus aircraft that had originally been purchased privately for air racing. They were allocated the Dominican military serials 401 to 405 (while a sixth Mustang reportedly crashed before it reached Dominican service). Many more Merlin-engined Mustangs were later obtained for service in this Caribbean country. Indeed, the love affair that the Dominicans subsequently developed with the Mustang resulted in the Dominican Republic being the longest-running user of the Mustang, the final Merlin-engined examples eventually being phased out of service in the 1980's.

Air Racing

It is a little known fact that a small number of Allison Mustangs were involved, under civil ownership, in air racing following World War Two. This was in addition to the much more substantial participation in air races by Merlin-powered Mustangs, which dominated the air racing scene in the US for several years following the end of the war.

In the pre-war era, air racing in the US had been a growing and impressive spectacle, attracting large crowds at a number of specific air race venues. The advent of the Second World War completely put an end to these activities, but with the end of the conflict and the drift back into something approaching pre-war normality (if such a thing was possible after such a destructive war), air racing was quite rapidly resurrected. This was in part due to the comparatively large number of increasingly unwanted (by the military), high-performance former warplanes that became 'war surplus' at the end of the war and passed into civil ownership. Although vast numbers of front-line combat aircraft were scrapped in the US following the end of the Second World War in 1945, nevertheless significant numbers were sold off into civil ownership. This included such high-performance types as the P-51 Mustang,

During 1946 the National Air Races of pre-war times were resurrected at Cleveland, Ohio. These took the form of races on a closed-circuit course with the aircraft competing in several laps around pylons. This sort of flying is very dangerous, with engine failure, the risk of collision, and the lack of any safe height to overcome aerodynamic or system failures being some of the chief hazards, and there had been some major accidents in the 1930's. Now the events were contested by high-performance former military aircraft. The most famous pylon race was the Thompson Trophy, of several laps around a closed-circuit course with pylons at the turns, which was contested in 1946 by a mixed-bag of former warplanes including several Mustangs. Also included in the National Air Races was a long distance 'dash' called the Bendix Trophy. Although these events were dominated by Merlin Mustangs and other types such as the Vought F4U Corsair naval fighter and its derivatives, a small number of Allison Mustangs found their way into the air racing scene during that period. Some published reports have claimed that these aircraft were actually of the P-51A type, but the tracing of their histories and original US military serial numbers suggests otherwise. Perhaps best-known amongst them was a handful of A-36A Apache/Invaders, which particularly contested in the 1947 and 1949 events at Cleveland. In 1947 an A-36A with the civil registration NX4E was involved, although it suffered a catastrophic engine failure and crashed. In 1949, flown by James Hannon, an A-36A registered NX39502 participated as 'Race 2'. This aircraft still exists, as a part of the collection of the National Museum of the USAF (previously known as the USAF Museum) at Wright-Patterson AFB, Ohio, where it wears its own correct original military serial number of 42-83665.

New Build

It might come as a surprise to many readers that in the early years of the twenty-first century, limited production of genuinely-new Mustangs was undertaken. Putting an aircraft type back into production is a costly affair, with the usual very necessary burocracy for a new aircraft type to also contend with, and the programme concerned was not without difficulties. This new production of the Mustang was undertaken by Tri-State Aviation of Wahpeton, to the south of Fargo, North Dakota. The company's proprietor, Gerry Beck, intended a production run of ten new-build Mustangs, and the first of these, with Beck at the controls, flew on 7 June 2006. The configuration chosen was that of the P-51A, with Allison V-1710 power, making these new Mustangs unusual in their own right, bearing in mind that few Allison-engined Mustangs currently exist. Original North American Aviation plans and blueprints were used as the basis of the work, and the first aircraft, civil registered as N8082U, performed well. Tri-State Aviation is well-known in the world of aircraft restoration in the US, working to a very high standard. Tragically, Gerry Beck was killed during July 2007 when he crashed in this new Mustang during the famous EAA AirVenture air show in Oshkosh, Wisconsin.

One of the Russian leased Mustang I's seen here during testing at the Air Forces Scientific Research Institute in June 1942.
(Photo: via MA Smith Collection)

The Mustang in Colour

Gracing the benign skies over Southern California, the NA-73X shows off its elegant and advanced lines. This photograph has sometimes been claimed as having been taken during the aircraft's first flight, but this seems highly unlikely, as North American Aviation would most probably have waited for success in the flight test programme of this shining new fighter before making a special photo shoot. In any case the addition of rudder stripes suggests that the picture was taken during the period leading up to the famous crash of this aircraft on 20 November 1940 - or possibly after the aircraft had been repaired following its accident *(Photo: NAA)*

The second production Mustang Mk.I, AG346, shows itself off in the clear air and blue sky of Southern California during the summer of 1941. This aircraft became the first Mustang to be delivered to Britain, in late October 1941, and wore the Dark Earth/Dark Green/Sky colour scheme shown, sprayed with American paint equivalents to the British shades. AG346 became a combat veteran, seeing a considerable amount of action with the RAF, and was active over Normandy in the post-Invasion period during mid-1944 *(Photo: NAA)*

AG345, the first production Mustang Mk.I, in flight against the backdrop of a blue California sky and showing underside details to advantage in this somewhat unusual view. In the event this aircraft was never delivered to Britain, but was retained by NAA for varied development work and related duties. It was painted in a Dark Green/Dark Earth/Sky colour scheme using American paint equivalents to British shades and specifications *(Photo: NAA)*

Well-known but nonetheless outstanding, this beautiful image shows Mustang Mk.I AG633 (named 'Eileen') of No.2 Squadron, Army Co-operation Command, during the summer of 1942. At that time this famous squadron was 'working-up' on the type, prior to its first combat operations with the Mustang later that year *(Photo: R.L. Ward Collection)*

The use of colour film by North American Aviation's photographers has given us an excellent record of the company's products at a time when many other organisations were using monochrome film for their publicity pictures. In one of the many photo shoots that NAA performed to showcase its products, this P-51 (Mustang Mk.IA equivalent) shows off its Dark Olive Drab/Neutral Grey colour scheme over Southern California. The P-51 version was armed with four 20mm cannons, two in each wing *(Photo: NAA)*

USAF Museum A-36A: This beautifully-restored A-36A is a part of the collection of the National Museum of the USAF (still better-known to almost everyone by its long-standing title of 'USAF Museum') at Wright-Patterson AFB, Ohio. It wears its own correct serial number of 42-83665, and was raced post-war as NX39502, but is otherwise painted to represent another A-36A that saw combat in southern Europe *(Photo: via USAF Museum)*

Allison V-1710: All early production versions of the Mustang, and several other major US fighters of that era including the P-38 Lightning, P-39 Airacobra, and P-40 Warhawk, were powered by the Allison V-1710. This engine type was the only properly developed inline aero engine in the US at that time, and it proved to be a successful power plant that nevertheless was rated in most of its production versions for low to medium-level optimum performance. This Allison periodical advertisement of the war years shows the V-1710 itself, plus a rather fanciful cartoon representing several Allison-engined fighters supporting an amphibious landing *(Photo: Malcolm V. Lowe Collection)*

Featuring in a number of publicity photographs, this P-51A, 43-6246, was operated in Orlando, Florida, at the Tactical Training Centre there alongside various other front-line combat aircraft. Like most if not all of its type, it wears Dark Olive Drab upper surfaces with Neutral Grey underneath, in this case in a heavily-worn finish *(Photo: USAAF)*

An A-36A used for wartime training in the southern US. This image is a useful reference for the flying clothing and survival equipment as worn by USAAF personnel in the pleasant climate and benign skies of the Continental US. The location has variously been described as Orlando or Baton Rouge *(Photo: USAAF)*

Although it is often claimed that this pilot is seen sitting in the cockpit of an A-36A, it is much more likely that the aircraft is in fact a P-51A. The latter featured the additional small vent window on the left-hand transparent windscreen panel as seen here, which was not normally fitted to the A-36A. The pilot is Charles McMillin, who as a Lt. Col. was one of the significant pilots in the 311th Fighter-Bomber (later Fighter) Group in the CBI. He eventually flew as an instructor in India, where it is believed this photograph was taken in 1945 *(Photo: USAAF)*

A North American Mustang Mk. IA on a test flight from NAA's Inglewood, California facility in October 1942. The painted-over serial number appears to be 41-37416, and records indicate that this aircraft was damaged during shipment to Europe in late 1943. *(Photo: via USAF Museum)*

USAF Museum A-36A: Another view of the Wright-Patterson aircraft which was obtained from Charles P. Doyle of Rosemount, Minnesota in 1971. Restored by the 148th Fighter-Interceptor Group, Minnesota Air National Guard, it is painted as the A-36A flown by Capt. Lawrence Dye, 522nd Fighter-Bomber Squadron, in Tunisia, Sicily and Italy.
(Photo: via USAF Museum)

A British North American NA-73 Mustang Mk.I (s/n AL968) being test-flown at Inglewood, California (USA) in October 1942. This aircraft was one of the original batch of 300 aircraft ordered by the Royal Air Force in December 1940 before the lend-lease act. Note that the fighter wears US national insignia as used by US forces up to April 1942. *(Photo: via USAF Museum)*

North American Mustang NA-91 fighters being serviced at NAA's Inglewood facility in California (USA) during October 1942. *(Photo: via USAF Museum)*

Colour Artwork

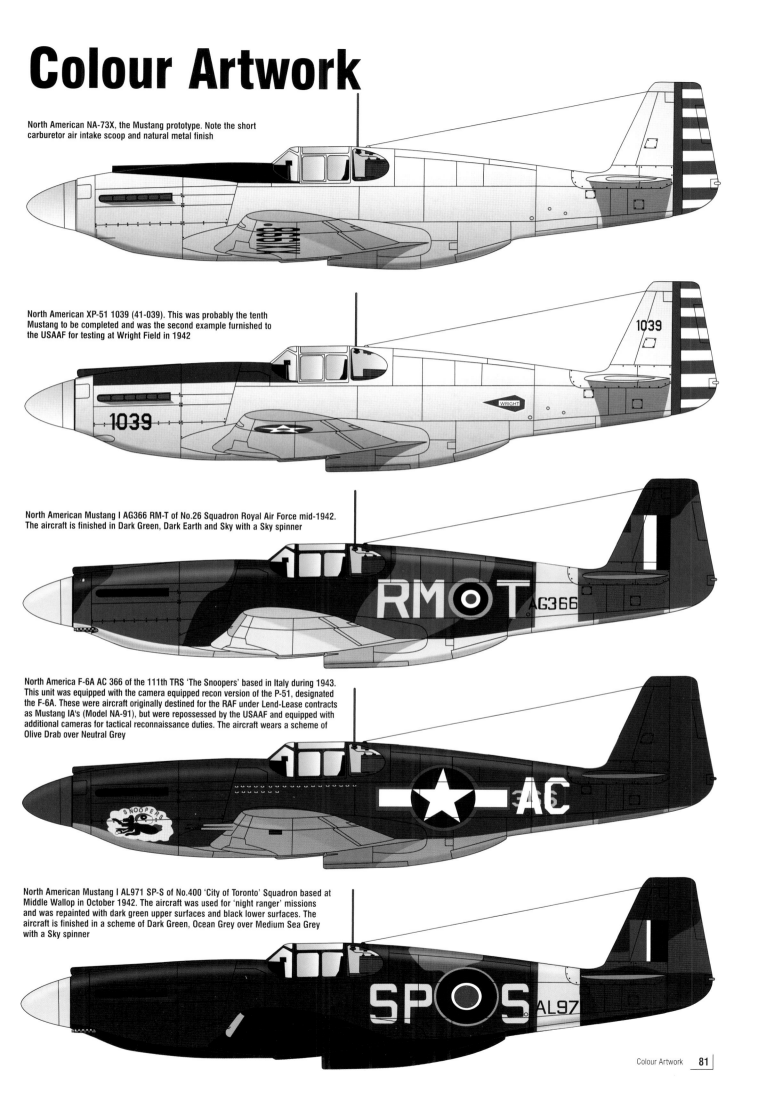

North American NA-73X, the Mustang prototype. Note the short
carburetor air intake scoop and natural metal finish

North American XP-51 1039 (41-039). This was probably the tenth
Mustang to be completed and was the second example furnished to
the USAAF for testing at Wright Field in 1942

North American Mustang I AG366 RM-T of No.26 Squadron Royal Air Force mid-1942.
The aircraft is finished in Dark Green, Dark Earth and Sky with a Sky spinner

North America F-6A AC 366 of the 111th TRS 'The Snoopers' based in Italy during 1943.
This unit was equipped with the camera equipped recon version of the P-51, designated
the F-6A. These were aircraft originally destined for the RAF under Lend-Lease contracts
as Mustang IA's (Model NA-91), but were repossessed by the USAAF and equipped with
additional cameras for tactical reconnaissance duties. The aircraft wears a scheme of
Olive Drab over Neutral Grey

North American Mustang I AL971 SP-S of No.400 'City of Toronto' Squadron based at
Middle Wallop in October 1942. The aircraft was used for 'night ranger' missions
and was repainted with dark green upper surfaces and black lower surfaces. The
aircraft is finished in a scheme of Dark Green, Ocean Grey over Medium Sea Grey
with a Sky spinner

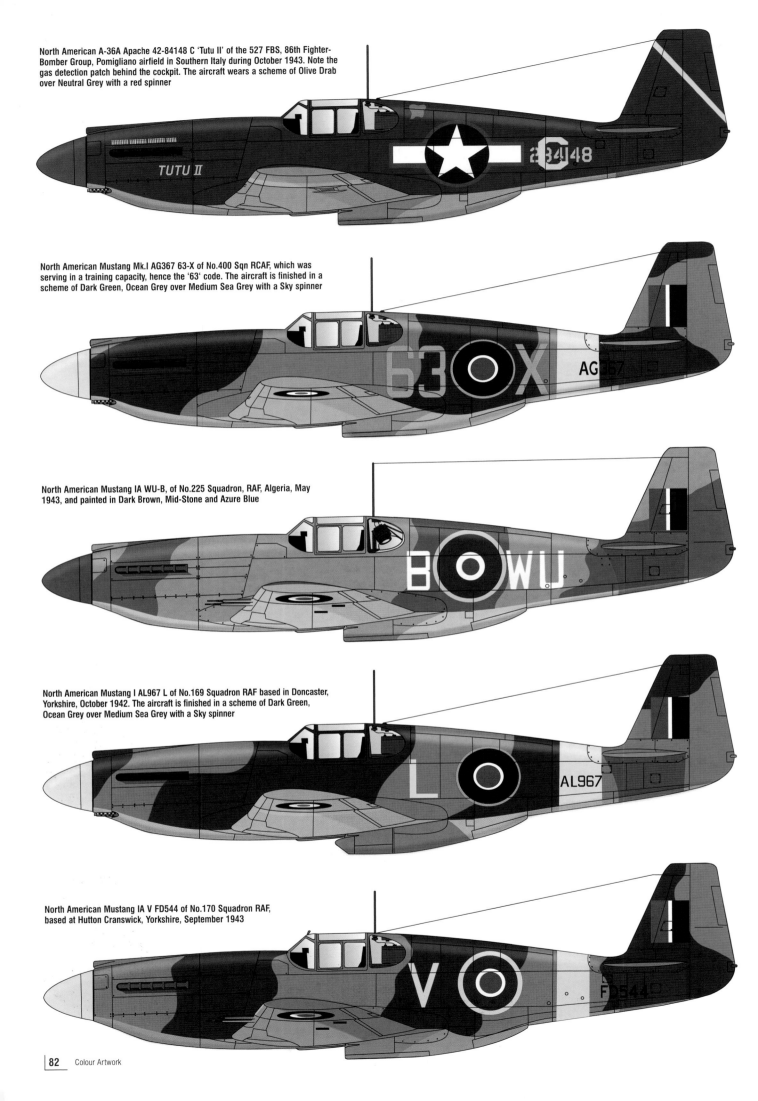

North American A-36A Apache 42-84148 C 'Tutu II' of the 527 FBS, 86th Fighter-Bomber Group, Pomigliano airfield in Southern Italy during October 1943. Note the gas detection patch behind the cockpit. The aircraft wears a scheme of Olive Drab over Neutral Grey with a red spinner

North American Mustang Mk.I AG367 63-X of No.400 Sqn RCAF, which was serving in a training capacity, hence the '63' code. The aircraft is finished in a scheme of Dark Green, Ocean Grey over Medium Sea Grey with a Sky spinner

North American Mustang IA WU-B, of No.225 Squadron, RAF, Algeria, May 1943, and painted in Dark Brown, Mid-Stone and Azure Blue

North American Mustang I AL967 L of No.169 Squadron RAF based in Doncaster, Yorkshire, October 1942. The aircraft is finished in a scheme of Dark Green, Ocean Grey over Medium Sea Grey with a Sky spinner

North American Mustang IA V FD544 of No.170 Squadron RAF, based at Hutton Cranswick, Yorkshire, September 1943

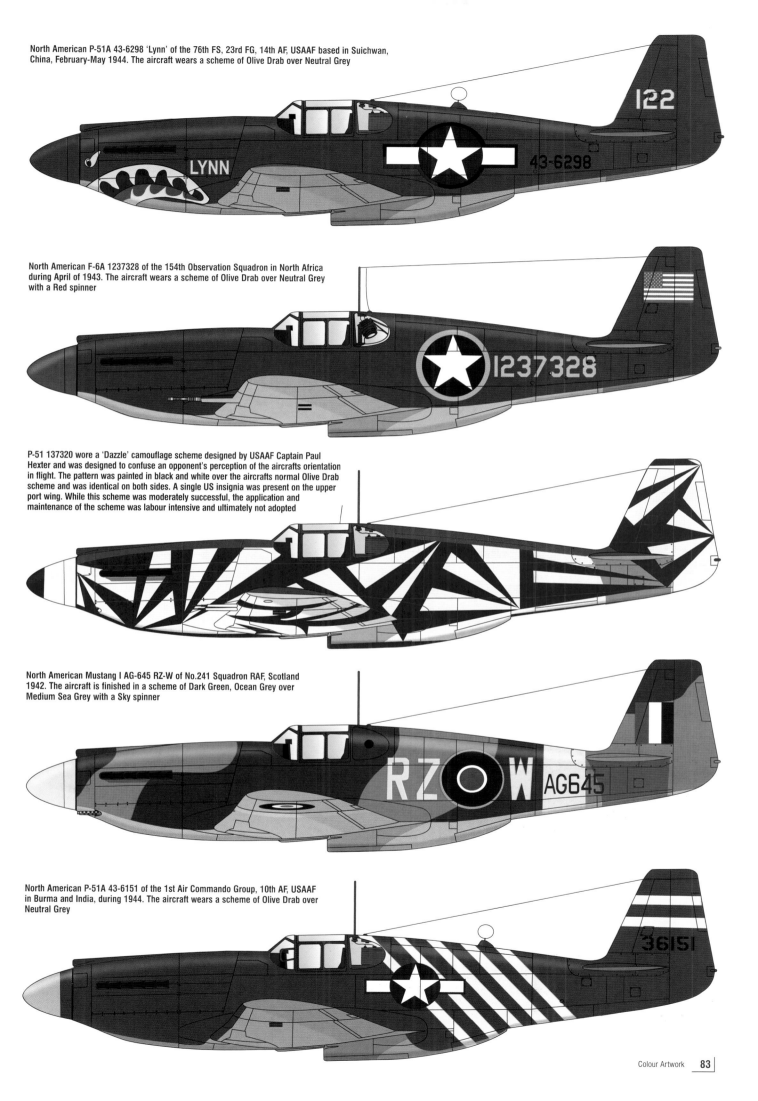

North American P-51A 43-6298 'Lynn' of the 76th FS, 23rd FG, 14th AF, USAAF based in Suichwan, China, February-May 1944. The aircraft wears a scheme of Olive Drab over Neutral Grey

North American F-6A 1237328 of the 154th Observation Squadron in North Africa during April of 1943. The aircraft wears a scheme of Olive Drab over Neutral Grey with a Red spinner

P-51 137320 wore a 'Dazzle' camouflage scheme designed by USAAF Captain Paul Hexter and was designed to confuse an opponent's perception of the aircrafts orientation in flight. The pattern was painted in black and white over the aircrafts normal Olive Drab scheme and was identical on both sides. A single US insignia was present on the upper port wing. While this scheme was moderately successful, the application and maintenance of the scheme was labour intensive and ultimately not adopted

North American Mustang I AG-645 RZ-W of No.241 Squadron RAF, Scotland 1942. The aircraft is finished in a scheme of Dark Green, Ocean Grey over Medium Sea Grey with a Sky spinner

North American P-51A 43-6151 of the 1st Air Commando Group, 10th AF, USAAF in Burma and India, during 1944. The aircraft wears a scheme of Olive Drab over Neutral Grey

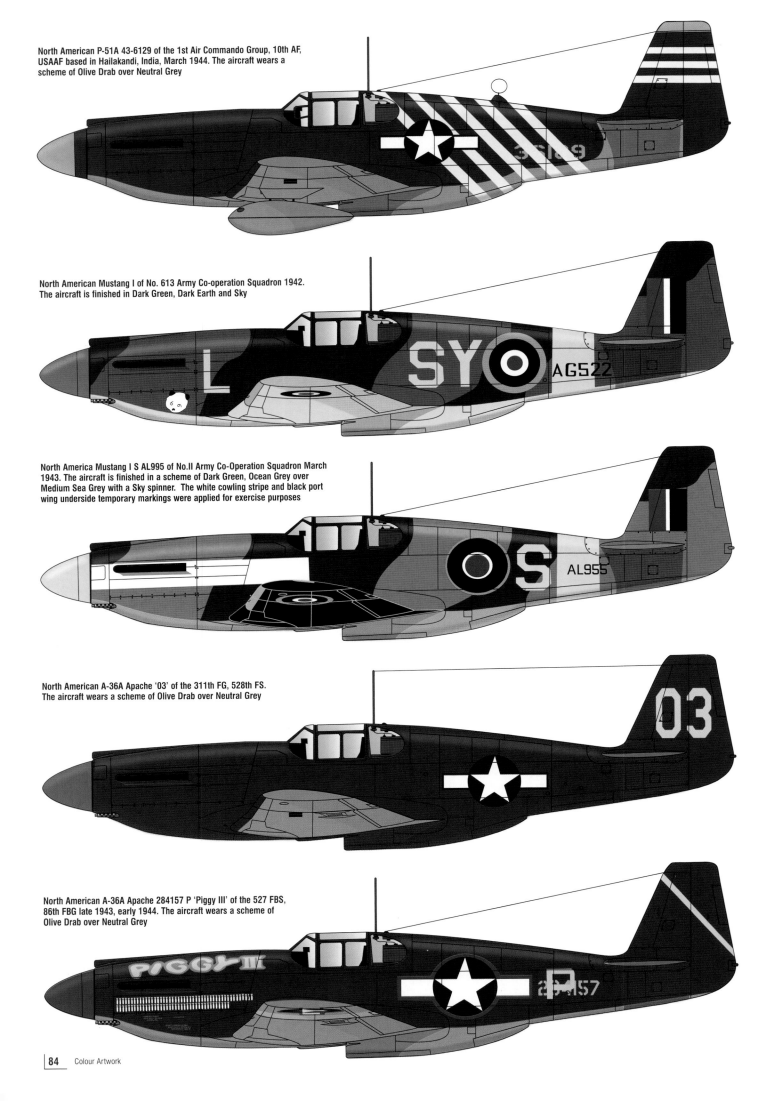

North American P-51A 43-6129 of the 1st Air Commando Group, 10th AF, USAAF based in Hailakandi, India, March 1944. The aircraft wears a scheme of Olive Drab over Neutral Grey

North American Mustang I of No. 613 Army Co-operation Squadron 1942. The aircraft is finished in Dark Green, Dark Earth and Sky

North America Mustang I S AL995 of No.II Army Co-Operation Squadron March 1943. The aircraft is finished in a scheme of Dark Green, Ocean Grey over Medium Sea Grey with a Sky spinner. The white cowling stripe and black port wing underside temporary markings were applied for exercise purposes

North American A-36A Apache '03' of the 311th FG, 528th FS. The aircraft wears a scheme of Olive Drab over Neutral Grey

North American A-36A Apache 284157 P 'Piggy III' of the 527 FBS, 86th FBG late 1943, early 1944. The aircraft wears a scheme of Olive Drab over Neutral Grey

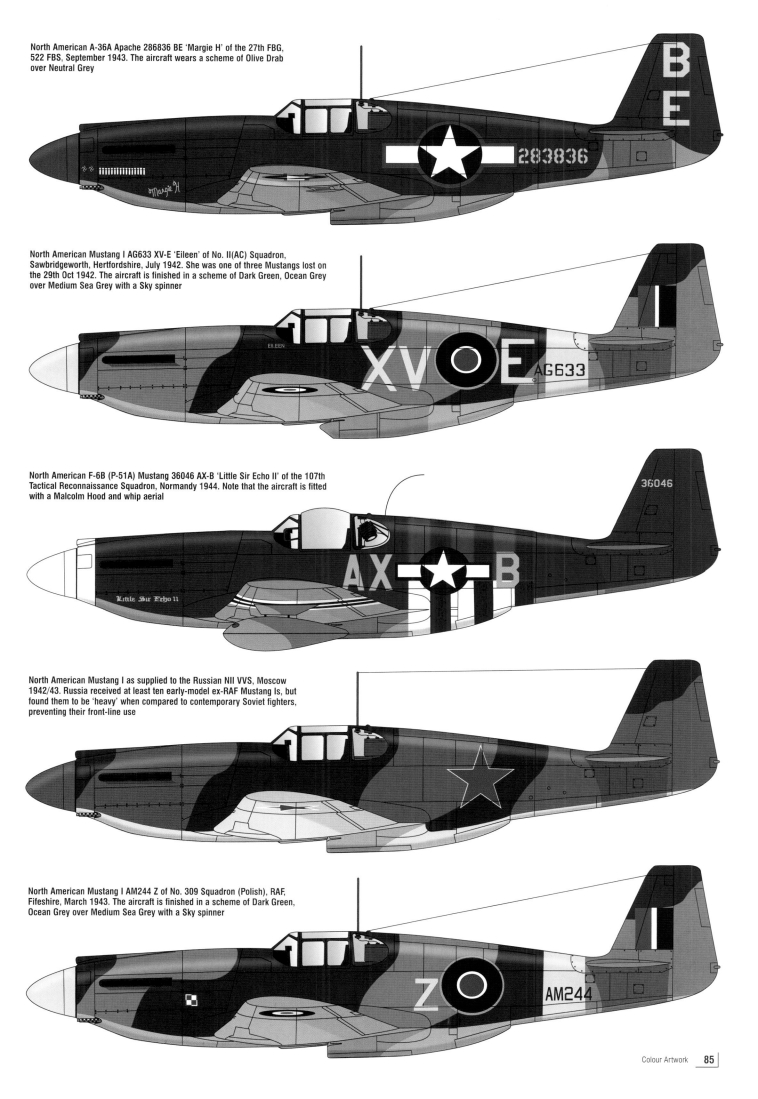

North American A-36A Apache 286836 BE 'Margie H' of the 27th FBG, 522 FBS, September 1943. The aircraft wears a scheme of Olive Drab over Neutral Grey

North American Mustang I AG633 XV-E 'Eileen' of No. II(AC) Squadron, Sawbridgeworth, Hertfordshire, July 1942. She was one of three Mustangs lost on the 29th Oct 1942. The aircraft is finished in a scheme of Dark Green, Ocean Grey over Medium Sea Grey with a Sky spinner

North American F-6B (P-51A) Mustang 36046 AX-B 'Little Sir Echo II' of the 107th Tactical Reconnaissance Squadron, Normandy 1944. Note that the aircraft is fitted with a Malcolm Hood and whip aerial

North American Mustang I as supplied to the Russian NII VVS, Moscow 1942/43. Russia received at least ten early-model ex-RAF Mustang Is, but found them to be 'heavy' when compared to contemporary Soviet fighters, preventing their front-line use

North American Mustang I AM244 Z of No. 309 Squadron (Polish), RAF, Fifeshire, March 1943. The aircraft is finished in a scheme of Dark Green, Ocean Grey over Medium Sea Grey with a Sky spinner

Modelling the Mustang in Popular Scales

Chapter 10

Building Allison Engined Mustangs

Vic Scheuerman and Neil Robinson illustrate the main external detail differences of the early Allison-engined Mustangs, using the Accurate Miniatures 1:48 scale kits as examples

North American Aviation's thoroughbred started life as a result of the company offering something 'a little better' to the British Direct Purchasing Commission, following initial discussions in April 1940, which resulted in this, then completely new fighter aircraft design, the NA-73, being produced as an alternative to North American Aviation building Curtiss P-40s for the RAF under licence, which was the original idea.

Although the NA-73 was also powered by an Allison engine, as

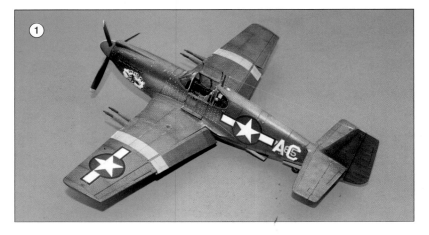

was the P-40, (the first engine designed to use ethylene glycol for cooling in lieu of water and the only US liquid-cooled production engine of the war, with 47,000 built), it was a much cleaner design that utilised the new laminar flow wing and perhaps benefited to some extent from Curtiss's research on using the now familiar under fuselage scoop to cool both the glycol and oil. Although the Mustang, (the British designation), was being produced for the British, the initial contract stipulated that two aircraft, (XP-51, 41-038 and 41-039), would be given to the Americans for testing.

The British Direct Purchasing Commission ordered 770 Allison-engined Mustangs for the RAF, in three distinct sub-types; Mk I, Mk Ia and Mk II, direct from the North American Aviation Company, and it has now become a part of aviation legend that it took North American only 117 days to design and build the NA-73, as the prototype was known, although it wasn't until May 1941 that it actually took to the air.

Flight testing soon revealed that whilst the basic design was good, with its innovative laminar flow wing aerofoil section, the 1150 hp Allison V-1710-39 engine failed to give the 'Mustang', (as the British named the type), sufficient high-altitude performance for the very demanding fighter-role over Northern Europe required by Fighter Command. However, its high maximum speed at lower levels, good handling characteristics and

86 Chapter 10

manoeuvrability, made it ideally suited for tactical reconnaissance duties and it was ordered by the RAF for its Army Co-operation Squadrons.

As the Mustang proved to be such a solid performer, the aircraft was also adopted by the United States Army Air Force. During the construction run of Allison-engined Mustangs, the American military used three variants, designated P-51, A-36 and P-51A, **(photos 1, 2 and 3)**, of the four main versions produced. The following is a brief overview of the detail differences and service use by the Americans, (and 'borrowed' aircraft by the RAF), of these versions.

Accurate Miniatures' 1:48 scale Allison Mustangs were simply a stunning debutant for the then new company. From their well-engineered layout, allowing the three basic 'American versions' to be made, to a complete and innovative cockpit, we modellers were in for a real treat. The interior includes separate sidewall consoles with details, battery rack and accessories in the aft section, proper curved 'floor', (ie the wing top), control column, gunsight, two separate levers for the port console, moulded rib detail on the fuselage walls, seat with separate two-piece framing and a clear instrument panel, (with rudder pedals attached), that allows the decals with the instrument faces printed to be viewed if so desired. The only thing that needs to be added is a seat harness. After assembly and careful painting one is rewarded with a great cockpit – that is unfortunately somewhat hidden with the sealed kit canopy.

Externally, Accurate Miniatures cater for the different wing configurations and external loads, with the A-36 carrying 500lb bombs and the P-51A getting nicely moulded drop tanks. Another option is the 'bulged' and 'normal' tyres with separate wheel inserts. All three kits offer the different fuselage cowlings for that specific variant and one decal option – the latter were used on the A-36 and P-51A kits featured in this article.

The perfect kit is yet to be made so there are some things to watch for. Whilst the kit propeller is accurate, although somewhat too thick for the P-51A, it is not entirely accurate for the other two versions. As mentioned previously, the kit canopy is closed and is thick and I would recommend replacing it with the Squadron/Signal SQ 9553 vacformed version if you wish to show off the interior. The only really weak part of these otherwise exceptional kits, are the instruction sheets. They include some of the poorest drawn efforts I have seen, and it hard to believe they come from the same company.

To borrow a phrase from Henry Ford: "You can paint your 'Allison American' any colour you like – as long as it is Olive Drab!" Well almost. There were at least two bare-metal P-51As, 43-6004 'Slick Chick' and 43-6178, and an early P-51 was painted in an experimental 'dazzle' splinter finish designed by Captain Paul Hexter.

At one time I found Olive Drab one of the most boring finishes to apply until I started to try to replicate the extreme weathering that this paint so rapidly faded to. For these specific builds, Testors Model Master enamels were selected and to offer that 'varied finish' four different colour shades were used, going from

mint to extreme fading – 1711 Olive Drab 34087, (post-war but provides some variation); 2050 Olive Drab (ANA 613); 2051 Faded Olive Drab; and 2071 RLM 02 Grau, **(photo 4)**.

As may be seen in the photos, the base coat is manipulated with random panels masked and sprayed with a different shade of Olive Drab and the lightest shade being used on the fabric areas, (except on the P-51 which was built first). The only trick is to lightly mist on the base Olive Drab near the end of the project when the decals are on, to both tone them down and to 'bind' all the Olive Drab shades together.

P-51/F-6A

This version was built under the first Lend-Lease Mustang order for the British, and covered 150 P-51s, (the American designation), even before the two XP-51s, (British supplied), were delivered. These aircraft differed from the original British aircraft in armament. Whilst the Mustang Mk I, (the British designation), sported two .50 calibre heavy machine guns in the nose chin and a further two in the wings along with four .30 calibre machine guns, the P-51 was armed with four Hispano-Suiza M2 20mm cannon. One other, minor, external change was the addition of the three-cluster American identification lights under the starboard wing. Of the total of 150 P-51s ordered, two were held back to be re-engined with the Roll-Royce Merlin, whilst the British received ninety-three under the designation Mustang Mk IA. Like the British, the Americans put cameras in their fifty-five diverted Lend-Lease P-51s and with this additional equipment, they were

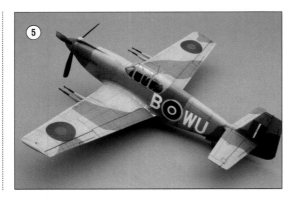

re-designated as F-6As.

The first F-6A to see operational service was 41-137328 of the 154th Observation Squadron of the 68th Observation Group. During 9 April 1943, whilst based in Sbeitla, Tunisia, North Africa, Lt Alfred Schwab, flew the first operational sortie – a reconnaissance flight over Kairouan airfield. Due to the very small number of P-51/F-6As produced, only thirty-five F-6As were sent to North Africa. The only other unit to use it operationally was the 111th Tactical Reconnaissance Squadron, also in North Africa. Some aircraft were retained in the United States for training, and in the case of the 'straight' P-51s, they went to the Aerial Reconnaissance School at Peterson Field, Colorado.

An interesting snippet here is that some of these diverted

aircraft were 'borrowed' back by the British. Operating in this area with the Spitfire Mk Vc for short range reconnaissance work was No 225 Squadron, RAF. For long range work they borrowed four F-6s and at least one was given 'proper' desert camouflage, (**photo 5**). Another RAF unit that was to benefit from this arrangement was No 14 Sqn, flying B-26 Marauder bombers. They would also use four F-6As, but this time the quad 20mm cannons would be used against German transport aircraft.

Whilst the Allison-engined Mustangs are sometimes looked at as 'inferior' to the Merlin-engined variants, one should keep a couple of things in mind. First, the Allison was the superior aircraft at the lower altitude and could even outdistance the vaunted Focke-Wulf 190A below 15,000 feet according RAF tests. The Allison Mustang was arguably the best low level reconnaissance platform used by the Allies during the entire war.

'Snoopers' – (AM kit AJ3400)

'Snoopers' is a well known F-6A flown by the 111th TR Squadron, 68th TR Group, used in North Africa and this model shows one of the marking variations, (**photo 6**). The markings are circa the fall of 1943 whilst the unit was in Algeria. A couple of interesting snippets here is that the US Navy sent eleven of their aviators to fly with the 111th to get some combat experience and that the first letter in the fuselage code designated the flight while the second letter identified the individual aircraft. In **photo 7**, the wing cannons, landing lights, (in both wings), and thin carburettor intake clearly identify this first operational version. Whilst this is the camera equipped F-6A, like most, it does not carry a camera behind the pilot for oblique shots, but has a single vertical camera in front of the tailwheel, (**photo 8**).

A-36 Apache

This particular version of the P-51 was created to get around funding restrictions. With money for Pursuit aircraft already allocated, by calling this variant an 'attack' aircraft and giving it the A-36 title, allowed the P-51 development to carry on. In time, 500 A-36s were ordered, (USAAF serials 42-83663 to 84162), making it the main American Allison version.

Unlike the previous versions, the British were not really interested in a dive bomber and only took one for testing; officially. To justify its attack title, dive brakes and 500 pound capacity bomb racks were added, while the armament was changed to six .50 calibre machine guns. The Allison V-1710-87 was used as it was thought the operating altitude would be below 12,000 feet and this version offered 1325hp at 3,000 feet.

Other external changes were that the carburettor scoop was widened to allow for the addition of an air filter, the landing lights were reduced to just one housing in the port wing but with two lights, the L-shaped pitot tube was changed to a boom configuration and moved to the edge of the starboard wing and the bottom air scoop lost its hinged door.

North American chose the name 'Apache' for this model, but as the British title of Mustang was now established, although it would unofficially be referred to as the 'Apache' in service and was

even given the mantle of 'Invader' by some units in the Mediterranean Theatre.

It was in this Theatre that the first operational mission was flown on 6 June 1943. The Island of Pantelleria, between Tunisia and Sicily, was subjected to a mass fighter-bomber assault by the 27th Fighter Bomber Group from Rasel Ma in French Morocco. It is worth adding here that one of the first 'Mustang' aces, (some sources say the only 'Allison' ace), actually flew the Allison A-36 that was supposed to be an attack version! 1/Lt M T Russo of the 522nd Fighter Bomber Squadron, claimed five enemy aircraft by 30 December 1943. The other Theatre unit using the A-36 was the 86th FBG and between these two Groups over 1000 sorties were flown in the first thirty-five days of operation. Overall, by war's end, the entire A-36 community had completed a total of 23,000 sorties.

The only other FB Group to use the A-36 was the 311th in India that also put their 'attack' aircraft to use as long-range fighter escorts. As per the P-51, some A-36s remained stateside for training and one of these units was the 88th Dive Bomb Squadron based at Key Field, Meridian, Mississippi.

Again we have aircraft borrowed from the Americans. In this case No 1437 Strategic Reconnaissance Flight RAF benefiting from six A-36s, with four of these receiving RAF serial numbers, (eg HK944), and taken on charge.

'White B' – (AM kit AJ3402)

'White B' of the 522nd Squadron of the 27th FG, proudly displays its missions as white bombs running along the fuselage, (photo 9). To fulfil its dive bomber mandate the A-36 had wing dive brakes added and these can be clearly seen in photograph 5. The other changes were the armament to four wing mounted and two chin mounted .50 cal heavy machine guns and the provision to carry up to a 500 pound bomb under each wing, (photos 10 and 11).

P-51A/F-6B

This final American Allison variant was similar to the A-36 minus the dive brakes and the 'chin' machine guns with the L-shaped pitot probe reintroduced and returned to the bottom of the starboard wing. The lightened gun load was also supplemented by a V-1710-81 rated at 1,125 hp at 18,000 in an attempt to improve its performance at higher altitudes. This, along with a new supercharger and slightly larger diameter propeller, gave this variant a top speed of 409 miles per hour at 11,000 feet. Whilst it still had underwing pylons, there were normally used to carry drop tanks to improve the range. A total of 310, (USAAF serials 42-6006 to 42-6312), were built with fifty going to the British, as Mustang Mk IIs. As with the P-51, some thirty-five aircraft were modified to carry a camera, and once modified, were designated F-6B and were used mainly by 9th AF units in Europe after the Normandy invasion. There were also two aircraft modified with retractable skis; 43-6003 and 43-6005.

Almost all of the P-51As went to the China-Burma-India (CBI) Theatre and North Africa. This time the baptism of fire for the P-51A was not in the latter, but in the CBI Theatre with the experienced A-36 equipped 311th during mid-1943. The P-51A would also be used on this front by Chennault's 23rd Fighter Group, 1st Air Commando, (air support for Ord Wingate's Raiders), and for a brief spell the 51st Fighter Group.

Whilst the Merlin-engined P-51 is recognised for its long-range escort missions in Europe; similar escorts were carried out a month earlier in CBI. The 311th escorted B-24 and B-25 bombers from Kurmitola, Bengal to Rangoon, Burma and back that was 450 miles one way, with their Allison's during November 1943. This was also the first mission to be flown with the 75 gallon metal drop tanks.

'Jackie' (AM kit AJ3410)

'Jackie' was the personal aircraft of Capt J J England, an 'ace' of the 530th Fighter Squadron, 311th Fighter Group, circa 1944, (photo 12). In photo 13, one can see the main difference from the previous model; no chin machine guns and with drop tanks being the normal underwing 'baggage', although triple 4.5 inch rocket launchers were also used by the 1st Air Commando in this

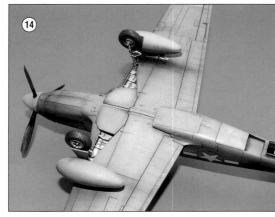

Theatre. As per the previous kits, the bottom Neutral Gray 43 received some weathering to match the wear and tear of the upper Olive Drab 41 surfaces and note the return of the L-shaped probe to the starboard wing, **(photo 14)**.

Modelling RAF Allison-engined Mustangs in 1:48 scale

The first RAF Mustangs reached the UK in October 1941 and began replacing Westland Lysanders and Curtiss Tomahawks of the RAF's Army Co-operation Squadrons in the following February. The armament of these early RAF Mk Is comprised two .50 inch machine guns in the lower nose and two .30 inch plus one .50 inch machine guns in each wing, **(photo 15)**. The USAAF gave the four 20mm cannon-armed sub-type the designation P–51. In British service, the 20mm cannon-armed P-51 was known as the Mustang Mk.IA, **(photo 16)**, which should not be confused with the P-51A, which had an uprated Allison engine and an armament of four .50 inch machine guns in the wings, and was designated Mustang Mk II in RAF service!

Fitted with an oblique F.24 camera behind the pilot's seat, the Mustang Mk I made its operational debut in May 1942 with No 26 Sqn, and five further units had re-equipped with the type by the summer, (Nos 2, 239, 400, 414 and 613 Squadrons).

The Accurate Miniatures' kits are absolute gems and are comparable to Tamiya and Hasegawa standards. Basically, AM's series of Mustang kits have individually moulded separate noses and wings reflecting the often subtle but noticeable variations amongst the different sub-types. The cannon-armed RAF Mustang Mk Ia or USAAF P-51 boxings provide the best starting point for an RAF version, although in both cases work will need to be done to the wings and nose.

The 'RAF boxed' Mustang Mk.IA kit is moulded in an easy-to-use pale grey plastic. The cockpit interior is very well detailed and the only alterations I made to what was supplied, was fitting a full height, armour plate, panel behind the pilot's seat from thin plastic card and substituting a circular spade-grip type control column for the kit's stick type – both of which modifications appear to be peculiar to these early RAF machines.

As recommended in the kit instructions, the cockpit interior was painted Interior Green 611 (FS 303187), and not Zinc Chromate – a minor point perhaps but worth noting. Whilst basic, the kit instructions are more than adequate for the job, with a written step-by-step building guide identifying and naming parts with informative sketches.

I made my Mustang Mk I from the USAAF P-51 mouldings, but I have since found out that the slightly bulged shape of the cowling top carburettor intake may be wrong – RAF Mk Is having straight-sided intakes.

The Canadian company Ultracast make a resin conversion set, 48031, to modify the Accurate Miniatures' Mustang Mk.IA, (kit 3410), in to an RAF Mk I, with replacement resin wing leading edge sections featuring the three gun ports; an undernose section with ports for the cowling guns; a pair of .50 inch cowling guns with perforated cooling jackets; and replacement propeller blades, **(photo 17)**.

Note the barrel on the port side of the lower nose extends level with the rear of the spinner, whilst the one on the starboard side only just protrudes clear of the cowling panelling. Many early Mustang Mk Is also featured exhaust manifolds without the flame-damping, 'fish-tails'; so I replaced my model's with the ones from a Monogram P-39 Airacobra.

I finished my model as AG366, RM•T of No 26 Sqn, which was originally delivered in the American DuPont paint colours Dark Earth 71-009 and Dark Green 71-003 upper surfaces with Sky Gray 71-021 undersides, and pre-May 1942 style, 1-3-5 ratio under wing and fuselage roundels and equal-width 24 inch wide x 27 inch high fin flashes.

This particular aircraft took part in 'Operation Jubilee', the large scale raid on the French harbour town of Dieppe, on August 1942, and by that time had been repainted, in either Ocean Grey

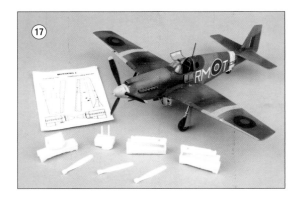

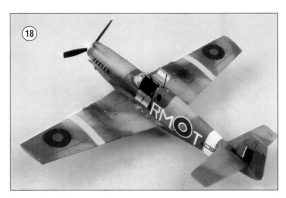

or Mixed Grey and Dark Green upper surfaces, possibly with Medium Sea Gray undersides, and the underwing and fuselage roundels had been updated in to the post-May 1942 style National marking II and III with 24 inch x 24 inch Tail fin marking (i) fin flashes.

The model was painted using Xtracolor paints throughout. X003 Medium Sea Grey under surfaces were applied first and when dry, masked out. A slightly lightened X004 Dark Sea Grey was then applied to the whole of the upper surfaces, (to represent Mixed Grey), and when that was dry, X001 Dark Green to the A Scheme pattern was applied. The spinner and rear fuselage band were painted in X007 Sky and the wing leading edges, from the gun ports to the wing tips, in X011 Trainer Yellow. All the national markings, the 24 inch high Sky code letters RM•T, and the black 8 inch high serial number AG366, came from the Xtradecal range, **(photo 18)**

From the beginning of July 1942, 12 inch wide Yellow chordwise bands were ordered to be applied around the wings of RAF Mustangs, (similar orders were issued to Typhoon Squadrons), as an additional recognition feature for the type's new and unfamiliar shape. The order was complied with rather reluctantly, in some cases with examples of 9 inch, or even 6 inch, wide bands being recorded. These Yellow bands were ordered to be removed in December 1942.

Cannon-armed Mustang Mk.IA

My second Allison Mustang was based on Accurate Miniatures' 'RAF Mustang Mk.IA' boxing, and was built virtually straight from the box. It was finished in the kit scheme, FD472, 'M' of No 268 Sqn, temporarily based at one of the Advanced Landing Grounds in mainland France in mid-June 1944, following the D-Day invasion.

By June 1944, these Mustangs had seen many months operational service, and had almost certainly undergone major servicing giving them the opportunity to be repainted in standard RAF paint shades of Ocean Grey and Dark Green upper surfaces with Medium Sea Grey undersides.

Most of the markings came from the kit decal sheet, but I replaced the fuselage roundels with some from the Xtradecal range, as the red centre of the kit's National marking IIIs were incorrectly proportioned, **(photo 19)**. I also hand painted on the 'invasion stripes' instead of applying the decal options in the kit, **(photo 20)**. It will be noted that 'invasion stripes' were not applied to the upper surfaces of the wings and fuselage, many of the Tactical Reconnaissance units foregoing this rapid identification feature to avoid compromising their camouflage in the low-level roles they performed.

Mah Sweet Eva Lee

Steve Evans builds Accurate Miniatures 1:48 P-51

North American P-51 Mustang
Manufacturer: Accurate Miniatures
Scale: 1:48
Kit Type: Plastic injection moulded

The whole project was a North American Aviation company response to the British Purchasing Commission asking them to undertake sub-contract building of the Curtiss P-40. North American said they could come up with something much better and true to their word, they did just that.

The cannon armed P-51 was the first version of this famous fighter to see service with the United States Army Air Force, a number having been kept back from a batch that was to be supplied to the Royal Air Force as the Mustang Mk.IA.

The Allison power plant of these early versions was unsuitable for high altitude work, which meant that nearly all of the first sub-types were used in the Army co-operation roles for ground

attack and close support missions. Many P-51s were converted to F-6As and used for long-range photo-reconnaissance; an aircraft of this type flew the first USAAF Mustang mission of the war.

Soon after, the British once again intervened and had the legendary Merlin engine shoe-horned into the slim nose of the P-51 airframe and the rest, as they say, is history.

The Kit

Accurate Miniatures certainly know how to make a kit appealing to the eye: some reasonable artwork on the top, a photo of a completed model on the bottom and a bit of Mustang history on the side in a number of languages. This history is nothing more than a quick gloss-over but interesting nonetheless. However, the real nice touches are on the inside; the box is split into an upper and lower half by a card separator that has a fine, four-view, line-drawing of the P-51 on it. In the upper half of the box are the three sprues of dark green plastic, which is hard and well formed, whilst below the separator are a single transparency sprue, the decal sheet and the two sheets of instructions. All in all a lovely piece of presentation (**See Photo 2**).

The green plastic parts are well formed without a single mould mark or ejection pin mark in an awkward spot, there is little flash and the detail work, both raised and recessed, is very fine indeed, especially the interior which is quite comprehensive.

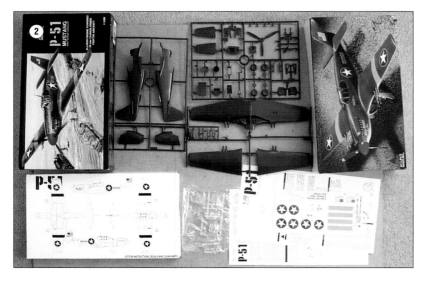

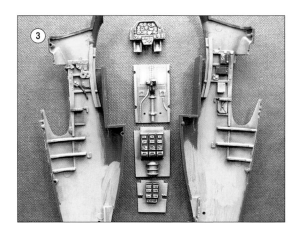

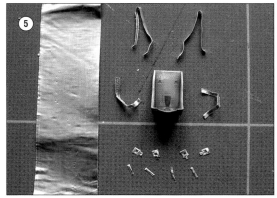

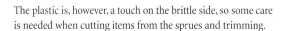

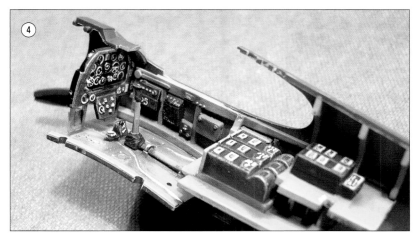

The plastic is, however, a touch on the brittle side, so some care is needed when cutting items from the sprues and trimming.

Instructions

The instruction sheets hark back to an older generation of kit, with only a few sketchy exploded diagrams and paragraphs of written directions, hints and tips. These instructions are at times a little bit confusing but anyone with even the slightest experience in modelling, will have no difficulty in working out what goes where.

The colours referred to within the instructions are all called up by their Federal stock codes so present no difficulties in finding a match.

Interestingly, the instructions also include, on the decal placement and painting sheet, a model paint reference chart that is a guide to the federal standard numbers and their closest match in a number of manufacturers' ranges: Model Master, MM Acrylic, Humbrol, Gunze Sangyo Aqueous, Mr Color, Tamiya and Polly S.

Construction

As is usual, construction begins with the interior, which is made up of 14 individual items that, once painted and weathered, build up into a good looking interior. The painting is straightforward and typically US, Interior Green and Zinc Chromate, black electrical boxes and batteries with silver pipes and wires (**See Photo 3**). A few strokes of black and dark grey pastels give the parts a bit of life and it all slots together quite nicely. The instrument panel however is something of a conundrum. It is moulded in clear plastic with a decal sheet to be used on its reverse side to represent the instruments. A reasonable idea perhaps but in practice this proves to be ineffective, so in the end I ditched the decal and treated the clear part just as I would have a normal item. A coat of matt black, dry brushed with grey to give it some definition then pick out the dial detail in white, yellow and red before filling in the dial faces with Clear Fix (**See Photo 4**).

The seat belts however were another problem. Not having an etched set to hand, I had to make them and to be honest I would much prefer not to. A few strips of aluminium self-adhesive tape (**See Photo 5**), painted in dark and light greys give a reasonable effect, but I'll definitely be leaving the canopy closed on this one (**See Photo 7**). You might have realised that I changed the shape of the belt buckles, as half way through fixing them in place, I realised the square ones were entirely the wrong shape.

Once all the interior parts were in place the fuselage halves were closed up around them and glued with a mixture of Liquid Poly and superglue, then set aside to dry overnight.

With the fuselage drying it was time to construct the wings. These go together nicely with no flash on any of the parts and minimal trimming required, remembering to take care with the brittle plastic. The only problem here was a slight warping of the upper wing components, both left and right, which required careful taping and clamping to set at the right angles. (**See Photo 8**).

Whilst all of the major components were now set aside to dry, I turned my attention to some of the other bits and pieces, notably the undercarriage units and the propeller.

The prop blades, as pointed out in one of my references, are the wrong shape, being more like the round-tipped type seen on many A-36s. They need careful trimming and filing to a much

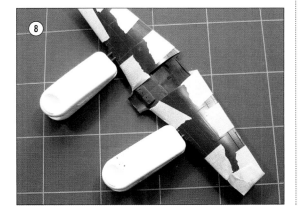

slimmer profile (**See Photos 9 & 10**).

The wheel units are provided in two types; standard and weighted, with separate wheel hubs which makes for easy painting of the units. The undercarriage legs themselves are reasonably well represented and once painted with Humbrol 56 (Aluminium) then highlighted with Chrome Silver, look pretty good.

Once the fuselage and wings were set, it was time to put them together and with a little trimming they slotted together well enough to dispense with any filler at the usual trouble spot, the wing root joint, and needing just a little bit of superglue at the lower nose joint to smooth out the contours. One area that did need close attention was the ventral intake and the fuselage joint. There was a slight mismatch in the left and right fuselage contours, added to a slightly oversize air intake, leaving this particular spot needing plenty of work to set right, but with a bit of filler and patience it smoothed out quite nicely (**See Photo 11**).

Another area that required a bit of patience was the carburettor intake on top of the engine cowling. If you set this item as the parts would have you, it drops downwards far too

much giving the nose a sort of 'broken' look. A smear of gel acrylate glue on its underside to hold it up and careful positioning gives a much better result.

The horizontal tailplanes slotted in without trouble, or filler and once the undercarriage doors were tacked into place and the tailwheel assembly masked out it was time to tackle the transparencies.

I always like to fit the transparencies pre-paint to give them a better 'built-in' look, which means careful masking up, priming with Johnsons Klear and setting into place. I know I've already said that the plastic is brittle but the transparent parts are viciously so, be VERY careful when cutting out these bits from the sprue; even with all the care I took, I still managed to crack one of the side windows. At least they all fitted well and have nice framework detailing.

Colour Options & Painting

One, would you like me to repeat that? One. Yep, that's right, you only get one choice but as it is totally representative of the type that is no problem. The basic colour scheme is the standard, for

the time, Olive Drab federal stock upper surfaces with Neutral Grey federal stock undersides. The rather bland scheme does have, however, a couple of redeeming features: the large American stars and stripes on the tail and the yellow theatre bands around the wings. Both of these marking were applied to 'Operation Torch' aircraft as recognition aids for Allied servicemen unfamiliar with US types.

The whole kit was given a couple of coats of Halfords Grey Primer which is a good representation of the darker position of the US Neutral Grey underside. The panels were highlighted with Polly Scale acrylic US Neutral Grey and the panel lines given a dusting of grey pastels and some general dirtying up. Some of the picture references of this type show them to be pretty beaten up and in some cases one step away from the scrap heap so there is plenty of license to go just about as far as you like with the weathering (**See Photos 12 & 13**).

This also applies, of course, to the upper surface which after a couple of coats of Humbrol 86 Light Olive were given much the same sort of treatment, with lighter panels and darker joint lines, this time with the inclusion of some darker exhaust stains (to be added to later, in the final assembly) and plenty of paint chipping, applied with a silver pencil (**See Photos 14–18**). After setting aside overnight to dry the whole thing was given a coat of gloss and set aside once more, in readiness for the decals.

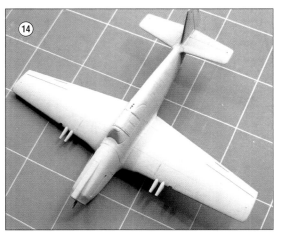

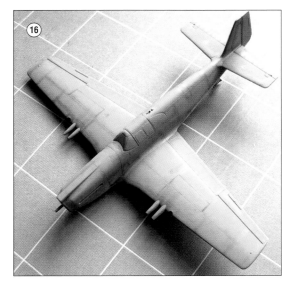

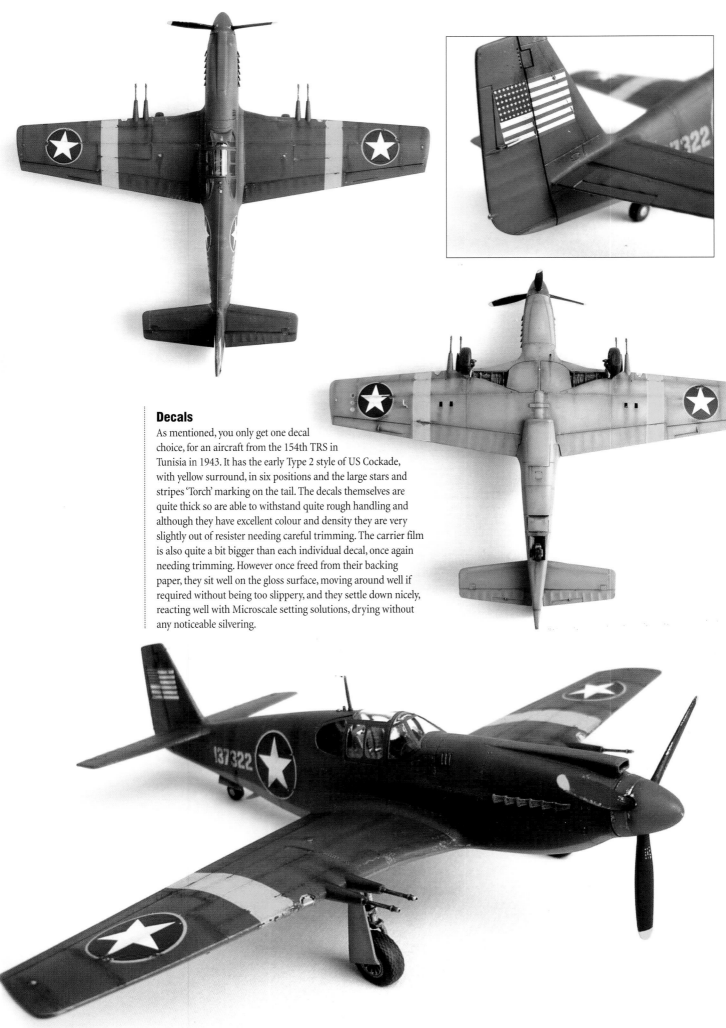

Decals

As mentioned, you only get one decal
choice, for an aircraft from the 154th TRS in
Tunisia in 1943. It has the early Type 2 style of US Cockade,
with yellow surround, in six positions and the large stars and
stripes 'Torch' marking on the tail. The decals themselves are
quite thick so are able to withstand quite rough handling and
although they have excellent colour and density they are very
slightly out of resister needing careful trimming. The carrier film
is also quite a bit bigger than each individual decal, once again
needing trimming. However once freed from their backing
paper, they sit well on the gloss surface, moving around well if
required without being too slippery, and they settle down nicely,
reacting well with Microscale setting solutions, drying without
any noticeable silvering.

Final Assembly

After giving the decals a good few hours to dry, it was out with the paints and pastels to grubby them up a little to match the rest of the paintwork. Then it was time to fit all the little bits left off earlier for fear of breakage, which included: main undercarriage units and doors, pitot tube, propeller and spinner (previously painted), wheels set at the correct angle, radio mast exhaust, landing lights in each wing and finally the cannon barrels.

These last items deserve a bit of describing. The kit-supplied items are of the wrong type, looking more like the British 20mm cannon fitted to the Hurricane IIc, with barrel finning (those 'fins' are springs - Ed). They should, of course, be the early US type with plain barrels, which were sourced from my spares box (I believe they came from the AMT/Ertl Havoc A-20G). The muzzles were hollowed out and all four were painted once in position.

After a couple of hours to let everything set properly the whole lot was given two coats of Humbrol matt enamel spray, the aerial wires attached (1lb fishing line), cockpit masking removed and the P-51 was complete.

Accuracy

The model measure 233mm span x 204mm length, which scales up to 11.18m span x 9.79m length. The official figures for this type are 11.27m span and 9.82m length which makes the finished model 1.8mm too narrow across the wings and 0.7mm too short. I call that pretty much spot on. As for its 'look' – it's unmistakably a Mustang, 'nuff said.

Conclusion

• Good points: Good detailing, reasonable fit and finish to all the parts, an accurate representation of the earliest P-51, a lovely interior and good presentation.
• Bad points: Brittle plastic, incorrect cannon barrels and propeller blade shape, out of register decals.

All in all this is a fine effort from Accurate Miniatures, the finished model captures the look and the lines of the Allison engined P-51 well. The kit goes together without any major problems and this would be a fine starting point for people who like to do plenty of detailing work as everything is in the right place and correctly proportioned. The bad points I've mentioned really are just niggles and in no way distracted from my enjoyment of making this model.

My only real gripe would be with the single colour/decal option; this aircraft is pretty much identical to the Mustang Ia and it would have been nice to have that option in the box.

1:32 A-36

Joachim Greer builds the HobbyCraft kit

North American A-36A Apache

Manufacturer: HobbyCraft

Scale: 1:32

Kit Type: Plastic injection moulded

Though her Merlin-powered siblings are much more in the limelight than the original Allison-powered aircraft one should never forget that without the latter there probably never would have been a P-51D flying over Berlin one day. Less well documented is that the Allison powered Mustangs, Apaches, or Invaders, gave good service during a critical phase of the conflict when victory for the Allies was by no means a certain outcome.

What is also true of this remarkable machine is that it was designed and flown in an incredibly short time, turned out to be a pretty good aircraft, was one of the fastest on the deck, and later, mated with the RR Merlin, became a legend. Now, as a result of recent new research, we have a 1:32 kit of this early P-51 from Hobbycraft of Canada.

The starboard console undergoing construction

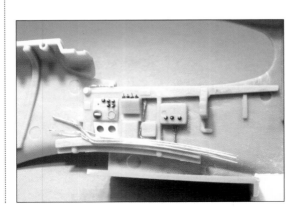

The kit

The first issue of the kit here in Germany was the 'Operation Torch' P-51. After opening the box there are four clear plastic bags each containing a sprue (three grey ones and one clear), one more bag with the decals and one loose decal of the US-flag. The panel lines are of the recessed type and very fine while most of the parts themselves seem to be rather on the thick side. The breakdown of parts suggests there will be some more versions, especially those with the nose mounted guns to follow. The main fuselage consists of four parts with a break at the firewall for the armed nose to be installed. Not all parts are to be used and some relate to the next release, the A-36, on sale at the time of writing.

The kit has its ups and downs. The cockpit contains separate sidewall details and a nicely moulded cockpit floor/wing top. Two different types of seats are included and there is a lot of radio equipment for the rear compartment. No engine is provided but there are two sets of hinged canopies, one opened and one in the closed position, and two sets of propellers are also included but one is the broad chord A-36 type.

No separate rudders or flaps are provided, which makes the overall number of parts quite modest. On the other hand the inclusion of both flattened and unflattened mainwheels is a nice feature, but the kit is missing the hinged forward radiator inlet typical of the Mustang I/P-51-2NA. All in all the relatively few detail parts are well moulded but seem to be on the slightly thick side at first impression. The decals are restricted to the main markings, omitting any stencils or instruments at all.

Getting Started

I started with the wings, joining upper and lower halves first. On my model the wing halves were slightly distorted, requiring some care while the glue cured. The wheel well is cast into the lower half of the wings and is slightly too shallow, while also missing the rearward space towards the main spar. After much consideration about how to detail the rather thick keel rib I realized that – contrary to all Merlin-engined Mustangs – the inner wheel well doors stayed locked on the Allison powered aircraft, even after the engine had been shut down for a considerable time, so no detailing of the inner wheel wells was necessary. At this early stage I also fixed the front fuselage halves to the rear ones.

Next I turned my attention to the cockpit. The seat was thinned and the outward curving seat pan was corrected to an inward curve. The sidewall frames were next glued to the inside of the cockpit walls (contrary to the instructions). With the addition of the throttle quadrant and its levers for mixture and propeller pitch, trim wheels, and other levers for landing gear and flaps the left console was soon looking busy. On the right console I added a few knobs and switches to the electrical systems and boxes. In general appearance both side consoles seemed to agree with my references and are acceptable.

One thing that greatly enhances the appearance of the consoles is the addition of those many cockpit placards typical for the P-51. Lacking any aftermarket parts it was time to scratch-build some, and when I say scratch I mean scratch! First I painted some small strips of sheet aluminium in the appropriate background colour (either red or black). After the colour had dried I took a scribing needle to scratch all the lettering and signs through the colour, revealing the bare aluminium below. The final result was cut to size and glued into place and from a small distance it looks good enough for me.

After all the cockpit details were finished I gave the whole assembley a coat of White Ensign Models Zinc Chromate Green, except for the seat, which was painted Interior Green to add some contrast. Then a wash with thinned oil-paints of black and burnt umber was applied and after this had dried thoroughly some dry-brushing was added. Pre-painted seat belts borrowed from Eduard's P-39 kit finished off the seat.

When dry fitting the fuselage halves I realized that now the cockpit floor was 1.5 mm too narrow in width, but this only

The radios were finished by adding some placards and dials

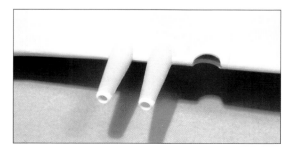

Styrene rings were glued over the gun fairing openings to allow a tidy appearance

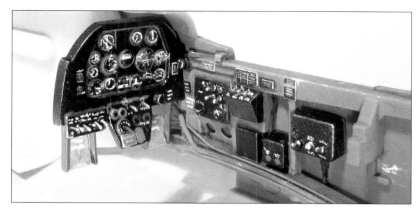

required some careful aligning while glueing the floor into the fuselage. This was done later when the fuselage halves were already glued together.

The radio compartment is very nicely represented, though like most of the kit very simplified. Here too, some additional knobs, dials and wires, carefully painted, do the job very well and make for a very nice compartment.

Finished starboard console with homemade placards in place

Not a masterpiece but necessary - the circular radiator for Allison-engined aircraft

The cockpit sub-assembley fits tidily into place

The windscreen was glued in place with cyanoacrylate after which some white glue was used as filler giving additional strength

The interior colour was sprayed first onto the masked clear parts

The Hasegawa outer rim fitted well into the wheel opening, enhancing the whole area

Wheels and Wheel Well Covers

Of the two sets provided I chose the flattened wheels, and although they are slightly too square when viewed from ahead the tyres have nice tread detail and do the job. The wheel rims are separate items and while the inner rims look good, the prominent outer ones are not acceptable. I used some from the old Hasegawa Mustang that have the correct diameter and this did the trick. The landing gear leg was used straight out of the box, only being cleaned up, scissor links drilled out, and brake lines added. It was a different story with the main gear doors. The kit parts were used as templates on some aluminium sheet, drawn around with a needle and then cut out. After that the outer part of the well covers was cut away and replaced with the shaped aluminium parts, using two-compound epoxy. These parts were then set aside for painting.

Radiator

As the P-51-2NA, and its British counterpart of course, were the only Mustangs to have a variable intake ramp for the radiator I

The pre-shading in full process. Maskol and salt were used to cover some chipped areas. Salt is on the port wing, Maskol on the starboard

Copper springs on small iron nails make for effective guns - at least when compared to the kit items

Humbrol MET 191 is applied to all areas of great wear and tear for later weathering

wanted to represent this feature in the partially lowered position. I cut both ramps out of the fuselage and inlet parts and sanded them to shape, adding sidewalls. Furthermore the cutouts were cleaned up and sidewall detail added. As the lowered intake ramp would allow a good look inside the fuselage, and as Hobbycraft has nothing to offer for this space, I bent a strip of sheet styrene to form a pipe, sealed both sides with some etched mesh, inserted a circular centrepiece with a different type of mesh, and managed somehow to fix it inside, although the matter was fraught. With this finished it was time to close the fuselage halves and add the pre-fabricated wings, which fit very tight and I had to remove a very little bit of plastic to avoid tension. This problem might not occur if you leave off the upper wing halves until the lower are glued to the fuselage.

The tailplanes were added and all of the main assemblies needed only the slightest touch of filler. With the windscreen and rear windows fixed and blended in it was time for my favourite part of the modelling:

Painting

First the clear parts were masked with one big piece of tape and then a white car primer was applied, after which I checked for any blemishes and scratches to be corrected. Now the canopy was masked properly with Parafilm and sprayed with the interior colour.

Humbrol Metallic Silver #191 was applied to all those surfaces subject to chipping - leading edges, wing walks and maintenance panels etc. Now Humbrol's Maskol and some wet salt were gently applied onto the silver colour before the next step – preshading.

White Ensign Models Neutral Grey and Olive Drab, lightened with 15% white, were applied in several thin coats carefully over the preshading. I applied the first two coats of the main colours to cover everything evenly, while the next two were applied

The Maskol and salt were now removed and all the scratches and chipping was now achieved, using different methods. The water-colour wash will be applied next

irregularly, making for a very attractive non-uniform result.

The Maskol and salt were now removed and Johnsons Future applied to the areas where decals were to be applied. Although these are slightly on the thick side they react well to setting solutions and the white really covers the background colour well. Only very slight silvering was noticed.

Next were the ID Markings, which consisted of 18" wide yellow identification bands on the wings and – according to the kit's instructions - horizontal tailplanes. I masked the areas with Tamiya tape and applied the yellow irregularly leaving different shades around the panel lines. Just before the yellow had dried I took a tissue dampened with white spirit and removed the paint partially from the leading edges.

Next I took out some painters' fleece and carpenters' steel

The right stuff (Tamiya's masking tape) on the wrong place. the ID stripes on the horizontal tail surfaces could not be confirmed by any reference

The masking tape was removed without any problems. Immediately after painting I partially removed the yellow paint from the leading edges with a cloth, dampened in white spirit

A dark brown water colour wash was applied next, applying the mix very generously. Alway try to wipe in the direction of the airflow when removing the excess

wool to work over all the areas prone to chipping and scratching, removing thin coats of paint here and there, adding fine scratches on the walking areas and the leading edges as well as the sharp edges of the wheel covers.

When this was finished to a satisfactory result the panel lines were dealt with next with water colours in different shades of black/brown. After the water colour had dried it was rubbed over with a dampened tissue leaving the colour in the recesses, and also dirtying-up the main colours to add to the used appearance of the aircraft. Everything was sealed with Testors Clear Coats, mixing gloss and dull 40/60.

To achieve the essential exhaust stain I first added a light grey into a mix of both Testors Clear Coats and sprayed the outside edges of the stains. Then the same mixture, replacing the grey with sand-yellow was sprayed into the centre of the stain, ending in a very nice result. After the paints had dried some panel lines were again picked out, using a light water colour wash, now

Detail on the canopy. Inner framing was added and the handles are PVA/white wood glue, a perfect medium to replicate all sorts of small knobs and handles

Heavy exhaust stains were typical for Allison engines. These were applied using light grey and sand, each thinned with white spirit and clear coat to give a more varnished effect

making the whole model looking really very worn.

Entering the final lap it was time to sit back, have a cup of coffee, look at the model, compare with references and shout out a loud a curse entirely unsuitable for the ears of my three-year old son. A golden rule in modelling is to check references twice before modelling and here I failed as I realized that 137322 did not have yellow bands around the tailplanes. Ok. Out with the wet and dry and some gentle rubbing removed most of the tailbands. Then the main colours were mixed again, hoping to match the correct shade, and applied over the affected areas.

Small Pieces

When looking at the opened canopy I decided to add some internal framing for a better appearance. The two locking handles were next added and a gear strut, that runs from the lower frame to actuate the locking mechanism, was simulated by a piece of stretched sprue. One very prominent and important handle is the small canopy safety pin on the upper left forward corner of the hinged part. This was made of copper wire and

Nav-light on spine and antenna mast fitted. The kit mast was too wide and did benefit from some thinning down. On my next P-51 I will omit the socket for the mast as this was not apparent on the real plane. Note the small spring in the rear quarter window

after everything else was painted in the appropriate colours, was given a coat of red enamel.

The P-51 had a rear view mirror and an auxiliary ring gunsight. The former part was made from plastic card and some self adhesive mirror foil – looking very convincing, while the latter was made of copper wire. One area that strained my nerves was the two rear window securing springs that run along the forward edge of the rear window. To produce these I took a very fine wire, locked a pin in my drilling tool locked the wire to the pin and switched on. This produced a very fine spring that could now be glued into position, taking me one and a half hours to do so, as two springs were crushed in the process and one ended up somewhere on the floor.

A similar technique was used on the guns. Here I produced springs in the above mentioned way, soldered them onto iron nails and filed them square afterwards. Then they were painted semi-gloss black, dry brushed with silver and dulled down with graphite.

Finally, as I wasn't happy with the antenna being too broad, this part was cut thinner. For the antenna wire I used invisible sewing thread and the last thing to do was to click the exhausts into place, having previously drilled out and painted them. These are among the poorer parts of the kit and should be replaced by some aftermarket items.

The radiator intake and exhaust doors were fixed in the lowered position as observed on many parked P-51s. There is a very prominent gap between the radiator door and the fuselage when the former is lowered. The guns and the exhausts were now fitted as well

Pitot tube fitted and ID Lights on outer starboard wing painted in their appropriate colours

Verdict

Now what can I finally say? I have a very nice looking Allison powered P-51 in my showcase looking every bit an early Mustang. Although the kit itself is quite simplified it will satisfy most modellers who want to add an early Mustang to their collection and is even suitable for the beginner. The lack of very fine detail is compensated by the nice surface and the panel lines and the outline looks every inch the part.

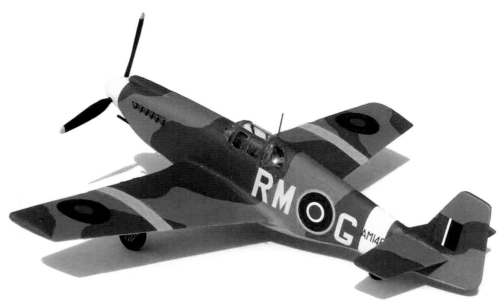

RAF Mustang Mk I

Ivor Ramsden builds the 1:72 Special Hobby kit

Mustang Mk I	
Manufacturer:	Special Hobby
Scale:	1:72
Kit Type:	Plastic injection moulded with etch

I don't know what the origin of this kit is, but the mouldings are also available from Smer. It includes spare wings, fuselage halves and tail, in fact almost a full airframe for different Mustang marks! sixteen resin parts provide a beautifully detailed cockpit, wheels and sections to graft into each wing to represent the six wing guns fitted to RAF aircraft. The instructions give a brief history, ten construction stages and two pages of colour scheme and markings drawings. Colour details are shown at each stage, with names and FS references being given throughout.

As with most limited-run kits this one needs careful assembly and several areas need attention, including the wing sections which need rubbing down vacform-style to give clean mating faces and a sharp trailing edge. The wing to fuselage joint needs trimming and the under-fuselage radiator fairing parts require some major smoothing, but unless you trim too enthusiastically no filler is required anywhere in the main assembly stages. Minor detail points to note are the inclusion of only one style of exhaust, whereas Mustang Is were seen with two distinctive styles. An extra landing light should be cut into the starboard wing and glazed with clear sprue or Kristal Kleer. The aileron trim tabs are moulded too far outboard but this can be rectified by filling and rescribing. The rear cockpit glazing is fitted with a very prominent bulge to clear the camera but I can't find any

photos of RAF Mustangs with this fitting. Most have the standard flush panel overpainted with a hole for the camera lens. Both under nose guns are too long, and note that the port gun protrudes further than the starboard one.

Decals are given for a 613 Squadron aircraft in the early Army Co-Operation scheme of Dark Earth, Dark Green and Sky and a 26 Squadron aircraft in the later grey and green scheme with yellow identification bands on the wings. My photographs show the 26 Sqn aircraft without the yellow bands and with its squadron codes and aircraft letter, RM-G, in similar sizes rather than with a larger G as depicted by the decals so I used Modeldecals to replace the letters. The kit decals are very good. They settled onto gloss surfaces without any help from decal solutions.

This kit is expensive and needs a lot of work but includes some lovely resin detail. Unfortunately for Special Hobby, the new P-51A from Academy is a cheaper option, which is much easier to build and is a more accurate basis, straight from the box, for an RAF Mustang I.

P-51 Mustang IA

Brian Derbyshire builds the 1:72 Academy kit

P-51 Mustang

Manufacturer: Academy
Scale: 1:72
Kit Type: Plastic injection moulded

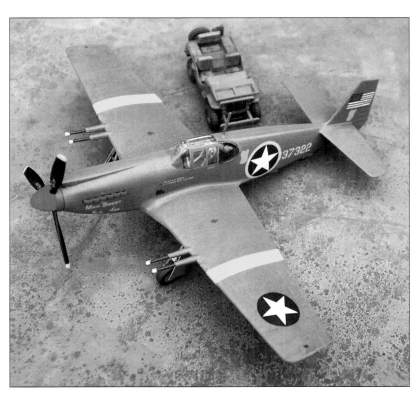

Academy's B and C versions of the Mustang, though lovely kits, are spoilt by gross inaccuracies. The 'just plain' P-51, however, stands head and kneecaps above both them and all previous 1:72 Allison-engined Mustang kits.

We've waited a long time for a decent Allison-Mustang, and this is it. The detail is beautiful. The cockpit floor is (correctly) cambered, with a nice seat, stick and panel. Transparencies are as good as I've ever seen in this scale, and even include a gunsight. You also get a radiator core, detailed both sides, and a four-part camera.

Dry-fit the floor into the starboard side and trim the forward location, or the fuselage halves will not close. Ease the fuselage locating pins, to avoid a step along the spine. Sand the inside faces of wing and rudder trailing-edges, or they'll be very thick. There are no pins on the wings, so it may be best to attach the lower wing to the fuselage first, and add the upper surfaces later. Once the radiator intake is installed and faired in, extend the scribed lines of the forward radiator door to the outside corners of the lip. Don't install the propeller into the spinner back-to-front. The tailplane tabs are very loose and need packing.

Instructions are clear, if you have the hang of them. Newcomers simply must read the key before starting — and it's placed as a footnote, not a header! See also Squadron/Signal's Fighting Colors by Davis and Greer for interior colours.

You get two options, both from the 68th TRG, which was the only USAAF Group to operate the type. Both aircraft are faded Olive Drab and Gray, enlivened by theatre markings — red spinners and yellow wing bands (which are provided). I was very happy with the transfers — thin and flexible, yet opaque. They stuck down well on their own, and the serials and stencilling — laid on Klear — were free from silvering.

Mah Sweet/Eva Lee of 154 OS has a double dose of those strangely-shaped gas detection panels to port, but probably not to starboard too, but we'll never know as both photos are of the port side. I reckon they'd be dull mustard yellow, so I overpainted mine in Zinc Chromate. Some sources claim that the red stripes of the tail flag were omitted, but this is debatable. Alas, the flags — correctly not handed — are modern, with 50 stars! I used very old 48-star AIR stock.

It is clear that the upper wing insignia were neither doubled up nor outlined in yellow, and from other photos I'd say that the underwing ones weren't either, though it was common on A-36s. The six (outlined) insignia supplied look fine on the fuselage, but I found a pair of plain 35in ones for the wings. Note that the outlines slightly overlap the forward ends of the serials. Photos also show a new, bulged transparency for the camera window, possibly cut away at its bottom rear. Also, the spinner appears to be red only over its front section, and the outboard wheel discs seem to be red too.

The other option is 137365, 'C' of A flight, 111 TRS. This one is six months down the line, and thus is even more worn. Again, the only photos are of the port side, and the markings shown are generally OK. However, the fuselage insignia, already outlined in darker blue, need a further and very crude outline in fresh olive drab, to represent the painting-out of the excessively wide red outline applied in Summer 1943. The rear half of the mission symbols should be duller, too — maybe they got some new paint. Cover with a thin wash of OD?

The only P-51-2 for which I have both port and starboard photos is coded BG and in her case the starboard codes are forward of the insignia. Was this also the case with AC? Certainly, if the insignia repainting left only the last four digits of the serial to port, it would leave only the first four (1373) to starboard, whether or not the code was painted over it.

Finally, if you cut up the '3s' from AC's serial to make a pair of '8s', and omit the artwork, you can produce 137328, otherwise

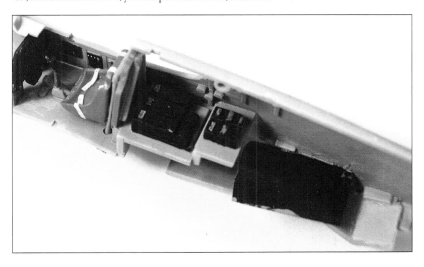

known as her squadron mate Mah Sweet. This aircraft flew the first-ever USAAF Mustang operation.

Years of staring and comparing have convinced me that the most accurate Mustang drawings to date are Arthur Bentley's. You'll find them in Osprey's Aces No. 7, and that's what I've worked to.

The P-51-2NA is generally excellent, though like all other pre-D Mustang kits in this scale there is no droop to the leading-edge extensions and there is as yet no easy cure. The wing plan is mostly accurate and the dihedral spot on — and it goes correctly right to the centreline.

The only thing that really spoils the kit's looks is the carburettor intake. Run a ruler along the upper nose of any side-view photo of an Allison-engined Mustang: the curve is always convex. The kit's intake fairing disappears at a kink just behind the exhausts. Build it up to run smoothly back to the firewall, and if you alter nothing else at all it'll look right.

For rivet-counters, the entire underside run from nose to rear of radiator is a tiny touch shallow. The nose and spinner base are a bit short on diameter, giving a rather pointy snout. The prop blades are too broad at the tips. The wings are 2mm short on total span, all outboard of the tip joint line (they can be fixed, but rounding-off the tip leading-edge looks nearly as good). The chordwise panel line at mid-aileron is 4mm too far inboard. The case ejector slots need extending forwards by about half their chord. The landing lamps are as deep above the wings as below. The U/C leg sockets are offset, which skews the wheels. There's no ducting for the radiator, so daylight shows through.

This is a marvellous kit, whose faults are outweighed by its virtues. I really enjoyed it.

'War Cry'

Italeri's Quarter Scale A-36A Apache by Dick Clark

A-36 Apache
Manufacturer: Italeri
Scale: 1:48
Kit Type: plastic injection moulded
Kit Number: 2729

This model is a reboxing of the Accurate Miniatures kit, dating from 1994, as can be seen by the engraving inside the lower wing section, but despite being nearly twenty-years old, this is a clean, crisply-moulded kit with 'all mod-cons'; finely engraved panel lines, very good interior detail and well-depicted rivets and fastenings. There is no flash and little in the way of mould-seams. Italeri have produced a new decal sheet offering four options: 'Priscilla', as featured on the box art, flown by Lt. Bert Benear, 526th FS, 86th FB, Corsica 1944; Herschel IV/Dotsie (as modelled here), flown by Lt. Donald 'Button' Smith, 312th FS, 86th FB, Tfarui (Algeria), 1943; 36081 flown by Lt. Bill Creech, 328th FS, 311th FB, 10th Air Force, Burma 1944; and HK944, 1437th

Strategic Reconnaissance Flight RAF, Foggia (Italy), 1943.

Construction begins in the cockpit and there are frames with moulded-on detail to be added to either cockpit sidewall, together with shelves for batteries and radio behind the cockpit. I added the sidewall detail before painting, but painted the cockpit and the radio and battery parts separately before adding the latter with CA glue. You need to use slow-setting CA and test-fit the fuselage halves together to ensure each shelf sits at the correct angle while the glue sets. Both floor and seat are well detailed. The kit includes a version of what seems to be Italeri's standard

generic seat-belt decal, which might just be acceptable in 1:72, but not really in this scale. So seat belts were acquired from an Eduard pre-coloured set (RAF pattern, to be honest, but they're better than nothing and I had them in stock!). The instrument panel/rudder pedals are moulded as one part, in clear plastic. I assume the idea was to have a decal for the instruments to go on behind the panel, but the decal isn't printed that way and that method would call for very careful painting of the panel around the instrument bezels. So I painted the panel in the normal way, then put the decal over the raised detail, using Micro-Set and -Sol to help the decal settle down. Once dry the decal was sealed in with matt varnish, and then a drop of 'Klear' was applied to each dial to simulate glass.

There is an inverted 'V' frame to add behind the seat, which doesn't fit especially well. With this and the floor-pan, I again held the fuselage sides together to ensure these parts set at the correct angle. Same goes for the vent panel under the rear of the fuselage, which is not such a precise fit. The tail wheel also has to be fitted before the fuselage halves are joined. Once everything was set in place, a wash was applied fairly roughly, switches and other details were picked out in white and red, and the fuselage halves joined permanently. This stage went well, with no more than a mere smear of filler being required although I did find one half was distorted, necessitating the use of tape and clamps to bring the tail end together. However, I would recommend not gluing the join underneath the cockpit, for reasons which will become clear.

The engine cowling is a separate assembly, presumably to allow for different engine/nose configurations to be fitted to the same fuselage. The machine-gun barrels below the prop have to be fitted at this stage, which makes for some awkward masking later on, but nothing too troublesome. I fitted the front of the intake on top of the cowling at this stage as this did need a touch of filler and filing to blend it in. The wing uppers fit to the one-piece lower, after drilling out the location-holes for the underwing pylons. My wing sections were badly distorted, needing more clamping and taping while the glue set - and I can only hope they pulled together into the correct shape.

When I came to fit the wings and the cowling to the fuselage, I discovered the problem caused by gluing the fuselage underneath the cockpit. I had used a clamp to close this join up, but this made the fuselage too narrow at the bottom, resulting in a gap at the wing roots and the front end being too narrow for the cowling at the wing roots. Clearly, if I had not gone to such lengths to close the fuselage up 'properly', this problem would not have arisen. As it was, I glued the wing along the starboard root (because the cowl fitted better that side) and allowed this to set, then pulled the front end of the fuselage out to close up the root as much as possible on the port side, clamping it down

Showing a good level of interior detail with the addition only of aftermarket seat belts.

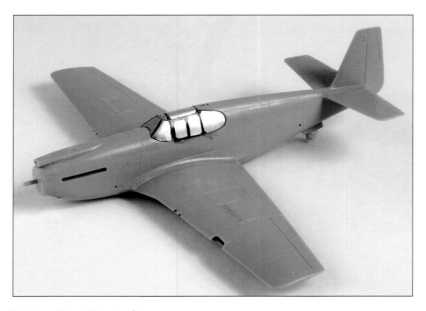

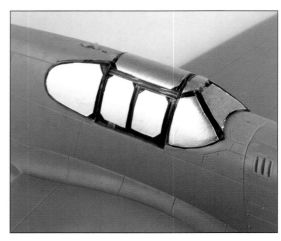

Close-up of the canopy masking.

Two views of the model ready for painting. Note the use of Bare-Metal Foil to mask the very fine canopy framing detail.

tightly while the glue set along that root. I was then able to fit the cowl such that the discrepancy barely showed. Thankfully the tailplanes fitted without any such problems!

The belly intake scoop fitted well, though it did need some attention with a rat-tail file to blend it in adjacent to the wing. The pylons went on with no trouble at all, but you do need to make sure they're on the correct wing as they are sided to allow for the dihedral. Last thing before painting was to mask and fit the glazing and, to be honest; I'd been putting this off. The glazing panels are very thin and crystal-clear, but the framing is extremely shallow. While this may be closely to scale, it doesn't make it easy to mask up. I used Bare-Metal Foil as this material burnishes down well over such fine detail, giving the best possible chance to cut accurately to the edges of the framing. Well, that's the theory. In practice it still was far from easy and,

particularly on the starboard side, hasn't gone as accurately as I'd have liked.

I then masked each panel off the model, and then fitted the panels working from the rear to the front - you have to do this because the rear side windows are a butt-fit to the fuselage. My method for fixing glazing - provided it fits accurately - is, after sealing each panel with a dip in 'Klear', to apply a little drop of CA glue here and there around the frame, fit the panel, allow it to set, and then run more 'Klear' around the frame to seal it all the way round. However, the main canopy doesn't fit accurately enough for this latter stage, having gaps at the bottom front and rear, so Humbrol Clear-Fix is a better option here. Note that the kit includes an optional Malcolm hood, which may be more appropriate for RAF versions, although there is no mention of it in the instructions.

The model was given a coat of grey primer and a few spots were given a bit more filling and sanding. I used Humbrol aerosol acrylics Sea Grey 27 underneath, Light Olive 86 with a light overspray of Olive Drab 155 for the upper surfaces. The Olive Drab was polished back to allow the lighter shade to show through patchily, then the whole model given a coat of Tamiya TS-13 Gloss Clear in preparation for decaling and the first stage

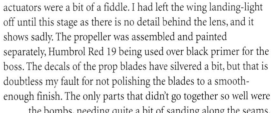

of weathering, a light wash to pick out some panel lines and the control surfaces.

I found the decals to be accurately printed and easy to apply, with the exception of the yellow wing stripes, which were difficult to work into the dive brake slots. I found I had to allow them to dry, then slit the decal over the slots with a scalpel and apply copious amounts of Micro-Sol. I found the same problem trying to get the US flag to settle on the starboard side of the fin. Also, the wing stripes are provided as separate upper and lower halves, resulting in an impossible-to-disguise join on the leading edge. I feel this would have been much better produced as a single piece to wrap around the leading edge. You may feel it would be better to mask and spray these stripes.

The decals include three rather random yellow objects which represent gas detection patches, which I left off. And a word of warning here as I would highly recommend separating the section of decal sheet for the version you are modelling, and the generic stencils, from the rest of the sheet. Even then be very careful you don't get mixed up. You see, the different versions are labeled A,B,C and D on the decal sheet and on the instructions but decals for the different versions and the stencils carry the same numbers on the decal sheet! Finally

Everything was sealed-in with a coat of Tamiya TS-80 Flat Clear. Further weathering was then applied, working a light grey fine pastel powder unevenly into the centre of some panels to lighten them a touch, and a darker powder to accentuate some of the panel joins a little more

All undercarriage parts, exhausts and aerials were painted on the sprues, although some parts do need to be removed from their sprues and taped to a piece of scrap cardboard. Everything fitted well, although the rear inner main door

actuators were a bit of a fiddle. I had left the wing landing-light off until this stage as there is no detail behind the lens, and it shows sadly. The propeller was assembled and painted separately, Humbrol Red 19 being used over black primer for the boss. The decals of the prop blades have silvered a bit, but that is doubtless my fault for not polishing the blades to a smooth-enough finish. The only parts that didn't go together so well were the bombs, needing quite a bit of sanding along the seams. A fishing-line aerial wire finished the model off.

Walk Around

Chapter 11

North American XP-51, 41-038, N51NA

On Display at the EAA Museum Oshkosh WI, USA

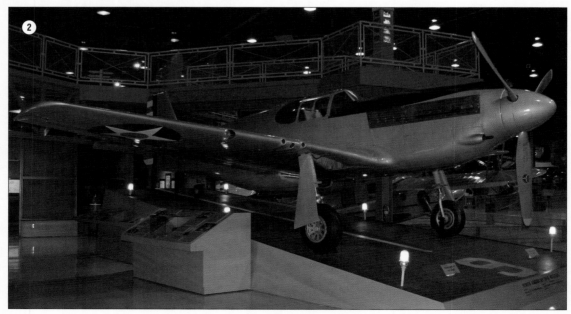

- **1** The clean lines of the XP-51 are very evident.
- **2** Note the gun fairings on the nose

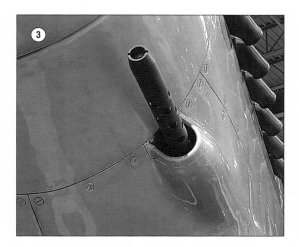

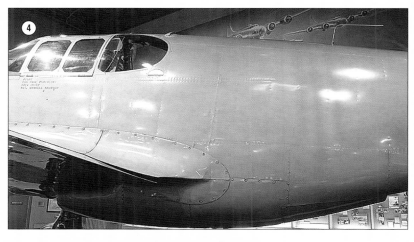

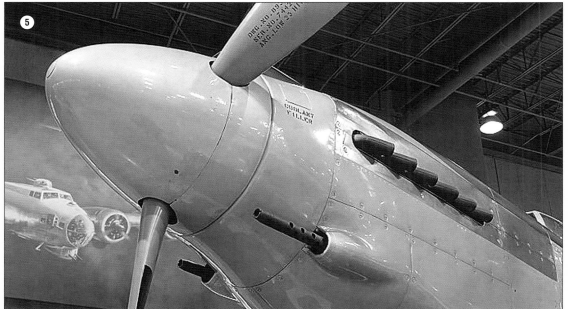

- 3 Close-up of the machine gun
- 4 The rear-mid fuselage
- 5 The nose and spinner
- 6 Underfuselage just behind the intake scoop
- 7 Landing gear and tyres
- 8 The wing machine gun fairings
- 9 Looking down on the canopy

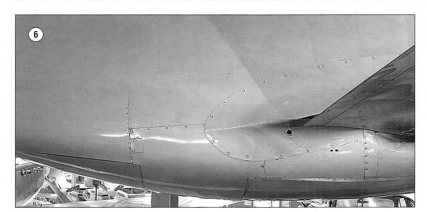

- **10** A close-up of the rear canopy glazing
- **11** Close in on the wing guns and fairings
- **12** Landing light
- **13** Mainwheel and tyre
- **14** Looking up under the wing
- **15** Close in on the canopy glazing
- **16** XP-51 41-039

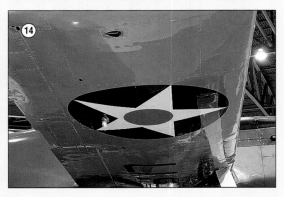

A-36 Apache

Photographs by John Bonnani

- **1** A-36 Preserved at the National Museum of the USAF in Dayton Ohio.
- **2** The aircraft is displayed with its dive brakes open
- **3** Looking up under the starboard wing

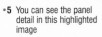

4 The A-36 framed by other exhibits and bathed in light

5 You can see the panel detail in this highlighted image

Section II – Nose and Forward Fuselage

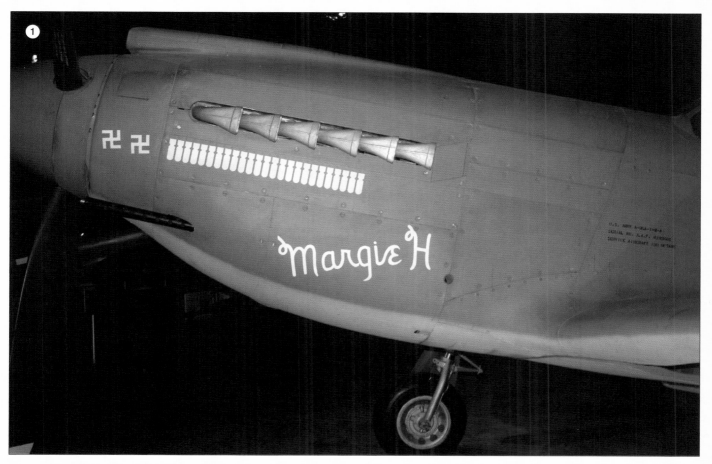

•1 Port side of the nose showing the Glycol filler cap and Data Block stencil

•2 Carburettor intake on top of the nose

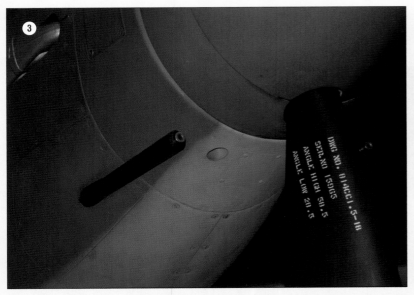

- **3** Starboard side .50 cal machine gun
- **4** Port side .50 cal machine gun
- **5** Close in on the starboard gun barrel
- **6** Close in on the port gun barrel
- **7** Port side engine exhausts and mission markings
- **8** Engine access panels around the exhausts on the port side
- **9** Close in on the fairing at the rear of the exhaust stack
- **10** Close in on the spinnier fairing

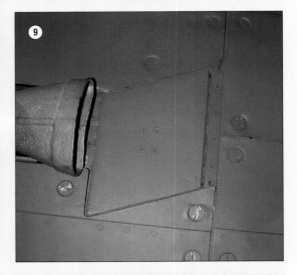

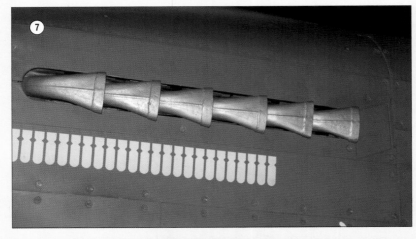

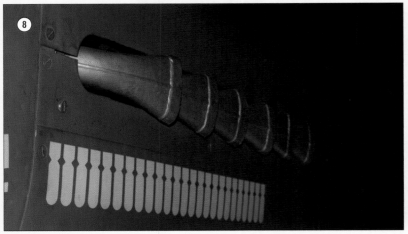

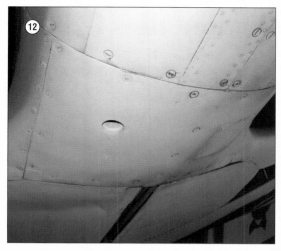

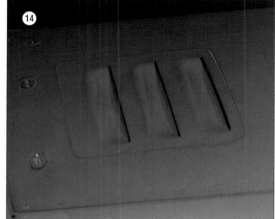

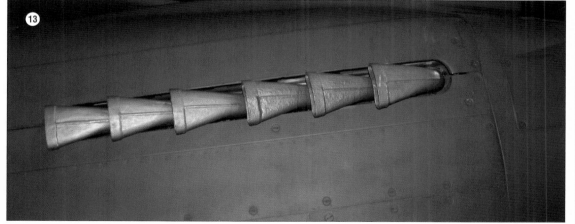

- **11** Looking up under the ose
- **12** Close in on the undernose access panels
- **13** Starboard side engine exhausts
- **14** Vent on the starboard side
- **15** Starboard vent in detail
- **16** Looking into the exhaust stack on the starboard side

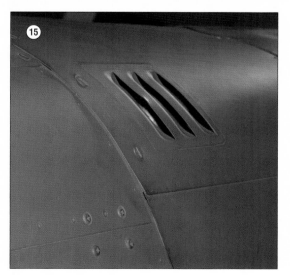

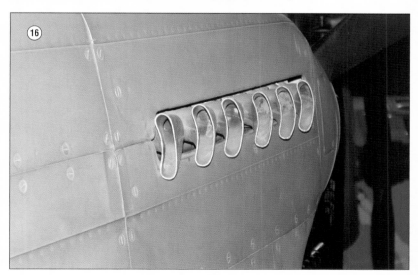

Section III – Canopy and Cockpit

- **1** Port side of the canopy
- **2** Overall view of the port side glazing. Note that this particular aircraft does not have the usual sliding panels or clear-view quarterlight.
- **3** Looking inside the rear glazing behind the seat
- **4** Pilots foot step
- **5** Note the wooden aerial mast
- **6** Ceramic connector
- **7** Starboard side rear glazing
- **8** Looking into the cockpit from the starboard side.

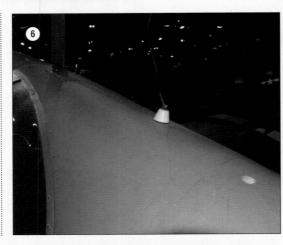

9

10

9 Pilots instrument panel

10 Looking into the cockpit from the port side

Section IV – Underfuselage Intake and Radiator

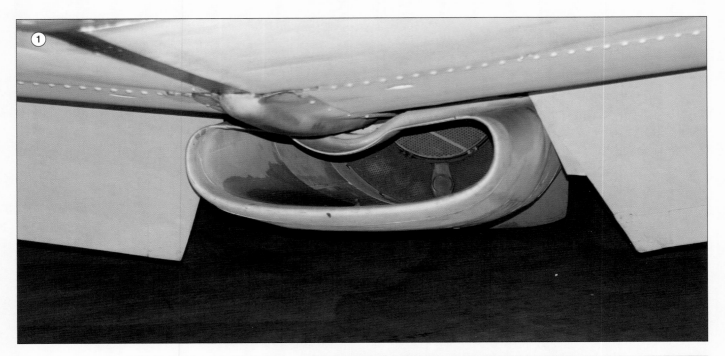

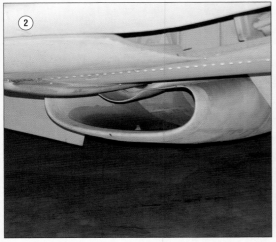

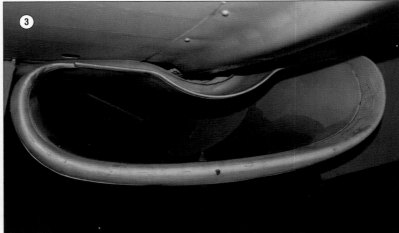

- **1** The fixed shape cooling intake with its internal cylinder radiator
- **2** The shape of the intake is well demonstrated here
- **3** Looking forward at the gap between fairing and fuselage
- **4** Looking straight into the intake

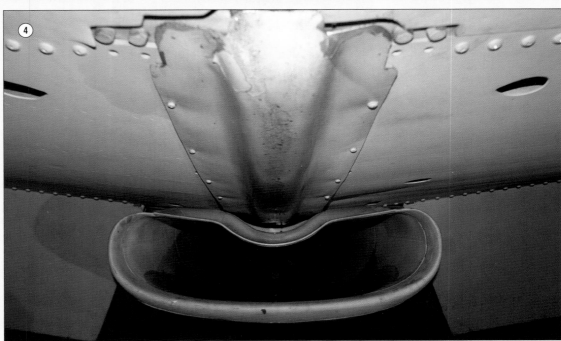

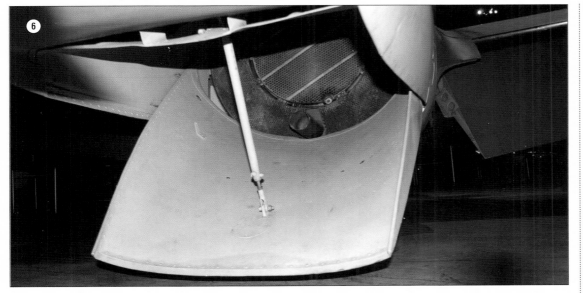

- **5** The aft end of the radiator view from the port side
- **6** The aft end of the radiator view from the starboard side
- **7** The shape of the rear fusealge to accomodate the radiator

Section V - Tail and Rudder

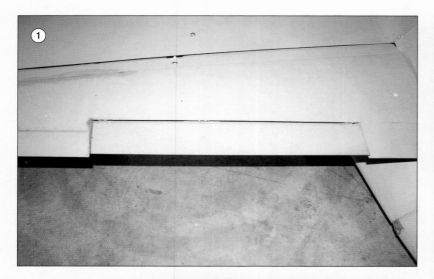

- 1 Port side tailplane and trim tab
- 2 Looking at the port side tailplane and rudder
- 3 Close in on the port side rudder and tailcode
- 4 Close in on the starbord side rudder and tailcode
- 5 Actuator tab located at the base of the rudder
- 6 Rudder trim tab

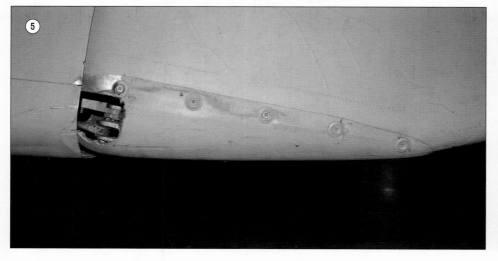

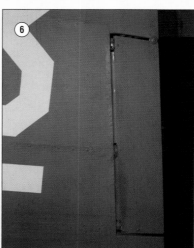

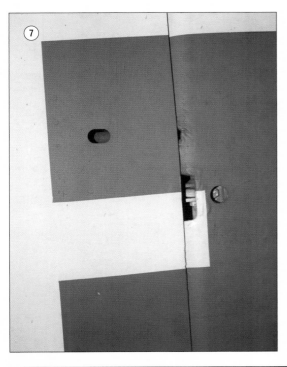

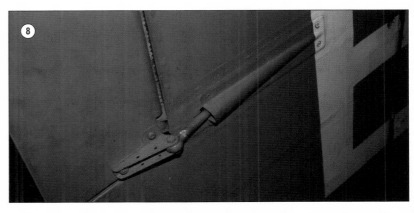

- **7** Starboard side of the rudder in close up
- **8** Starboard side of the rudder showing acutaor and fairing
- **9** Starboard side tailplane
- **10** Close in on the panel shape and detailing at the base of the rudder
- **11** Starboard side base of the rudder
- **12** Panel details under the starboard tailplane
- **13** Panel details under the port tailplane
- **14** Radio antennae fairing

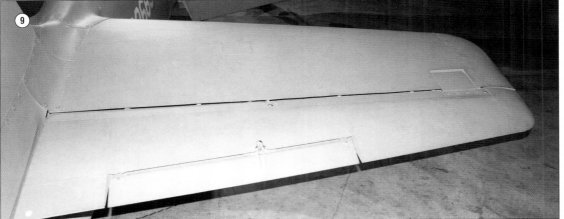

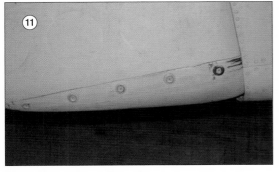

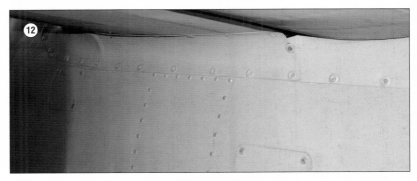

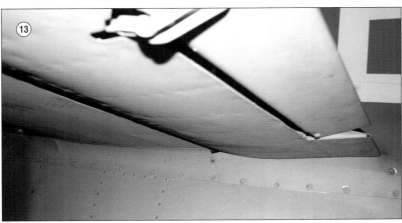

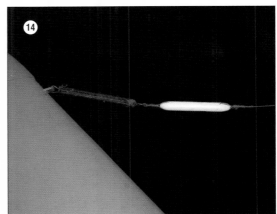

Section VI - Wheels and Wheelwells

- 1 Port mainwheel
- 2 Port mainwheel and tyre
- 3 Port mainwheel with door detail
- 4 Starboard mainwheel

- **5** Starboard mainwheel with door detail
- **6** Head on view of the starboard mainwheel
- **7** Rear view of the starboard mainwheel
- **8** Port mainwheel door exterior

• **9** Close in on the wheel hub

• **10** Oleo linkage

• **11** Oleo linkage from the rear

• **12** Looking up inside the mainwheel door

• **13** Hydraulic line detail

• **14** Looking up into the port mainwheel well

• **15** Port wheel well detail

• **16** Hydraulic hub

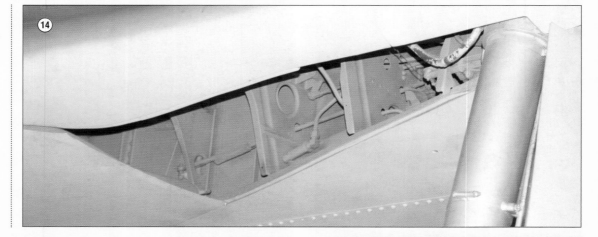

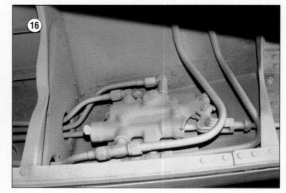

- **17** Looking up inside the starboard wheel well
- **18** Internal structure and hydraulic pipes in detail
- **19** Interior structure detail
- **20** Tailwheel and door
- **21** Tailwheel in detail
- **22** Rear view of the tailwheel
- **23** Tailwheel door on the port side

Section VII - Wings, Guns and Dive Brakes

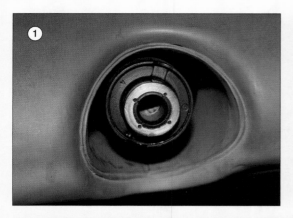

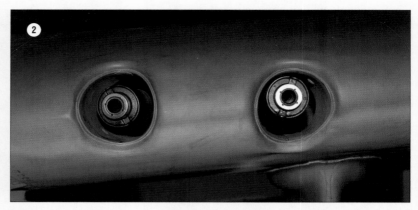

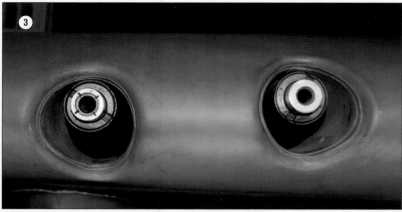

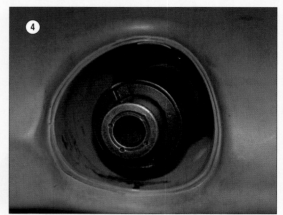

- **1** Close in on one of the wing mounted .50 calibre guns
- **2** Note how the outer gun is lower in the wing
- **3** Close in on the wing guns and their fairings
- **4** Note the shape of the gun fairing
- **5** Port side guns in situ
- **6** Close in on one of the wing mounted landing lights
- **7** Twin lights fitted to the port wing
- **8** Head on view of the bomb rack fairing

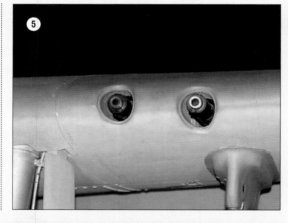

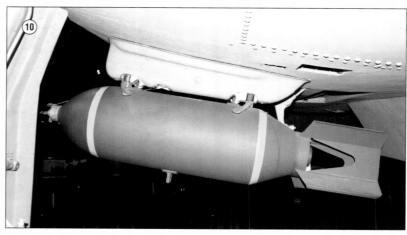

- 9 Close in on the bomb rack
- 10 Side view of port side bomb rack
- 11 Side view of starboard side bomb rack
- 12 Lowered wing flap detail
- 13 Port upper wing detail showing dive brake fairing
- 14 Port open dive brake
- 15 Rear view of the port dive brake

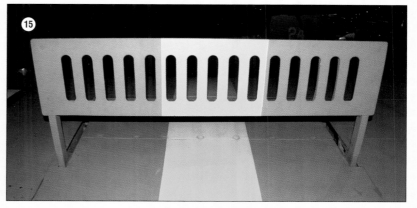

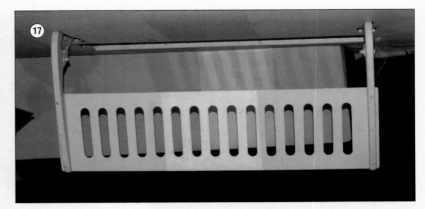

- **16** Head on view of port dive brake
- **17** Lover port dive brake
- **18** Lower starboard dive brake
- **19** Head on view of lower port dive brake
- **20** Looking upwards to the port underfuselage dive brake housing
- **21** Looking upwards to the starboard underfuselage dive brake housing
- **22** Port side dive brake housing

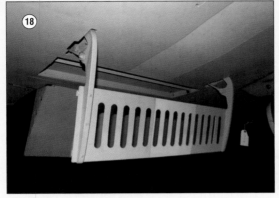

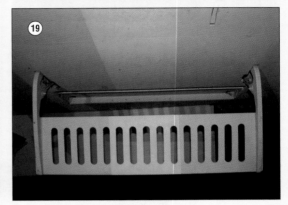

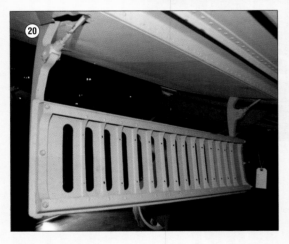

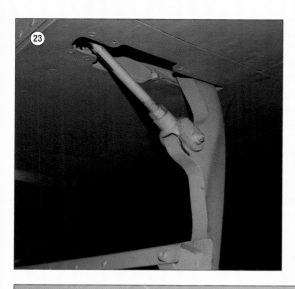

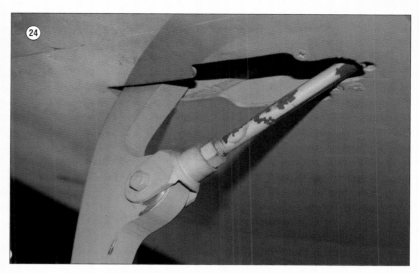

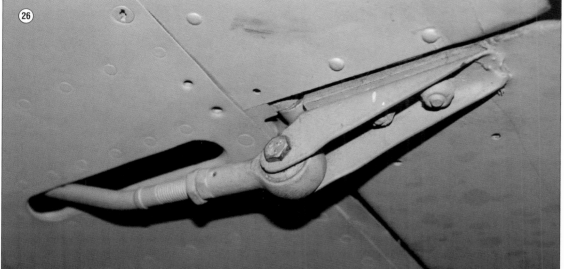

- **23** Dive brake actuator port side
- **24** Dive brake actuator starboard side
- **25** Red port side lamp
- **26** Flap actuator
- **27** Fuel filler
- **28** Starboard upper side blue lamp
- **29** Starboard lower side blue lamp

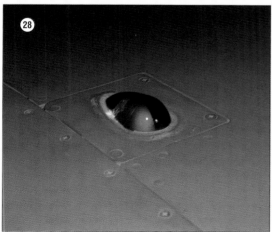

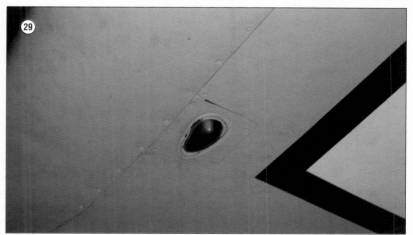

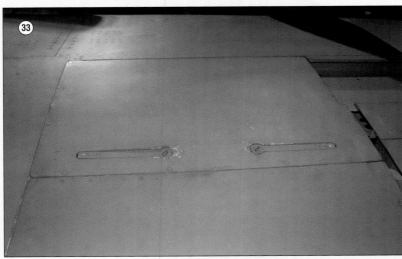

- **30** Underwing lights
- **31** Flap actuator starboard side
- **32** Starbord flap in detail
- **33** Upper wing panel detail
- **34** Wing pitot tube

Section VIII – A-36 'Mrs Virginia' – Planes of Fame

• **1** A great view of an A-36 with engine panels removed

• **2** A superb view of the Allison engine is afforded here

Technical Diagrams

Courtesy of John Dienst

Chapter 12

Three View of A-36A and P-51A

Three View of Mustang I

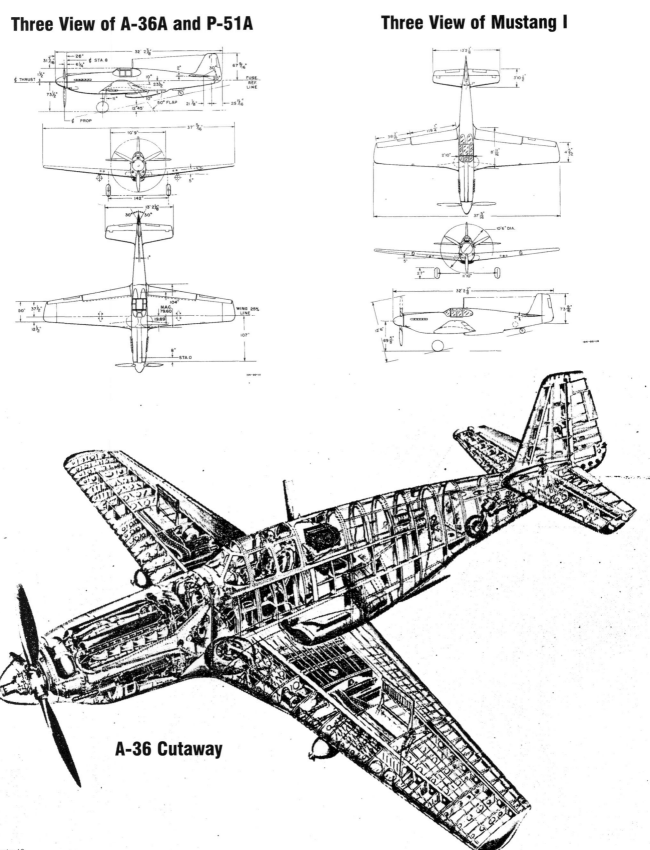

A-36 Cutaway

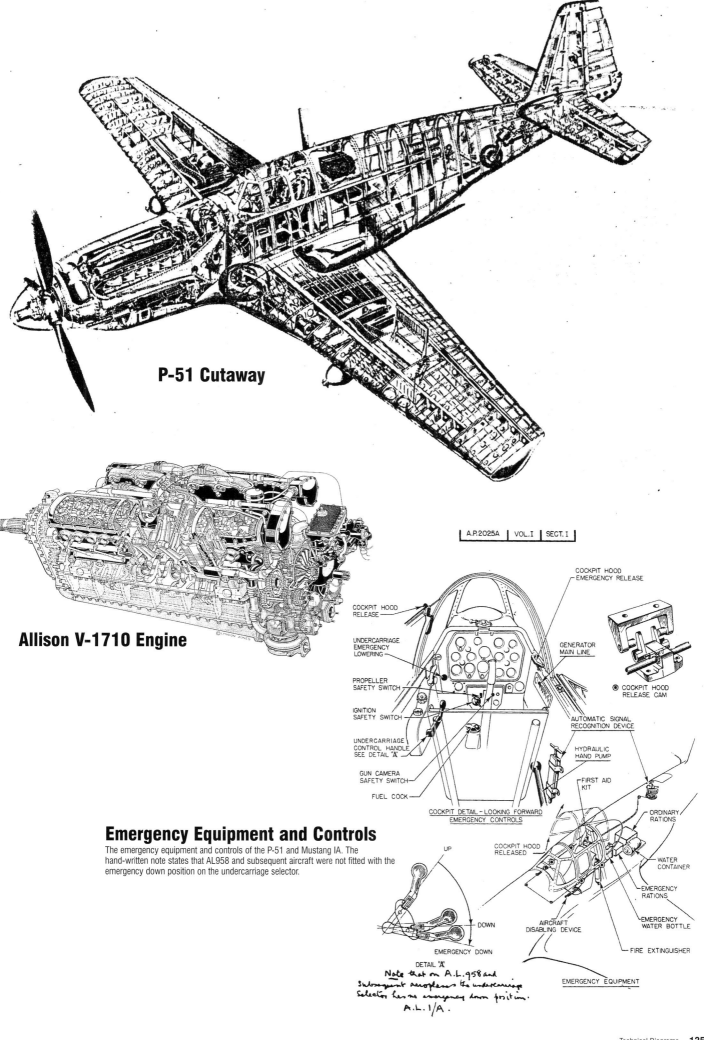

P-51 Cutaway

Allison V-1710 Engine

A.P.2025A | VOL. I | SECT. I

COCKPIT HOOD RELEASE

COCKPIT HOOD EMERGENCY RELEASE

UNDERCARRIAGE EMERGENCY LOWERING

GENERATOR MAIN LINE

PROPELLER SAFETY SWITCH

IGNITION SAFETY SWITCH

COCKPIT HOOD RELEASE CAM

UNDERCARRIAGE CONTROL HANDLE SEE DETAIL "A"

AUTOMATIC SIGNAL RECOGNITION DEVICE

GUN CAMERA SAFETY SWITCH

HYDRAULIC HAND PUMP

FUEL COCK

FIRST AID KIT

ORDINARY RATIONS

COCKPIT DETAIL - LOOKING FORWARD EMERGENCY CONTROLS

COCKPIT HOOD RELEASED

WATER CONTAINER

Emergency Equipment and Controls

The emergency equipment and controls of the P-51 and Mustang IA. The hand-written note states that AL958 and subsequent aircraft were not fitted with the emergency down position on the undercarriage selector.

UP

DOWN

EMERGENCY DOWN

DETAIL "A"

EMERGENCY RATIONS

AIRCRAFT DISABLING DEVICE

EMERGENCY WATER BOTTLE

FIRE EXTINGUISHER

EMERGENCY EQUIPMENT

Note that on A.L.958 and subsequent aeroplanes the undercarriage selector has no emergency down position. A.L.1/A.

Major Assembles A-36A and P-51A

REF. NO.	PART NO.	TITLE
1	73-44025	Propeller Spinner
2	73-31011	Engine Nose Cowling
3	83-31073	Engine Top Cowling
4	73-31071	Engine Intermediate Cowling
5	91-310155	Engine Bottom Cowling
6	73-31098	Engine Bottom Aft Cowling
7	73-31099	Engine Bottom Intermediate Aft Cowling
8	73-310100	Engine Upper Intermediate Aft Cowling
9	73-31072	Engine Top Aft Cowling
10	83-31826	Cockpit Hood Windshield Assembly
11	73-31102-20	Firewall
12	91-31107	Fuselage Side Panel
13	73-31848-10	Cockpit Hood Exit Hatch Left Side
14	73-31835	Cockpit Hood Exit Hatch Right Side
15	73-31829	Cockpit Hood Exit Hatch Upper
16	91-31122	Fuselage Top Deck
17	73-31830	Cockpit Hood Aft
18	83-310119	Radiator Air Scoop Forward Fairing
19	83-31022	Radiator Air Duct Forward
20	91-31024	Radiator Air Scoop Forward
21	83-310108	Aft Air Duct Upper Dome
22	73-31025	Radiator Air Scoop Aft
23	73-46050	Radiator
24	73-310106	Radiator Bottom Cover

REF. NO.	PART NO.	TITLE
25	73-31108	Fuselage Rear Section
26	73-31066	Tail Wheel Door
27	91-34101	Tail Wheel Strut
28	73-21001	Horizontal Stabilizer
29	73-22001	Elevator
30	83-22004	Elevator Trim Tab
31	73-23001	Vertical Stabilizer
32	73-24001	Rudder
33	83-24004	Rudder Trim Tab
34	73-14011	Wing Tip RH
35	73-14060	Fuel Tank Door
36	73-14101	Wing Rib Station 0
37	73-10023	Wing Center Bulkhead
38	91-14001	Outer Panel
39	73-14032	Landing Gear Access Door
40	91-14050	Armament Bay Door
41	73-18001	Wing Flap
42	91-14121	Landing Light Cover
43	73-16001	Aileron
44	83-16005	Aileron Trim Tab
45	91-14729	Cannon Fairing
46	83-14011	Wing Tip LH
47	73-33301	Landing Gear Fairing Door
48	73-33102	Landing Gear Strut
49	73-33302	Landing Gear Fairing

Major Assembles Mustang I

REF. NO.	PART NO.	TITLE	REF. NO.	PART NO.	TITLE
1	73-44002	Spinner (on Airplane Serial Nos. AG345 to AG367 & AG369 to AG377, Incl.)	23	73-31024	Radiator Air Scoop Forward
			24	73-310108	Aft Air Duct Upper Dome
	73-44025	Spinner (on Airplane Serial Nos. AG368 & AG378 & Subsequent)	25	73-31025	Radiator Air Scoop Aft
			26	73-46003	Radiator
2	73-31012	Engine Nose Cowling	27	73-310106	Radiator Bottom Cover
3	73-31073	Engine Top Forward Cowling	28	73-31108	Fuselage Aft Frame
4	73-31073-2	Engine Top Forward Cowling	29	73-31066	Tail Wheel Door
5	73-31071-16	Engine Center Side Cowling	30	73-34101	Tail Wheel Strut
6	73-31071	Engine Center Side Cowling	31	73-21001	Horizontal Stabilizer
7	73-31074	Engine Lower Forward Cowling	32	73-22001	Elevator
8	73-31068	Engine Lower Center Cowling	33	73-22004	Elevator Trim Tab
9	73-31098	Engine Lower Aft Cowling	34	73-23001	Vertical Stabilizer
10	73-31099	Engine Lower Intermediate Aft Cowling	35	73-24001	Rudder
			36	73-24004	Rudder Trim Tab
11	73-310100	Engine Upper Intermediate Aft Cowling	37	73-14011	Right Wing Tip
			38	73-14060	Wing Fuel Tank Cover
12	73-31072	Engine Top Aft	39	73-14101	Wing Rib Station 0
13	73-31826	Cockpit Enclosure Windshield Assembly	40	73-10023	Wing Center Bulkhead
			41	73-14000	Wing
14	73-31104	Firewall	42	73-14032	Landing Gear Access Door
	73-31102	Firewall Armor Plate	43	73-14050-2	Wing Guns Access Door
15	73-31111	Forward Fuselage Frame	44	73-14050-4	Wing Ammunition Access Door
16	73-31848	Cockpit Enclosure Exit Hatch Left Side	45	73-18001	Wing Flap
17	73-31835	Cockpit Enclosure Exit Hatch Right Side	46	73-14122	Landing Light Recess Cover
			47	73-16001	Aileron
18	73-31829	Cockpit Enclosure Exit Hatch Upper	48	73-16005	Aileron Trim Tab
19	73-31111-39	Fuselage Top Deck	49	73-14024-7	Camera Access Door
20	73-31830	Cockpit Enclosure Aft	50	73-14024	Left Wing Tip
21	73-310119	Radiator Air Scoop Forward Fairing	51	73-33301	Landing Gear Fairing Door
22	73-31022	Radiator Air Duct Forward	52	73-33102	Landing Gear Shock Strut
			53	73-33302	Landing Gear Fairing

Major Assembles Mustang P-51A

REF. NO.	PART NO.	TITLE	REF. NO.	PART NO.	TITLE
1	73-44025	Propeller Spinner	25	73-31108	Fuselage Rear Section
2	73-31011	Engine Nose Cowling	26	73-31066	Tail Wheel Door
3	83-31073	Engine Top Cowling	27	91-34101	Tail Wheel Strut
4	73-31071	Engine Intermediate Cowling	28	73-21001	Horizontal Stabilizer
5	91-310155	Engine Bottom Cowling	29	73-22001	Elevator
6	73-31098	Engine Bottom Aft Cowling	30	83-22004	Elevator Trim Tab
7	73-31099	Engine Bottom Intermediate Aft Cowling	31	73-23001	Vertical Stabilizer
8	73-310100	Engine Upper Intermediate Aft Cowling	32	73-24001	Rudder
9	73-31072	Engine Top Aft Cowling	33	83-24004	Rudder Trim Tab
10	83-31826	Cockpit Hood Windshield Assembly	34	73-14011	Wing Tip RH
11	73-31102-20	Firewall	35	73-14060	Fuel Tank Door
12	91-31107	Fuselage Side Panel	36	73-14101	Wing Rib Station 0
13	73-31848-10	Cockpit Hood Exit Hatch Left Side	37	73-10023	Wing Center Bulkhead
14	73-31835	Cockpit Hood Exit Hatch Right Side	38	91-14001	Outer Panel
15	73-31829	Cockpit Hood Exit Hatch Upper	39	73-14032	Landing Gear Access Door
16	91-31122	Fuselage Top Deck	40	91-14050	Armament Bay Door
17	73-31830	Cockpit Hood Aft	41	73-18001	Wing Flap
18	83-310119	Radiator Air Scoop Forward Fairing	42	91-14121	Landing Light Cover
19	83-31022	Radiator Air Duct Forward	43	73-16001	Aileron
20	91-31024	Radiator Air Scoop Forward	44	83-16005	Aileron Trim Tab
21	83-310108	Aft Air Duct Upper Dome	45	91-14729	Cannon Fairing
22	73-31025	Radiator Air Scoop Aft	46	83-14011	Wing Tip LH
23	73-46050	Radiator	47	73-33301	Landing Gear Fairing Door
24	73-310106	Radiator Bottom Cover	48	73-33102	Landing Gear Strut
			49	73-33302	Landing Gear Fairing

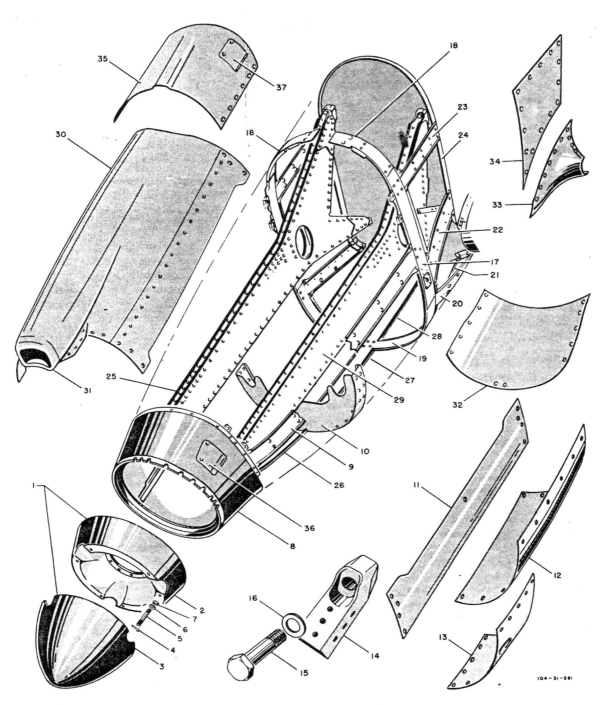

Typical Engine Cowling Formers Allison Engine

REF. NO.	PART NO.	TITLE		REF. NO.	PART NO.	TITLE		REF. NO.	PART NO.	TITLE
1	73-44002-10	Spinner Complete—Prop. (Used on Airplanes AC42-83663 to AC42-83762)		10	97-31055	Bulkhead—Engine Removable Cowling Lower Center Complete		18	83-31041-1	Former—Engine Removable Cowling Top Rear Complete RH
	99-44002	Spinner Complete—Prop. (Used on Airplanes AC42-83763 & Subs.)		11	73-31071	Cowling—Engine Removable Center Side Complete LH			83-31041	Former—Engine Removable Cowling Top Rear Complete LH
	AN7-10A	Bolt			73-31071-1	Cowling—Engine Removable Center Side Complete RH		19	73-31044	Former—Cowling Lower Rear Comp.
	2W1-29-28-6	Washer		12	73-31068	Cowling—Engine Removable Lower Center Complete LH		20	73-31096	Former—Cowling Lower Interm. Rear Complete LH
	AC365-720	Nut			73-31068-1	Cowling—Engine Removable Lower Center Complete RH		21	73-31096-1	Former—Cowling Lower Interm. Rear Complete RH
	2W1-16-24-63	Washer		13	73-310155-50	Cowling—Engine Removable Lower Front Complete LH		22	73-310101	Former—Cowling Upper Interm. Rear Complete LH
	AN4-6A	Bolt (Used Only on 7344002-10)			73-310155-51	Cowling—Engine Removable Lower Front Complete RH			73-310101-1	Former—Cowling Upper Interm. Rear Complete RH
	AN4-7A	Bolt (Used Only on 99-44002)		14	73-31919	Fitting—Engine Mount Attaching Upper LH		23	73-31038	Former—Cowling Hor. Side Rear Complete LH
	AC365-428	Nut (Used Only on 73-44002-10)			73-31919-1	Fitting—Engine Mount Attaching Upper RH			73-31038-1	Former—Cowling Hor. Side Rear Complete RH
	AC365-52A	Nut (Used Only on 99-44002)			73-31920	Fitting—Engine Mount Attaching Lower LH		24	73-31102-30	Firewall—Armor Plate Complete
2	73-44002-6	Spinner—Rear Section		15	73-31910	Bolt—Engine Mount Attaching		25	73-31901-1	Engine Mount Complete RH
	99-44002-3	Spinner—Rear Section			73-31912	Nut		26	83-31056	Former—Cowling Bottom Front Complete
3	73-44002-7	Spinner—Front Section		16	73-31913	Washer		27	73-31057	Former—Cowling Bottom Center Complete
	99-44002-4	Spinner—Front Section			73-31359	Bushing		28	73-31075	Former—Cowling Bottom Rear
4	AN380-3-4	Pin		17	73-31043-100	Former—Removable Cowling Side Rear Complete LH		29	73-31901	Engine Mount Complete LH
5	73-44024	Stud			73-31043-1	Former—Removable Cowling Side Rear Complete RH		30	83-31073-100	Cowling—Removable Top Front Comp.
6	AN960-516	Washer						31	73-310146	Edge—Fus. Carb. Air Scoop Leading
7	AC365-524	Nut						32	73-31098	Cowling—Lower Rear
8	73-31011-100	Cowling—Engine Removable Nose Comp.						33	73-31099	Cowling—Lower Rear Left Side
9	73-31037	Former LH							73-31099-1	Cowling—Lower Rear Right Side
	73-31037-1	Former RH						34	73-310100	Cowling—Rear Left Side
									73-310100-1	Cowling—Rear Right Side
								35	73-31072	Cowling—Upper Rear
								36	91-31086	Door—Cowling Access Front
								37	73-31089	Door—Cowling Access Rear

Typical Engine Mount Structure Allison Engine

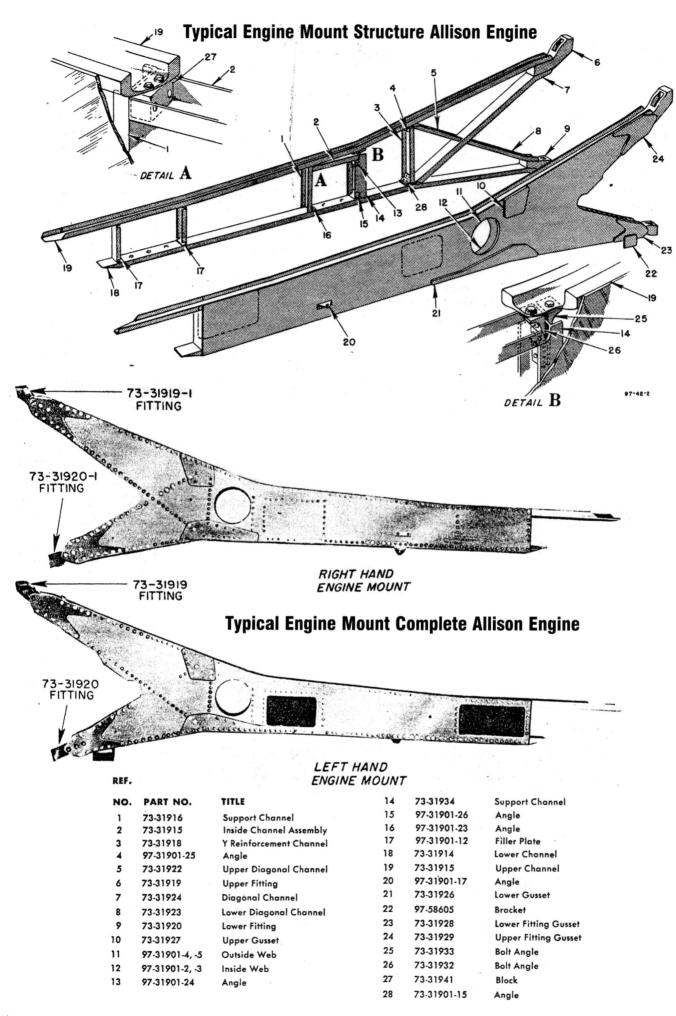

DETAIL A

DETAIL B

97-42-2

73-31919-1
FITTING

73-31920-1
FITTING

RIGHT HAND
ENGINE MOUNT

Typical Engine Mount Complete Allison Engine

73-31919
FITTING

73-31920
FITTING

LEFT HAND
ENGINE MOUNT

REF. NO.	PART NO.	TITLE
1	73-31916	Support Channel
2	73-31915	Inside Channel Assembly
3	73-31918	Y Reinforcement Channel
4	97-31901-25	Angle
5	73-31922	Upper Diagonal Channel
6	73-31919	Upper Fitting
7	73-31924	Diagonal Channel
8	73-31923	Lower Diagonal Channel
9	73-31920	Lower Fitting
10	73-31927	Upper Gusset
11	97-31901-4, -5	Outside Web
12	97-31901-2, -3	Inside Web
13	97-31901-24	Angle
14	73-31934	Support Channel
15	97-31901-26	Angle
16	97-31901-23	Angle
17	97-31901-12	Filler Plate
18	73-31914	Lower Channel
19	73-31915	Upper Channel
20	97-31901-17	Angle
21	73-31926	Lower Gusset
22	97-58605	Bracket
23	73-31928	Lower Fitting Gusset
24	73-31929	Upper Fitting Gusset
25	73-31933	Bolt Angle
26	73-31932	Bolt Angle
27	73-31941	Block
28	73-31901-15	Angle

Front Fuselage Structure – Mustang I, P-51 and A-36A

REF. NO.	PART NO.	TITLE
1	73-31144	Frame—Sta. 232 Lower
	73-31144-1	Frame—Sta. 232 Lower
2	73-31143	Frame—Sta. 216 Lower
	73-31143-1	Frame—Sta. 216 Lower
3	73-31102-30	Firewall Assembly—Armor Plate Comp.
4	73-31317	Former Assembly—Sta. 184 to 200
	73-31317-1	Former Assembly—Sta. 184 to 200
5	73-31204	Channel—Sta. 89 to 104 LH
	73-31204-1	Channel—Sta. 89 to 104 RH
6	73-31213	Frame Assembly—Sta. 89¾
7	73-33525	Bracket—Ldg. Gr. Lock Mech. Cont. Rod Fus. Longeron
8	73-31157	Frame—Sta. 114⁷⁄₁₆
9	-73-31158-10	Frame—Sta. 133
10	73-31218	Angle Assembly—Sta. 104 to 133
11	73-31216-11	Frame—Sta. 116¼ to 122¼
12	73-31216-10	Frame—Sta. 116¼ to 122¼
13	73-31156-10	Frame Assembly—Sta. 104 Left
14	73-31185	Former Assembly—Nose-over Structure Fwd.
	73-31185-3	Former—Nose-over Structure Fwd.
15	*91-31160	Frame Assembly—Sta. 157½
	*91-31160-1	Frame Assembly—Sta. 157½
16	*91-31161	Frame Assembly—Sta. 168
	*91-31217	Frame Assembly—Sta. 168
17	73-31162	Frame Assembly—Sta. 184
	73-31162-1	Frame Assembly—Sta. 184
18	†97-31163	Frame Assembly—Sta. 200
	†97-31163-1	Frame Assembly—Sta. 200
19	†97-31307	Frame Sta. 208
	†97-31316	Frame Sta. 208
20	†97-31164	Frame Assembly—Sta. 216 Left
	†97-31164-1	Frame Assembly—Sta. 216 Right
21	†97-31315	Former—Sta. 224
	†97-31315-1	Former—Sta. 224
22	73-31165	Frame—Sta. 232
	73-31165-1	Frame—Sta. 232
23	73-31314	Former—Sta. 240
	73-31314-1	Former—Sta. 240
24	73-31286-2	Frame Assembly—Sta. 248
	73-31286-3	Frame Assembly—Sta. 248
25	73-31225	Frame Assembly—Sta. 89¾
26	73-31155	Frame Assembly—Sta. 104
27	73-31214	Frame Assembly—Sta. 116 Right
28	*91-31174-10	Frame Assembly—Sta. 130½ Right
29	73-31184	Former Assembly—Nose-over Structure Aft
	73-31184-3	Former Assembly—Nose-over Structure Aft
30	73-31152	Frame Assembly—Sta. 205⅝₁₆
	73-31152-1	Frame Assembly—Sta. 205⅝₁₆
31	†97-31079-26	Strip—Sta. 205⅝₁₆ to 232
32	†97-31141	Frame Assembly—Sta. 180
	†97-31141-1	Frame Assembly—Sta. 180
33	†97-31139	Frame Assembly—Sta. 162
	†97-31139-1	Frame Assembly—Sta. 162
34	†97-41322	Frame—Sta. 232
35	73-31262	Support—Radio Switch Box
36	73-31188	Beam Assembly—Sta. 168
37	73-31243	Channel—Sta. 180 to 205⅝₁₆
	73-31243-1	Channel—Sta. 180 to 205⅝₁₆
38	73-31319	Frame—Sta. 184
39	73-31320	Frame Assembly—Sta. 200
40	†97-31079-27	Channel Assembly—Sta. 180
	†97-31079-28	Channel Assembly—Sta. 180
41	97-31321	Frame—Sta. 216
42	†97-31147	Frame—Sta. 241

* Use 73 prefix for Mustang I.
† Use 73 prefix for Mustang I and P-51.

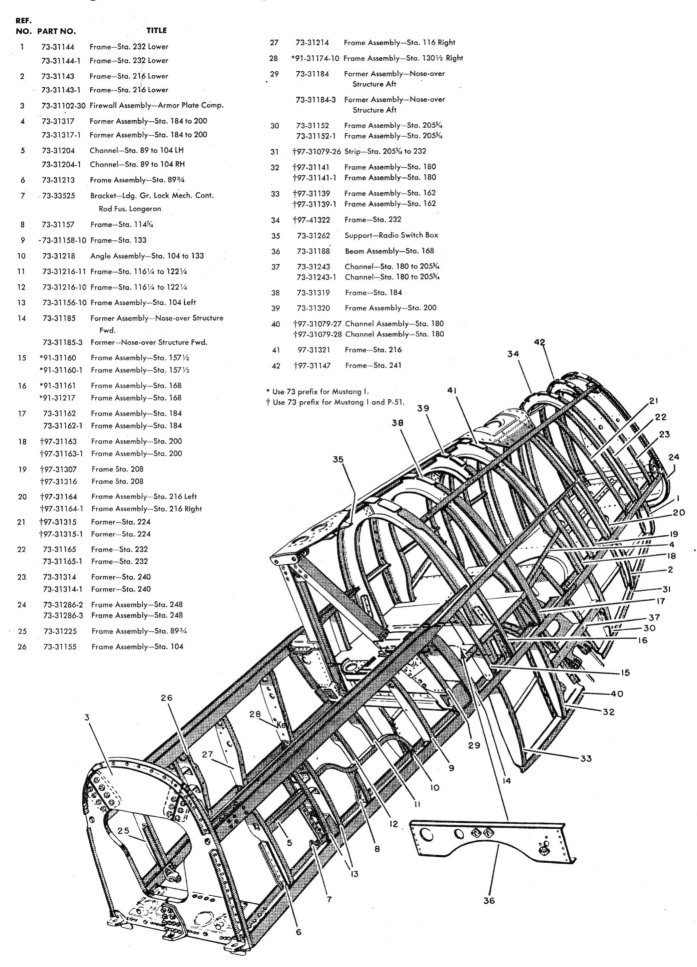

Fuselage Structure - P-51A

REF. NO.	PART NO.	TITLE
1	99-31144	Frame—Station 232 Lower
	99-31144-1	Frame—Station 232 Lower
2	99-31143	Frame—Station 216 Lower
	99-31143-1	Frame—Station 216 Lower
3	99-31102	Firewall—Armor Plate Complete
4	99-31145	Frame—Sta. 192 LH
	99-31145-1	Frame—Sta. 192 RH
5	73-31204	Channel—Sta. 89¾ to 104
6	73-31213-200	Frame—Sta. 89¾
7	99-310176	Channel—Sta. 162 to 182⅝
8	73-31157	Frame—Sta. 114⁷⁄₁₆
9	73-31158-10	Frame—Sta. 133
10	73-31218	Angle—Sta. 104 to 133
11	73-31216	Frame—Sta. 116¼ to 122¼
12	73-31216-1	Frame—Sta. 116¼ to 122¼
13	73-31156-10	Frame—Sta. 104 Left
14	73-31185	Former Assem.—Nose-over Structure Forward
	73-31185-3	Former—Nose-over Structure Forward
15	73-31160	Frame—Sta. 157½
	73-31160-1	Frame—Sta. 157½
16	91-31161	Frame—Sta. 168
	91-31217	Frame—Sta. 168
17	73-31162	Frame—Sta. 184
	73-31162-1	Frame—Sta. 184
18	97-31163	Frame—Sta. 200
	97-31163-1	Frame—Sta. 200
19	97-31307	Frame—Sta. 208
	97-31316	Frame—Sta. 208
20	97-31164	Frame—Sta. 216
	97-31164-1	Frame—Sta. 216
21	97-31315	Former—Sta. 224
	97-31315-1	Former—Sta. 224
22	99-31165	Frame—Sta. 232
	99-31165-1	Frame—Sta. 232
23	73-31314	Former—Sta. 240
	73-31314-1	Former—Sta. 240
24	73-31286-2	Frame—Sta. 248
	73-31286-2	Frame—Sta. 248
25	73-31225	Frame—Sta. 89¾
26	73-31155	Frame—Sta. 104 Right
27	73-31214	Frame—Sta. 116
28	91-31174-10	Frame—Sta. 130½
29	73-31184	Former—Nose-over Structure Aft
	73-31184-3	Former—Nose-over Structure Aft
30	99-31163	Frame—Sta. 200
	99-31163-1	Frame—Sta. 200
31	99-31079-16	Strip—Sta. 205⁵⁄₁₆ to 232

REF. NO.	PART NO.	TITLE
32	99-31141	Frame—Sta. 182⅝
	99-31208	Channel—Sta. 162 to 200 Lower LH
	99-31208-1	Channel—Sta. 162 to 200 Lower RH
	99-31141-1	Frame—Sta. 182⅝
33	99-31146	Frame—Sta. 162 LH
	99-31146-1	Frame—Sta. 162 RH
34	99-31322	Frame—Sta. 232
35	73-31262	Support—Radio Switch Box
36	99-31188	Beam—Sta. 168
37	99-31150	Frame—Sta. 196 LH
	99-31150-1	Frame—Sta. 196 RH
38	73-31319	Frame—Sta. 184
39	97-31320	Frame—Sta. 200
40	99-31148	Frame—Sta. 182⅝ LH
	99-31148-1	Frame—Sta. 182⅝ RH
41	99-31321	Frame—Sta. 216
42	99-31147	Beam—Sta. 162 Lower Front
	99-31149	Beam—Sta. 182⅝ Lower Rear
43	97-31151	Channel—Sta. 216 to 232 LH
	97-31151-1	Channel—Sta. 216 to 232 RH
44	99-31142	Frame—Sta. 208 LH
	99-31142-1	Frame—Sta. 208 RH
45	99-31317	Former—Sta. 192 to 200 LH
	99-31317-1	Former—Sta. 192 to 200 RH
46	99-31381	Channel—Hydraulic Strut Attaching

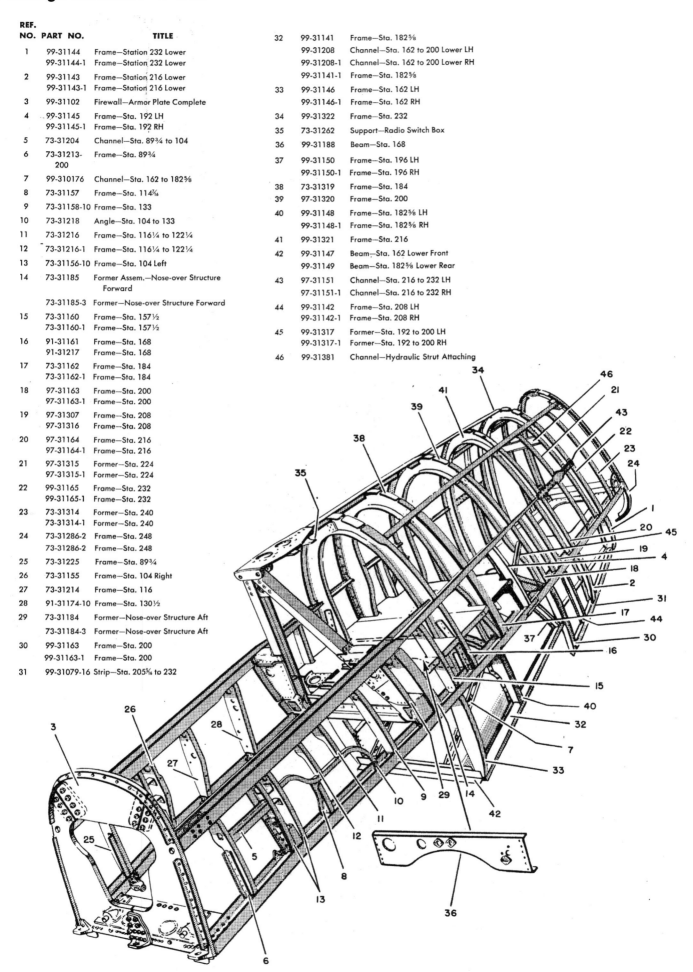

Typical Cockpit Enclosure Early Mustangs

DETAIL **A**

DETAIL **B**

NOTE:
DETAIL B APPLICABLE ONLY
TO P-5IC (60 AIRPLANES)

102-31-112A

REF. NO.	PART NO.	TITLE
1	83-31826-300	Windshield Assem.—Cockpit Encl.
	83-31828	Glass—Windshield ont Armor Plate
	83-318180	Glass—Windshield Upper
	83-31827-1	Glass—Windshield Side RH
	99-31827-2	Glass—Windshield Side LH
	99-31827	Glass Assem.—Windshield Side LH
2	99-318141	Pin—Side Glass Handle
3	99-318140	Handle—Left Side Glass Door Latch
4	99-318139	Bracket—Side Glass Door Latch
5	99-318135-3	Retainer—Side Glass Inner
6	99-31827-3	Transparent Sheet—Left Side Glass Door
7	99-318135-2	Retainer—Side Glass Inner
8	99-318137	Hinge—Side Glass Door
	7S5-6-8	Screw
	7S5-6-9	Screw
	AN936-A6	Washer
	AN365-632	Nut
9	99-318138	Fitting—Side Glass Door Latch
10	99-318105	Hook Assem.—Side Glass Open Position
	99-318102	Hook—Side Glass Open Position
	73-52448	Spring—Side Glass Open Position Hook
	7S4-8-8	Screw
	AC365-832	Nut
11	73-31848-20	Panel Assem.—Cockpit Encl. LH
12	102-31830	Panel Assem.—Cockpit Enclosure Rear LH
13	102-31830-1	Panel Assem.—Cockpit Enclosure Rear RH
14	73-318144-2	Panel Assem.—Exit Hatch Top & Right Side
	73-31835-10	Panel Assem.—Exit Hatch RH
15	73-31829	Panel Assem.—Exit Hatch Upper
16	73-31271-2	Pin—Side Panel Attaching
	73-31271-4	Pin—Side Panel Attaching
17	83-318182	Nut—Retainer Attachment Front
	AC365-832	Nut—Retainer Attachment Rear
18	73-31271	Fitting—Exit Hatch Attaching RH
	73-31271-3	Fitting—Exit Hatch Attaching LH
19	83-318179	Shim—Exit Hatch Attaching Retainer
20	7S5-8-8	Screw—Front
	5C4-832-10	Screw—Rear
	AN936-A416	Washer—Front

Cockpit and Rear Fuselage

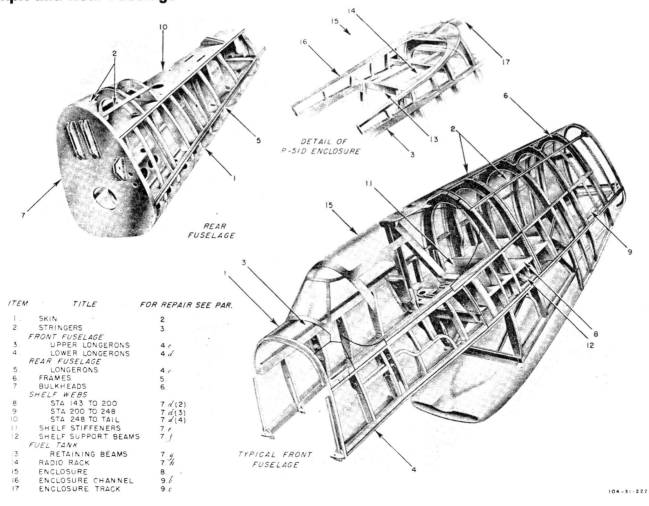

DETAIL OF
P-5ID ENCLOSURE

REAR
FUSELAGE

TYPICAL FRONT
FUSELAGE

ITEM	TITLE	FOR REPAIR SEE PAR.
1	SKIN	2
2	STRINGERS	3
	FRONT FUSELAGE	
3	UPPER LONGERONS	4 c
4	LOWER LONGERONS	4 d
	REAR FUSELAGE	
5	LONGERONS	4 e
6	FRAMES	5
7	BULKHEADS	6
	SHELF WEBS	
8	STA 143 TO 200	7 d (2)
9	STA 200 TO 248	7 d (3)
10	STA 248 TO TAIL	7 d (4)
11	SHELF STIFFENERS	7 e
12	SHELF SUPPORT BEAMS	7 f
	FUEL TANK	
13	RETAINING BEAMS	7 g
14	RADIO RACK	7 h
15	ENCLOSURE	8
16	ENCLOSURE CHANNEL	9 b
17	ENCLOSURE TRACK	9 c

104-31-222

Fuselage Shelves and Supporting Beams - Mustang I, P-51 and A-36A

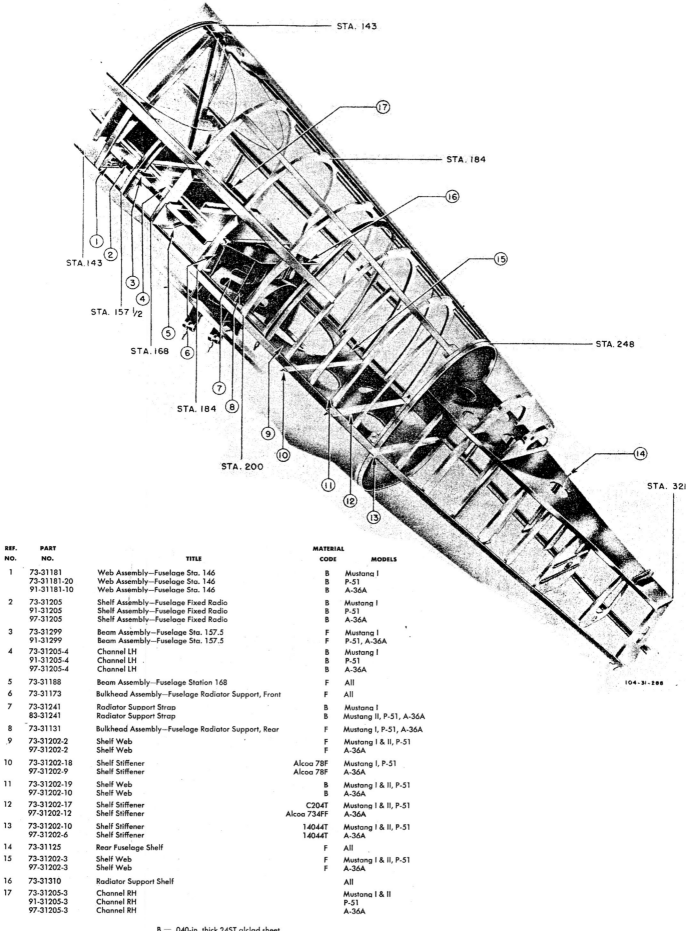

REF. NO.	PART NO.	TITLE	MATERIAL CODE	MODELS
1	73-31181	Web Assembly—Fuselage Sta. 146	B	Mustang I
	73-31181-20	Web Assembly—Fuselage Sta. 146	B	P-51
	91-31181-10	Web Assembly—Fuselage Sta. 146	B	A-36A
2	73-31205	Shelf Assembly—Fuselage Fixed Radio	B	Mustang I
	91-31205	Shelf Assembly—Fuselage Fixed Radio	B	P-51
	97-31205	Shelf Assembly—Fuselage Fixed Radio	B	A-36A
3	73-31299	Beam Assembly—Fuselage Sta. 157.5	F	Mustang I
	91-31299	Beam Assembly—Fuselage Sta. 157.5	F	P-51, A-36A
4	73-31205-4	Channel LH	B	Mustang I
	91-31205-4	Channel LH	B	P-51
	97-31205-4	Channel LH	B	A-36A
5	73-31188	Beam Assembly—Fuselage Station 168	F	All
6	73-31173	Bulkhead Assembly—Fuselage Radiator Support, Front	F	All
7	73-31241	Radiator Support Strap	B	Mustang I
	83-31241	Radiator Support Strap	B	Mustang II, P-51, A-36A
8	73-31131	Bulkhead Assembly—Fuselage Radiator Support, Rear	F	Mustang I, P-51, A-36A
9	73-31202-2	Shelf Web	F	Mustang I & II, P-51
	97-31202-2	Shelf Web	F	A-36A
10	73-31202-18	Shelf Stiffener	Alcoa 78F	Mustang I, P-51
	97-31202-9	Shelf Stiffener	Alcoa 78F	A-36A
11	73-31202-19	Shelf Web	B	Mustang I & II, P-51
	97-31202-10	Shelf Web	B	A-36A
12	73-31202-17	Shelf Stiffener	C204T	Mustang I & II, P-51
	97-31202-12	Shelf Stiffener	Alcoa 734FF	A-36A
13	73-31202-10	Shelf Stiffener	14044T	Mustang I & II, P-51
	97-31202-6	Shelf Stiffener	14044T	A-36A
14	73-31125	Rear Fuselage Shelf	F	All
15	73-31202-3	Shelf Web	F	Mustang I & II, P-51
	97-31202-3	Shelf Web	F	A-36A
16	73-31310	Radiator Support Shelf		All
17	73-31205-3	Channel RH		Mustang I & II
	91-31205-3	Channel RH		P-51
	97-31205-3	Channel RH		A-36A

B = .040-in. thick 24ST alclad sheet
F = .081-in. thick 24ST alclad sheet

Typical Front Fuselage Rivited Assemblies

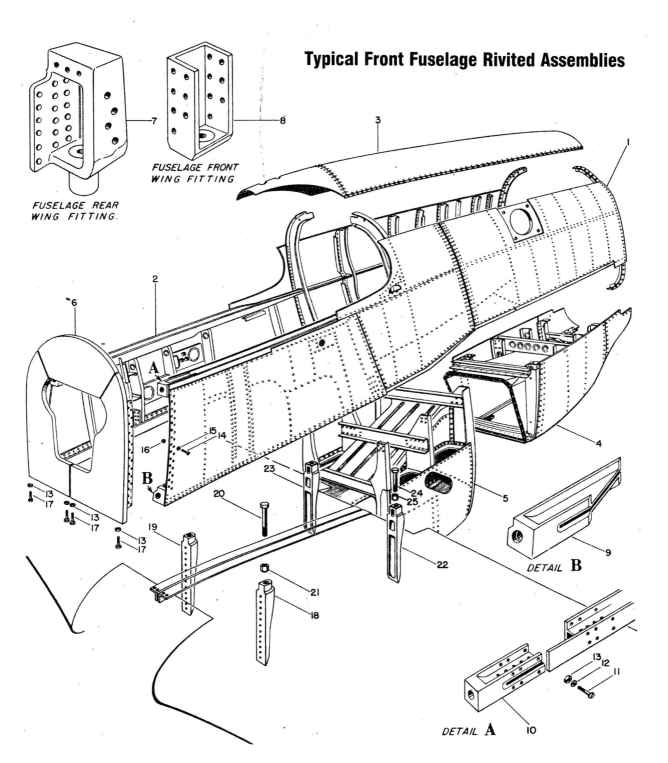

FUSELAGE REAR
WING FITTING.

FUSELAGE FRONT
WING FITTING

DETAIL B

DETAIL A

REF. NO.	PART NO.	TITLE
	* 102-31111-100	Fuselage Assem.—Forward Complete
1	* 102-31107-100	Side Assem.—Fuselage LH
2	* 102-31107-101	Side Assem.—Fuselage RH
3	* 99-31122	Deck Assem.—Fuselage Forward Upper
4	* 102-31079	Covered Assem.—Fuselage Sta. 202 to 248
5	* 102-31016	Covered Assem.—Fuselage Sta. 159 to 182.75 Lower
6	* 102-31102	Firewall Assem.—Armor Plate Complete
7	* 102-31177	Fitting—Nose-over Structure Lower LH
	102-31177-1	Fitting—Nose-over Structure Lower RH
8	* 102-31178	Fitting—Fuselage Sta. 104 Front Spar Attaching LH
	102-31178-1	Fitting—Fuselage Sta. 104 Front Spar Attaching RH
9	* 102-31402	Fitting—Fuselage Lower Longeron to Firewall LH
	102-31402-1	Fitting—Fuselage Lower Longeron to Firewall RH
10	73-31119	Fitting—Fuselage Upper Longeron to Firewall LH
	73-31119-1	Fitting—Fuselage Upper Longeron to Firewall RH
11	7S2-524-15	Screw

REF. NO.	PART NO.	TITLE
12	AN960-516L	Washer
13	AC365-524	Nut
14	7S6-1032-9	Screw
15	AN960-10	Washer
16	AC365-1032	Nut
17	AN5-11A	Bolt
	AN960-516	Washer
18	73-14007	Fitting—Front Spar to Fuselage LH
19	73-14007-1	Fitting—Front Spar to Fuselage RH
20	AN12-41A	Bolt
	2W1-50-34-125	Washer
21	AC365-1216	Nut
22	73-14006	Fitting—Rear Spar to Fuselage LH
23	73-14006-1	Fitting—Rear Spar to Fuselage RH
24	AN10-34A	Bolt
	91-14716	Washer—Wing Rear Attaching Bolt
25	AC365-1018	Nut

* Substitute 73 prefix for Mustang, 91 prefix for P-51, 97 prefix for A-36, 99 prefix for P-51A.

Fuselage Stringer Locations - Early Airplanes

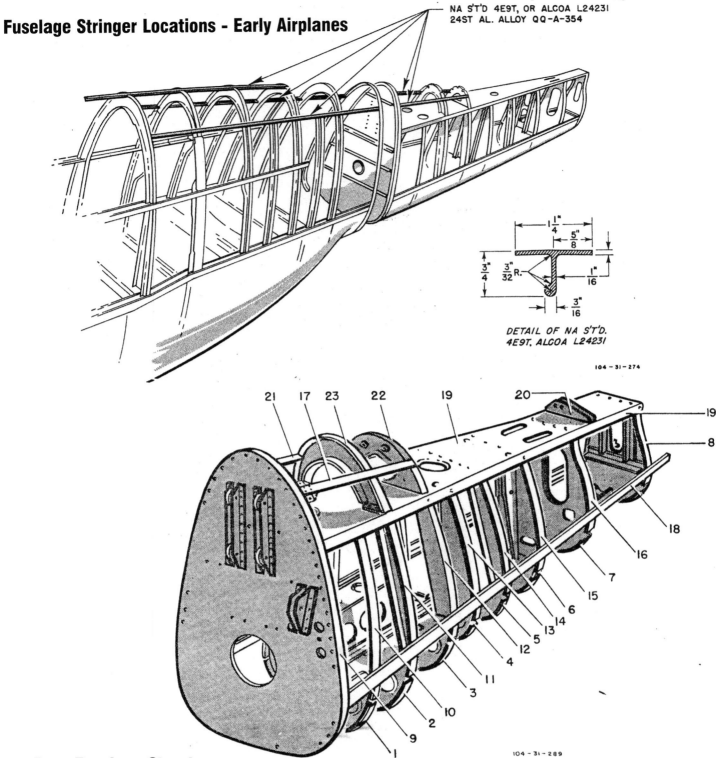

NA S'T'D 4E9T, OR ALCOA L24231
24ST AL. ALLOY QQ-A-354

DETAIL OF NA S'T'D.
4E9T, ALCOA L24231

104-31-274

104-31-289

Rear Fuselage Structure

REF. NO.	PART NO.	TITLE
1	73-31110-14	Frame—Fus. Sta. 256 Rear Section Lower LH (A)
	73-31110-15	Frame—Fus. Sta. 256 Rear Section Lower RH (A)
2	73-31110-16	Frame—Fus. Sta. 264 Rear Section Lower LH (A)
	73-31110-17	Frame—Fus. Sta. 264 Rear Section Lower RH (A)
3	73-31110-18	Frame—Fus. Sta. 272.5 Rear Section Lower LH (A)
	73-31110-19	Frame—Fus. Sta. 272.5 Rear Section Lower RH (A)
4	73-31187	Frame—Fus. Sta. 281 Rear Section Lower (B)
5	73-31197	Frame—Fus. Sta. 291 Rear Section Lower (B)
6	73-31199	Frame—Fus. Sta. 300 Rear Section Lower (C)
7	73-31200	Frame—Fus. Sta. 311.5 Rear Section Lower (B)
8	73-31172	Frame—Fus. Sta. 321 Rear Section Lower (D)
9	*97-31186	Frame—Fus. Sta. 248 Rear (E)
10	73-31334	Angle—Fus. Sta. 256 Rear Section Center LH (F)
	73-31334-1	Angle—Fus. Sta. 256 Rear Section Center RH (F)
11	73-31167	Frame—Fus. Sta. 264 Rear Section Center LH (A)
	73-31167-1	Frame—Fus. Sta. 264 Rear Section Center RH (A)
12	*97-31166	Frame—Fus. Sta. 273.5 Rear Section Center LH (D)

REF. NO.	PART NO.	TITLE
	*97-31166-1	Frame—Fus. Sta. 273.5 Rear Section Center RH (D)
13	*97-31168	Frame—Fus. Sta. 281 Rear Section Center LH (B), (G)
	*97-31168-1	Frame—Fus. Sta. 281 Rear Section Center RH (B), (G)
14	73-31169	Frame—Fus. Sta. 291 Rear Section Center LH (B)
	73-31169-1	Frame—Fus. Sta. 291 Rear Section Center RH (B)
15	*97-31170	Frame—Fus. Sta. 300 Rear Section Center (D)
16	73-31171	Frame—Fus. Sta. 311.5 Rear Section Center (A)
17	*97-31108-3	Stringer—Sta. 248 to 273.5 LH (I)
	*97-31108-4	Stringer—Sta. 248 to 273.5 RH (I)
18	73-31110-6	Longeron—Rear Section Lower LH
	73-31110-7	Longeron—Rear Section Lower RH
19	73-31125	Bulkhead—Fus. Sta. 248 to 321 Rear Section Upper (H)
20	73-31228	Bracket—Fus. Sta. 311½ Rudder Trim Tab Pulley Upper (D)
21	*97-31108-4	Stringer—Fus. Sta. 248 to 273.5 Rear Section Upper RH
22	73-31370	Frame—Fus. Sta. 273½ Rear Section Upper (B)
23	73-31175	Frame—Fus. Sta. 264 Rear Section Upper (A)

DESCRIPTION	AAF MATERIAL SPEC.	REMARKS
A = 24SO Alclad H.T.	QQ-A-362	.032" Thick
B = 24SO Alclad H.T.	QQ-A-362	.040" Thick
C = 24SO Alclad H.T.	QQ-A-362	.064" Thick
D = 24SO Alclad H.T.	QQ-A-362	.051" Thick
E = 24ST Alclad	QQ-A-362	.032" Thick
F = 24SO Al Alloy H.T.	QQ-A-354	Alcoa K5290 Extr.
G = 24SO Alclad H.T.	QQ-A-362	.102" Thick
H = 24SO Alclad H.T.	QQ-A-362	.081" Thick
I = 24ST Al Alloy	QQ-A-354	Alcoa L24231 Extr. (NAA Standard C283T)

* Substitute 73 prefix for models prior to A-36A.

Typical Radiator Air Scoop - A-36A and Early Airplanes

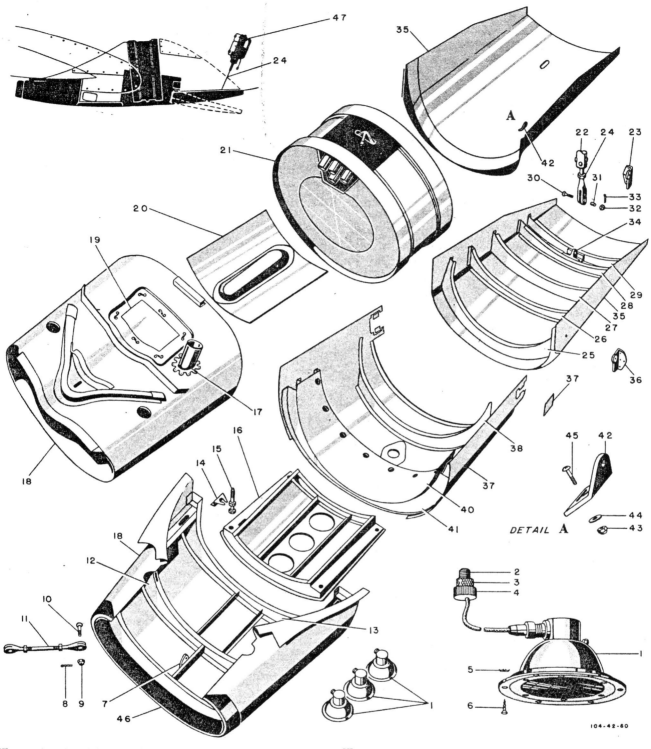

DETAIL A

104-42-60

REF. NO.	PART NO.	TITLE
1	Spec. 32374	Lamp Type E-2 (Red), (G.F.E.)
	Spec. 32374	Lamp Type E-2 (Green), (G.F.E.)
	Spec. 32374	Lamp Type E-2 (Amber), (G.F.E.)
2	38A1531	Plug
3	2W1N-16-21-125	Washer—Plain
4	AN3054-6	Plug
5	AC366F-632	Nut Plate (Tinnerman)
6	#21803-6-6	Screw (Parker-Kalon)
7	91-31076	Fitting—Fus. Sta. 142¼ Front Rad. Air Scoop to Wing Attach't.
8	AN380-2-2	Pin
9	AN310-4	Nut
10	AN4-7	Bolt
11	*99-31080	Clevis—Fus. Sta. 145½ Front Rad. Air Scoop to Wing Attaching
12	*97-310204	Frame—Fus. Sta. 148½ Rad. Air Duct
13	*97-310205	Frame—Fus. Sta. 162 Rad. Air Duct
14	*97-310169	Keeper—Fus. Sta. 162 to 180 Lower Access
15	*97-310168	Bolt—Fus. Sta. 162 to 180 Lower Access Cover Attaching
16	*97-31021	Cover—Fus. Sta. 162 to 180 Lower Access
17	73-53333	Tube—Ventilating System Air Scoop Intake
18	*97-310119	Fairing—Fus. Rad. Air Scoop Front Removable
19	*97-310141	Cover—Fus. Rad. Air Scoop Fairing Access
20	*97-31021-2	Skin—Fus. Sta. 162 to 180 Lower Access Cover
21	83-46050	Radiator Assembly
22	*97-46059	Rod—Rear Air Scoop Operating
23	73-31020	Fitting—Fus. Rad. Rear Air Scoop Hinge LH
	73-31020-1	Fitting—Fus. Rad. Rear Air Scoop Hinge RH
24	AN486-2	Clevis

REF. NO.	PART NO.	TITLE
25	*97-31025-4	Frame—Scoop Fus. Rad. Air Rear Scoop
26	*97-31025-5	Frame—Scoop Fus. Rad. Air Rear Scoop
27	*97-31025-6	Frame—Scoop Fus. Rad. Air Rear Scoop
28	*97-31025-7	Frame—Scoop Fus. Rad. Air Rear Scoop
29	*97-31025-8	Frame—Scoop Fus. Rad. Air Rear Scoop
30	AN4-13	Bolt
31	4B14-4-29	Bushing—Spacer
32	AN310-4	Nut
33	AN380-2-2	Pin
34	*97-31010	Fitting—Fus. Rad. Air Scoop Strut Attaching
35	*97-31025	Scoop—Fus. Rad. Air Rear

REF. NO.	PART NO.	TITLE
36	73-31019	Fitting—Fus. Rad. Rear Scoop Fus. Hinge LH
	73-31019-1	Fitting—Fus. Rad. Rear Scoop Fus. Hinge RH
37	*97-310106-11	Cover—Fus. Rad. Access RH
	*97-310106-12	Cover—Fus. Rad. Access LH
38	73-31340	Frame—Fus. Sta. 200³⁄₃₂ Guide Support
39	*97-310106	Cover—Fus. Rad. Access
40	*97-310166	Frame—Fus. Rad. Access Cover Interm.
41	*97-310165	Frame—Fus. Rad. Access Cover Front
42	*97-46017	Clip—Rad. Air Scoop Pos. Ind. Cable Attaching
43	AC366F832	Nut
44	AN960-8	Washer
45	752-8-7	Screw
46	*97-310223	Edge—Fus. Rad. Air Duct Front Removable Fairing Lower (Including Bolts and Washers)
47	*97-58052	Panel Assembly—Hyd. Preselective Scoop Control Mech.

* Substitute 73 prefix for Mustang; 91 prefix for P-51.

Radiator Air Scoop - P-51A

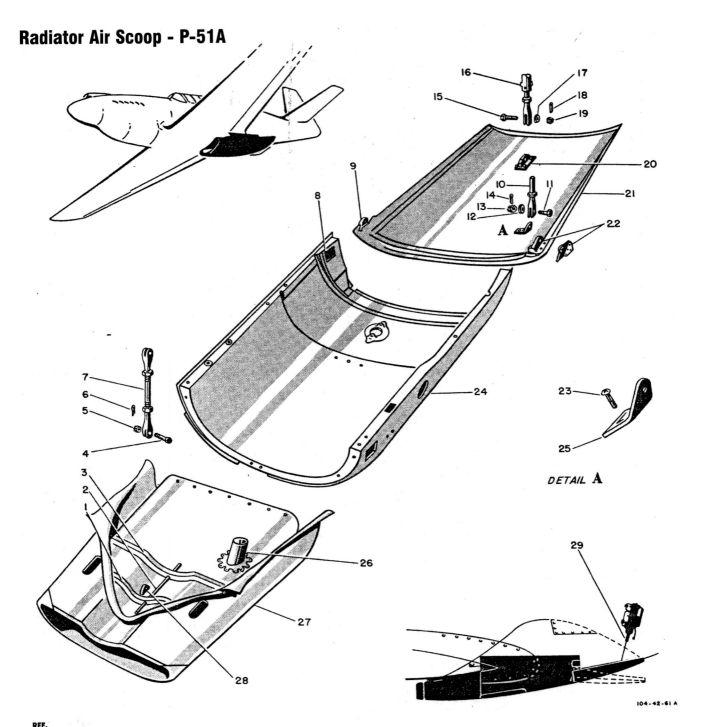

DETAIL A

104-42-61 A

REF. NO.	PART NO.	TITLE
1	97-31048	Stiffener—Fuselage Sta. 142⅞ Radiator Air Duct Top Skin
2	99-54025	Tube—Battery Vent Intake
3	99-31049	Stiffener—Fus. Sta. 148½ Radiator Air Duct Top Skin
4	AN4-7	Bolt
5	AN310-4	Nut
6	AN380-2-2	Pin
7	99-31080	Clevis—Fuselage Sta. 145¼ Front Radiator Air Scoop to Wing Attaching
8	99-31340	Frame—Fuselage Sta. 197¹⁵⁄₁₆ Lower Canted
9	99-31020-1	Fitting—Fuselage Radiator Rear Air Scoop Hinge RH
10	99-58760	Rod—Hydraulic Preselective Scoop Control Arm Actuating
11	AN3-6	Bolt
12	AN960-10	Washer
13	AN310-3	Nut
14	AN380-2-2	Pin
15	AN24-13	Bolt
16	99-58487	Rod—Hydraulic Radiator Air Scoop Operating Strut
17	AN960-416L	Washer
18	AN380-2-2	Pin
19	AN320-4	Nut
20	99-31010	Fitting—Fuselage Radiator Air Scoop Strut Attaching
	AC365-1032	Nut
	AN960-10	Washer
	7S6-1032-22	Screw—100° Recessed Flat Head
	7S6-1032-20	Screw—100° Recessed Flat Head
21	99-31025	Scoop—Fus. Radiator Air Rear
22	99-31020	Fitting—Fus. Radiator Rear Air Scoop Hinge LH
23	21803-8-8	Screw
24	99-31016	Cover—Fus. Sta. 162 to 200¾ Radiator Access
25	99-58752	Angle—Hydraulic Preselective Control Scoop Attaching
26	73-53333	Tube—Ventilator System Air Scoop Intake
27	99-310119	Fairing—Fus. Radiator Air Scoop Front Removable
28	99-31084	Fitting—Fus. Sta. 145½ Front Radiator Air Scoop to Wing Attaching
29	99-58040	Strut—Hydraulic Radiator Air Scoop Operating

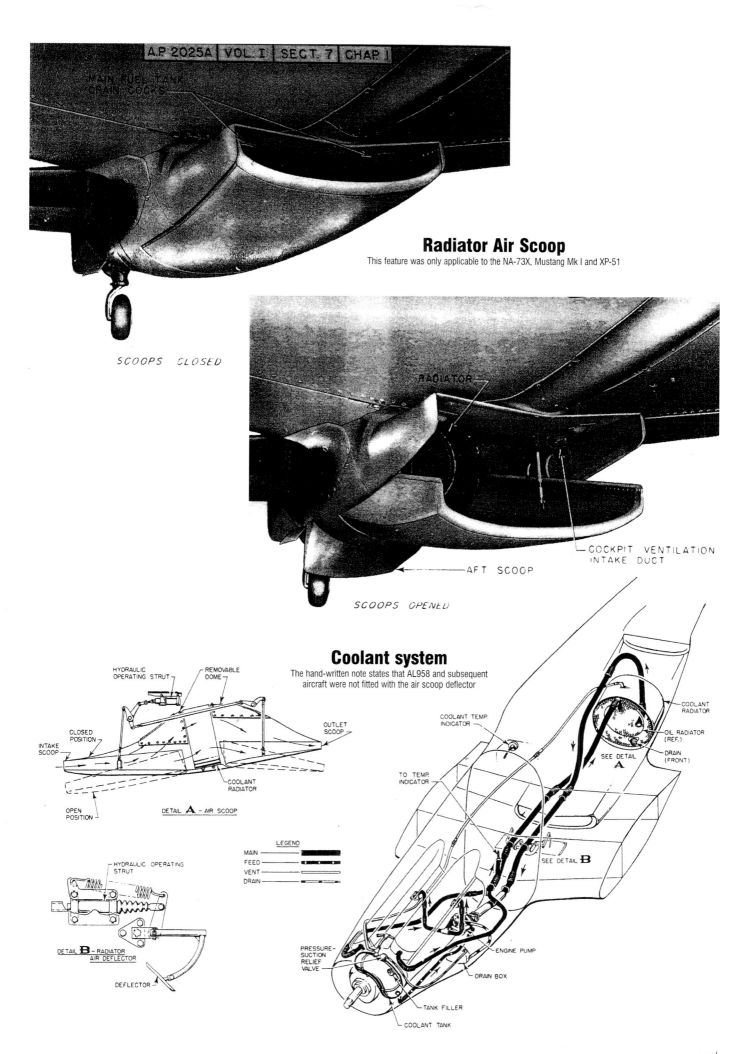

MAIN FUEL TANK
DRAIN COCKS

Radiator Air Scoop
This feature was only applicable to the NA-73X, Mustang Mk I and XP-51

SCOOPS CLOSED

RADIATOR

COCKPIT VENTILATION
INTAKE DUCT

AFT SCOOP

SCOOPS OPENED

Coolant system
The hand-written note states that AL958 and subsequent
aircraft were not fitted with the air scoop deflector

HYDRAULIC
OPERATING STRUT

REMOVABLE
DOME

CLOSED
POSITION

OUTLET
SCOOP

INTAKE
SCOOP

COOLANT
RADIATOR

OPEN
POSITION

DETAIL **A** - AIR SCOOP

COOLANT TEMP.
INDICATOR

TO TEMP.
INDICATOR

SEE DETAIL **A**

COOLANT
RADIATOR

OIL RADIATOR
(REF.)

DRAIN
(FRONT)

SEE DETAIL **B**

LEGEND
MAIN
FEED
VENT
DRAIN

HYDRAULIC OPERATING
STRUT

DETAIL **B** - RADIATOR
AIR DEFLECTOR

DEFLECTOR

PRESSURE-
SUCTION
RELIEF
VALVE

ENGINE PUMP

DRAIN BOX

TANK FILLER

COOLANT TANK

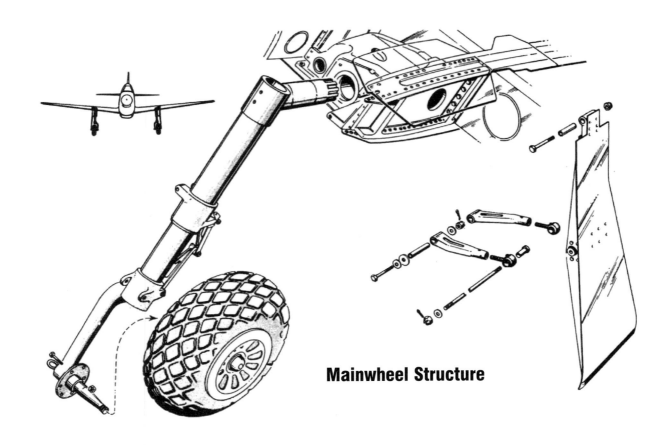

Mainwheel Structure

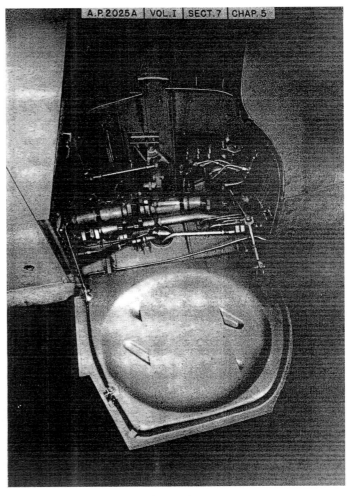

Port and starboard wheel wheels looking outboard

REFER TO N.A. DWGS. 73-3400
AND 73-34101

The Tail Wheel Assembly

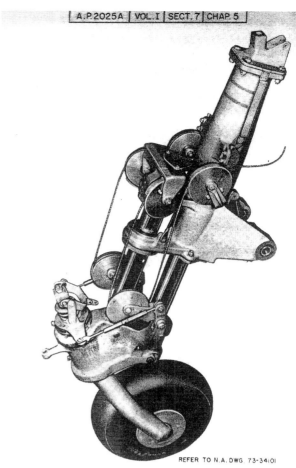

REFER TO N.A. DWG. 73-34101

The Tail Wheel Unit

Typical Cockpit

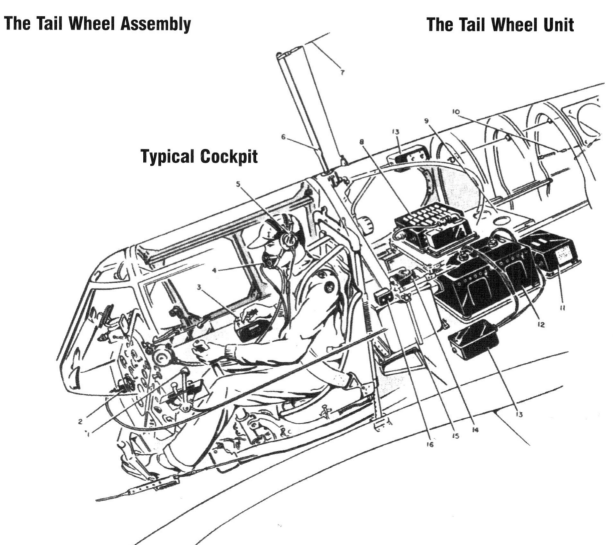

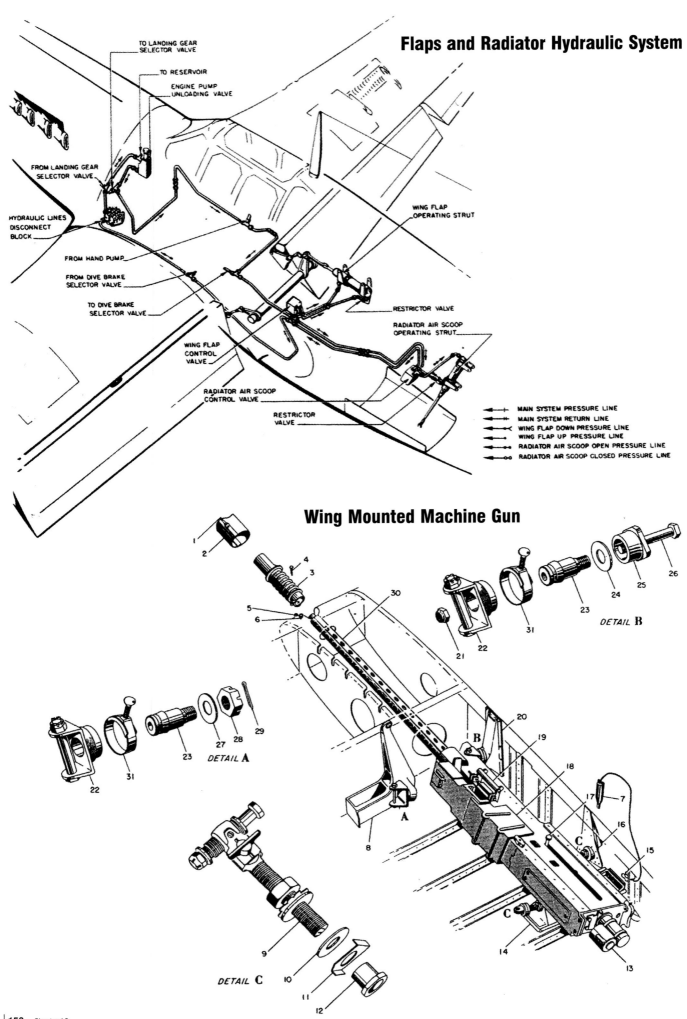

Flaps and Radiator Hydraulic System

TO LANDING GEAR SELECTOR VALVE

TO RESERVOIR

ENGINE PUMP UNLOADING VALVE

FROM LANDING GEAR SELECTOR VALVE

HYDRAULIC LINES DISCONNECT BLOCK

FROM HAND PUMP

FROM DIVE BRAKE SELECTOR VALVE

TO DIVE BRAKE SELECTOR VALVE

WING FLAP CONTROL VALVE

RADIATOR AIR SCOOP CONTROL VALVE

RESTRICTOR VALVE

WING FLAP OPERATING STRUT

RESTRICTOR VALVE

RADIATOR AIR SCOOP OPERATING STRUT

MAIN SYSTEM PRESSURE LINE
MAIN SYSTEM RETURN LINE
WING FLAP DOWN PRESSURE LINE
WING FLAP UP PRESSURE LINE
RADIATOR AIR SCOOP OPEN PRESSURE LINE
RADIATOR AIR SCOOP CLOSED PRESSURE LINE

Wing Mounted Machine Gun

DETAIL B

DETAIL A

DETAIL C

Cockpit Starboard Sidewall

A.P. 2025A | VOL. I | SECT. II | CHAP. 4

Gun Installation

A.P. 2025A | VOL. I | SECT. II | CHAP. I

AMMUNITION FEED CHUTES

GUN HEATER

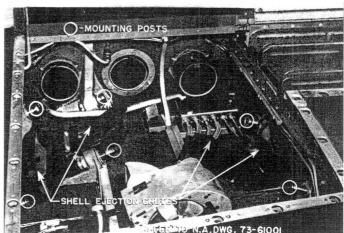

MOUNTING POSTS

SHELL EJECTION CHUTES

REFER TO N.A.DWG. 73-61001

Oxygen Installation and Valves

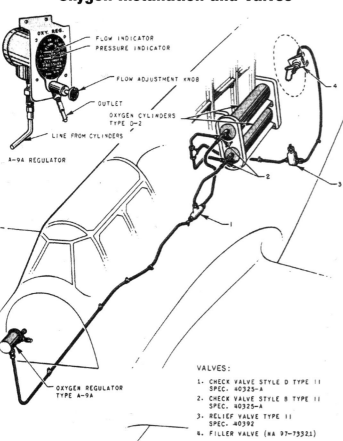

OXY. REG.

FLOW INDICATOR
PRESSURE INDICATOR

FLOW ADJUSTMENT KNOB

OUTLET
OXYGEN CYLINDERS
TYPE D-2

LINE FROM CYLINDERS

A-9A REGULATOR

4

2

3

1

OXYGEN REGULATOR
TYPE A-9A

VALVES:

1. CHECK VALVE STYLE D TYPE II
   SPEC. 40325-A
2. CHECK VALVE STYLE B TYPE II
   SPEC. 40325-A
3. RELIEF VALVE TYPE II
   SPEC. 40392
4. FILLER VALVE (NA 97-73321)

Dive Brake Hydraulic System

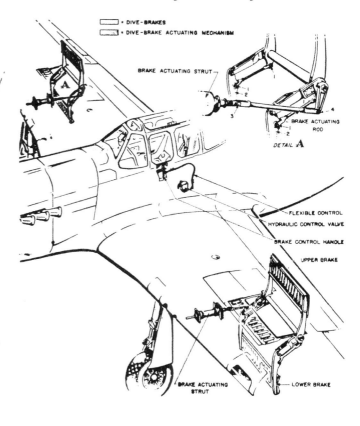

☐ = DIVE-BRAKES
☐ = DIVE-BRAKE ACTUATING MECHANISM

BRAKE ACTUATING STRUT

BRAKE ACTUATING
ROD

DETAIL A

FLEXIBLE CONTROL

HYDRAULIC CONTROL VALVE

BRAKE CONTROL HANDLE

UPPER BRAKE

BRAKE ACTUATING
STRUT

LOWER BRAKE

Cockpit Instrument Panel

1. Cockpit flourescent light
2. Winshield defroster
3. Gun sight
4. Ring and Bead gun sight (shown stowed)
5. Windshield de-icer spray controller
6. Cockpit flourescent light
7. LH gun charging handle
8. Magnetic compass
9. Clock
10. Suction gauge
11. Manifold pressure gauge
12. RH gun charging handle
13. Throttle
14. Accelerometer
15. Remote contactor
16. Altimeter
17. Turn indicator
18. Artificial horizon
19. Tachometer
20. Oxygen flow indicator

21. Canopy emergency release handle
22. Propeller constant speed control
23. Landing gear - emergency lower control
24. Landing gear – electrical position indicator
25. Air speed indicator
26. Turn and bank indicator
27. Rate of climb indicator
28. Coolant temperature indicator
29. Oil temperature/fuel and oil gauge
30. Oxygen flow regulator
31. Carburetor air temp control
32. Contractor heater switch
33. Parking brake handle
34. Automatic flare discharge unit
35. Gun camera safety switch
36. Gun heater switch
37. Bomb nose arming switch
38. Bomb tail arming switch
39. Bomb safety switch
40. Propeller selector switch

41. Propellor circuit breaker button
42. Oil dilution switch
43. Compass light an rheostat control #1
44. Compass light an rheostat control #2
45. Engine primer control
46. Hydraulic pressure gauge
47. Instrument static selector valve
48. Bomb control handle
49. Ignition switch
50. Starter switch
51. Fuel booster pump switch
52. Gun sight and rheostat control
53. LH flourescent ligh control
54. Landing gear control handle
55. Leg length adjustment pins
56. Main fuel system selector valve
57. Auxilliary fuel system selector valve
58. Cockpit cold-air ventilation valve
59. Surface control lock
60. Hydraulic hand-pump

Cockpit Port Side Key

47. Windscreen defrosting control
48. Port fuselage gun charging handle
49. Clock
50. Suction indicator
51. Optical gun sight
52. Gun selector control
53. Optical gun sight lamp rheostat
54. Airspeed indicator
55. Artificial horizon
56. Mixture control
57. Undercarriage emergency down
58. Undercarriage visual position indicator
59. Altimeter
60. Turn indicator
61. Throttle control
62. Manual propeller pitch control
63. Hydraulic system pitch control*

64. Fuselage gun heater control
65. Parking brake
66. Engine control quadrant friction disc
67. Wing flap and radiator air scoop mechanical
    indicators
68. Undercarriage selector handle
69. Elevator trimming tabs control
70. Tail wheel lock control
71. Air scoop deflector control*
72. Port fuel tank gauge
73. Radiator air scoop control
74. Wing flap control
75. Cold air control
76. Undercarriage mechanical indicators
77. Port aileron trimming tabs control
78. Port cockpit light
79. TR.9D radio control

80. Rudder trimming tabs control
81. Propeller pitch control switch
82. Propeller safety switch
83. Engine starter control switch
84. Gun camera safety switch
85. Oil dilution switch
86. Undercarriage warning horn cut-out
87. Ignition switch
88. Instrument panel lights rheostat
89. Cockpit lamps rheostat
90. Flight instrument lights rheostat
91. Port sliding window control
92. Fuel selector valve control
93. Port rudder and brake pedal

*These two controls are not fitted to AL958 and
subsequent aircraft

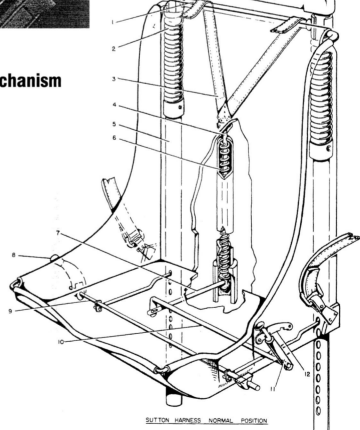

The photo at top left contains: **A.P.2025A | PILOT'S NOTES | VOL.I | SECT. I**

Cockpit Starboard Side Key

1. Engine unit
2. Glycol temperature indicator
3. Starboard fuselage gun charging handle
4. Rate of climb indicator
5. Engine tachometer
6. Engine priming pump
7. Manifold pressure indicator
8. Vacuum system selector switch
9. Cockpit hood emergency release control
10. Radio control
11. Upper and lower identification lamps control
12. Undercarriage doors position indicator lights
13. Remote contactor
14. Spare lamps container
15. Forward switch panel
16. Control column
17. Starboard brake and rudder pedal
18. Starboard switch panel
19. Map and data case
20. Aperiodic compass
21. Cold air control valve
22. Surface controls locking gear
23. Oxygen system regulator
24. Mounting brackets for the radio control unit
25. Starboard cockpit lamp
26. Mounting socket for oxygen pipe
27. Starboard sliding window control
28. Stowage for aircraft disabling device
29. Starboard fuel tank gauge
30. Radio R3003 control unit
24v supply plug box
31. Radio jack plug
32. Radio R3003 remote control switch
33. Sutton harness stowage hook
34. Radio R3303 remote control switch
35. Warm air control
36. Hydraulic system hand pump
37. Automatic recognition device control
38. Starboard formation keeping (flood) lamp
39. Generator ammeter
40. Generator main line switch
41. Port landing lamp switch
42. Starboard landing lamp switch
43. Navigation lamp switch
44. Formation-keeping (flood) lamp
45. Pressure head heater switch
46. Aeroplane check-off list holder

Pilot's seat and its operating mechanism

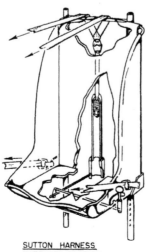

SUTTON HARNESS
EXTENDED POSITION

SUTTON HARNESS NORMAL POSITION

Allison Engined Mustang Specifications

A part from the obvious alterations in armament from one version to the next within the production run of Allison-engined Mustangs, and the various changes that turned the type into a dive-bomber and ground attack aircraft as the A-36A Invader, there were few if any major alterations to the basic layout of the Mustang in its Allison-powered versions. Without doubt, one of the yardsticks by which a successful aircraft design can be judged, is the amount that its airframe is altered by necessity during production – and therefore in the case of the Allison-engined Mustang, there were few significant alterations that actually 'needed' to be made to the size and general layout of the Allison-Mustang throughout its production run.

Nevertheless, there still have been a number of anomalies within published sources over the years as to what the size of the Allison-engined Mustang really was. This has partly arisen due to the understandable tendency in many publications to round off the wingspan and lose the 5/16-inch over 37 feet. However, as related elsewhere in this book, that 5/16-inch (closely equivalent to 0.3-inch) nevertheless existed in the official Manuals for the P-51 - with which the aircraft was maintained and looked after in the field. It is therefore included without hesitation in the following specification summaries.

Specifications - NA-73X

Dimensions	Span 37 ft 0.3 in (11.29 m); length 32 ft 2.65 in (9.82 m); height 12 ft 2 in (3.71 m)
Power plant	One Allison V-1710-F3R inline piston engine, producing 1,150 hp
Weights	Loaded 8,633 lb (3,916 kg)
Performance	Maximum speed 382 mph (615 km/h) at 13,700 ft (4,176 m); range c. 750 miles (1,207 km); service ceiling 32,000 ft (9,754 m)

Specifications - P-51A Mustang

Dimensions	Span 37 ft 0.3 in (11.29 m); length 32 ft 2.88 in (9.83 m); height 13 ft 8 in (4.17 m)
Power plant	One Allison V-1710-81 inline piston engine, producing 1,200 hp
Armament	Four 0.5-inch machine guns, plus underwing stores including drop tanks or unguided rockets, or two 500 lb (227 kg) bombs
Weights	Empty 6,850 lb (3,107 kg); loaded 10,600 lb (4,808 kg)
Performance	Maximum speed 390 mph (627 km/h) at 12,000 ft (3,658 m); range c. 1,250 miles (2,012 km) with drop tanks; service ceiling 31,000 ft (9,449 m)

Specifications - A-36A Invader

Dimensions	Span 37 ft 0.3 in (11.29 m); length 32 ft 2.88 in (9.83 m); height 13 ft 8 in (4.17 m)
Power plant	One Allison V-1710-87 inline piston engine, producing 1,325 hp
Armament	Six 0.5-inch machine guns, plus underwing stores including drop tanks, or two 500 lb (227 kg) bombs
Weights	Empty 7,240 lb (3,284 kg); loaded 10,000 lb (4,536 kg)
Performance	Maximum speed 368 mph (592 km/h) at 14,000 ft (4,267 m); range c. 1,250 miles (2,012 km) with drop tanks; service ceiling c. 31,000 ft (9,449 m)

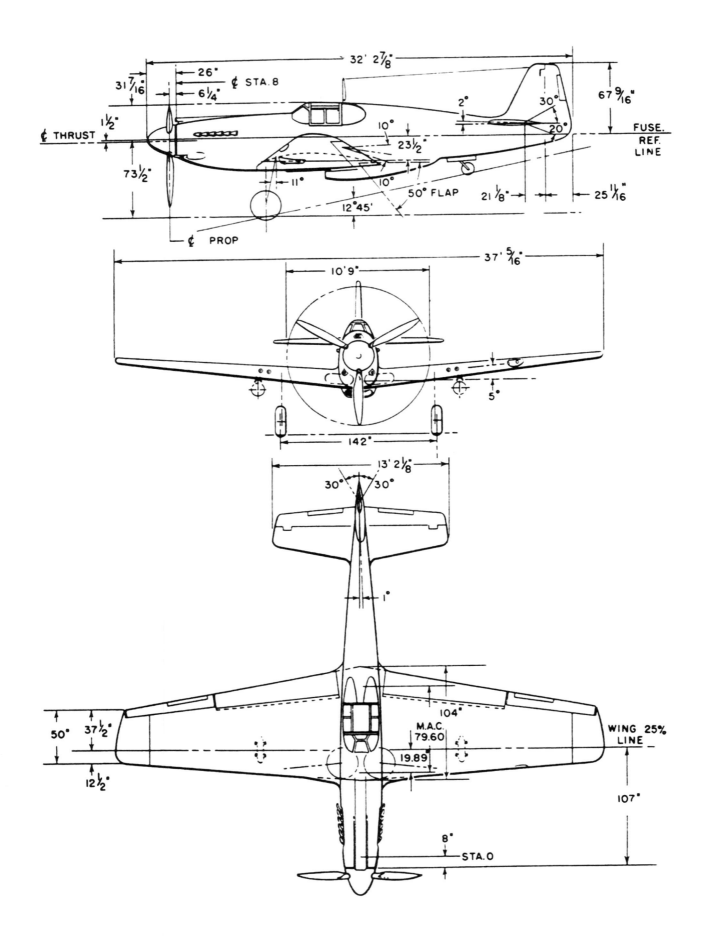

Figure 2—Airplane Three-view Dimensions

Power for the Allison Mustang

The Allison V-1710

All the early marks of Mustang were powered by the inline, liquid-cooled Allison V-1710 engine. Basically a V12 inline power plant, the V-1710 was the engine used in several major US Army Air Corps/Army Air Force fighters in its straightforward production, basic supercharged form during the early and mid-World War Two period. Amongst these were most of the members of the long-running and extensive Curtiss P-40 series - as well as the Bell P-39 Airacobra – although the engine installation in the P-39 was unconventional, being in the mid-fuselage position behind the cockpit and driving the aircraft's propeller via an extension shaft. In its turbo-supercharged form (i.e., with supercharging using power provided by the redirection of the engine's exhaust), the type powered the Lockheed P-38 Lightning twin-engined fighter. There had been some intention by Bell for the P-39 also to have turbo-supercharging, but in the event this was not installed in production Airacobras. The US Army had specified that the V-1710 was to be developed as a single-stage supercharged engine and, if a higher altitude capability was ever required, a newly developed turbo-supercharger could be used as was featured in the Curtiss X/YP-37 development series (forerunners of the P-40 line), P-38 Lightning, and prototype XP-39.

Never given a name and so always known as the V-1710 or simply very often as 'the Allison engine', this power plant was originally developed during the early 1930's, although work by James Allison's Indianapolis, Indiana-based company on engines for aviation applications had started in the mid-1920's. An important reason for the creation of the V-1710 (it eventually had a displacement of 1,710 cu in, hence its name) was – believe it or not - as a potential power plant for U.S. Navy airships. Inline engine development in the United States was slow during the 1930's and only the V-1710 amongst several programmes was developed to anything like its real potential. Even then this engine type suffered from development problems and application difficulties when it matured as a fighter engine in the mid- to late 1930's. Nevertheless, in its various production forms it gave valuable service as the power plant for several US-built fighters, and eventually proved to be a generally reliable power plant that (except for its application in the P-38) was optimised for low to medium-level operations. It was developed from the first to use ethylene glycol rather than water for its cooling, a feature that resulted in the possibility for a smaller radiator than would have been required with simple water cooling due to the glycol being able to carry far greater heat than ordinary water. Allison also performed important work on the design and

Annotated illustration from an Allison manual/handbook on the V-1710 engine, showing relevant parts and equipment
(Photo: Allison)

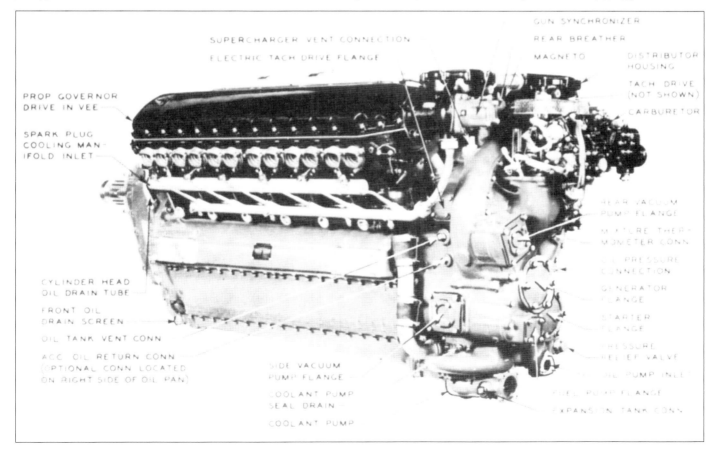

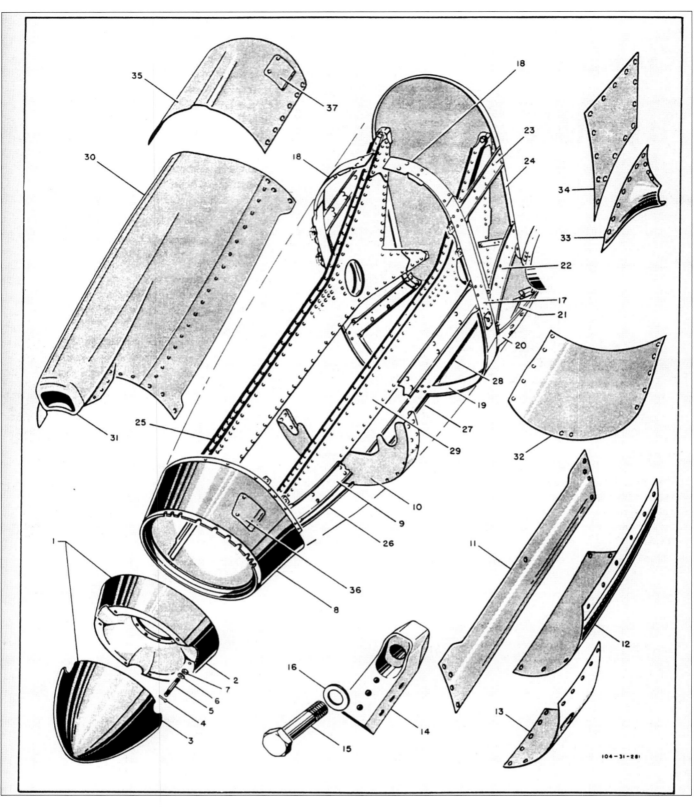

An illustration from a manufacturer's type manual/handbook showing the various engine cowling panels including removable items for the Allison-engined Mustangs, plus the framework that held the panels in place when fitted, and the engine bearers *(Photo: NAA)*

development of steel-backed, bronze-lined engine bearings, actually being one of the leaders in the field in this aspect of piston engine development.

The first V-1710 prototype engine ran in 1931, but interest in the large military airship in the US was curtailed following the loss of the airship USS Macon in 1935. During the development of the V-1710 Allison became a part of the giant General Motors empire, and in the mid-1930's Allison considerably extended its production facilities in the expectation of large orders for the V-1710, which eventually matured into a viable and ultimately successful fighter engine. This was partly due to demand fostered by the development of the P-40 series, via the Curtiss

XP-37 which was a development of the radial-engined Curtiss P-36 and was fitted with a turbo-supercharged V-1710. Although that particular combination did not lead to a production series, the Allison engine in simple supercharged form (as opposed to turbo-supercharged) subsequently went on to power not only the vast Curtiss P-40 series, but also the Bell P-39 Airacobra and P-63 Kingcobra and, with turbo-charging, the Lockheed P-38 Lightning. With turbo-charging, the P-38 was comparatively capable at high altitudes, but the type really came into its own not at high altitude over Europe (where it was used as a bomber escort fighter for a time) but in the Pacific, where combat tended to be at lower levels.

The V-1710 was central to the early story of the Mustang as well, and was the motor of choice for the North American Aviation engineers and designers when development work on the Mustang began in the spring of 1940. There were various series of the V-1710, including the 'F' series which powered the Allison-Mustangs and the P-40 Warhawk/Kittyhawk series. The V-1710-39 of 1,150 hp (commercial name V-1710-F3R) powered the Mustang Mk I/IA and P-51 production models, as well as the NA-73X prototype; the V-1710-81 (commercial – F20R) of 1,200 hp was installed in the Mustang Mk II and the P-51A; and the V-1710-87 (commercial –F21R) of 1,325 hp powered the A-36A Invader. None of these engines was optimised for high-altitude work, but they were more than adequate for the lower altitudes at which these early Mustangs operated. Later, the V-1710 made a brief reappearance in the Mustang story. Much later, the V-1710-119 powered the lightweight experimental XP-51J Mustang, and the V-1710-143/145 was the engine type for the later production F-82 Twin Mustang versions – but that is another story entirely.

A particular feature of the overall engine installation of the V-1710 in the Mustang was its excellent streamlined nature. Allison and North American worked hard on this aspect of the Mustang's design, and it is another of the enduring design innovations of the Mustang that such a successful and well thought out design was incorporated in the Mustang's layout. Ease of access for maintenance was also of great importance and here again the Mustang was well ahead of some of its peers, with many removable panels and access to most of the engine's major parts and equipment. This facet of aircraft design can always be improved, however, and on the revised installation for the Packard Merlin engine of later Mustang versions this aspect was further enhanced.

Allison as an engine designer and manufacturer flourished after World War Two, and came to be a significant manufacturer of jet engines, originally derived from other manufacturers' products. The company was also involved

successfully in turboprop design and development. Ironically, bearing in mind the fact that the Rolls-Royce Merlin replaced the Allison V-1710 in the Mustang, in 1993 Rolls-Royce acquired Allison, and the company remains to this day a part of the Rolls-Royce organisation as Rolls-Royce North America. Over the years there have been a number of published estimates as to how many V-1710 engines were actually manufactured. However, the generally-accepted figure of some 47,000 has always appeared to this author to be a low estimate. Indeed, the Allison Company in its advertising can be seen to have claimed the manufacture of more than 50,000 of these engines in their various series. A more recent figure made available by Rolls-Royce (and contained in writings published by the excellent Rolls-Royce Historical Trust) suggests that the real total was approximately 70,000 V-1710 examples of all marks, with some 48,700 being of the 'F' series. This seems to be a much more reliable figure. All subsequent Mustang versions, from the P-51B onwards for the USAAF, and the Mustang Mk III onwards for the RAF and Commonwealth (except for those noted earlier in this section), were powered by the famous Rolls-Royce Merlin in its American-produced, Packard V-1650 Merlin form.

The port side of the Allison engine fitment in the Mustang, showing the overall very neat installation. The engine bearers and the framework for holding the removable cowling panels in place when they were fitted are also visible *(Photo: NAA)*

Allison-Engined Mustang Armament

A remarkable fact about the Allison-Mustang is that virtually every version of the Allison-powered Mustang line featured a different armament fit to the previous one. Originally, during the initial design phases of what became the Mustang, the British were offered two alternative configurations for the new fighter. One would have a full armament of eight machine guns (two 0.5-in in the lower nose and one of these machine guns in each wing, plus two further 0.303-in machine guns in each wing). Alternatively, a lighter-armed configuration (known to NAA as the P-509 layout) was proposed, in which only four guns would be installed, with no armour protection.

The first production version for Britain was the Mustang Mk I. As pointed out earlier in this book, the armament that the British chose for this initial Mustang mark consisted of eight machine guns - two Browning 0.5-in in the lower nose, synchronised and firing through the propeller arc, and one of these machine guns in each wing, plus two further 0.3-in machine guns in each wing, outboard of the wing 0.5-in machine guns. Interestingly there has

been some debate as to whether all of these aircraft were armed with 0.3-in or 0.303-in machine guns in their outboard wing positions. The 0.303-in machine gun was a British weapon, whereas the 0.3-in was American. Documentation on this point that dates from the time suggests quite strongly that the weapons were 0.3-in, although there has been suggestion since the war that some aircraft were fitted with 0.303-in machine guns following delivery to Britain. Certainly the testing and trials of the new aircraft that were carried out at Boscombe Down on the Mk I suggested that the eight-gun armament consisted of 0.5-in and 0.3-in machine guns. The pilots at Boscombe Down also discovered a fact that was much appreciated by pilots who flew the aircraft in combat, namely that it was a good, stable gun platform, with little vibration when the guns were fired.

The initial Mustangs that were supplied to Britain under Lend-Lease were known to the British as the Mustang Mk IA. These aircraft were significantly different from the previous 620 Mk I aircraft that Britain had actually paid for, in that they were armed

A posed but nonetheless valuable image showing the arming of an early RAF Mustang. Noteworthy are the generous gun bay panels, which allowed excellent access to the wing guns and ammunition bays. Although this is a staged publicity photograph, it does show the type of teamwork that was necessary to keep these combat aircraft operational
(Photo: via Chris Ellis)

with four 20 mm cannons, two being installed in each wing. The eight machine gun armament of the original Mustangs was thus dispensed with, and the considerable fire power of the four 20 mm cannons of the Mustang IA was subsequently to prove equally destructive against ground targets. The forward part of the barrels of these weapons protruded very prominently forward of the wing leading edge of each wing, with a very visible fairing around each.

Britain also received fifty Mustangs from the P-51A production run which were designated Mustang Mk II by the British. The P-51A was significant in being the first Mustang to introduce an internal armament that was comprised solely of wing-mounted 0.5-in machine guns – a combination that was highly significant for later Mustang versions. As for US Mustangs, the first two were designated XP-51, and were standard Mustang Mk Is in all but their paint job and some equipment details. They therefore theoretically had the same armament as the Mustang Mk I, but in practice many photographs show these aircraft either devoid of all weapons or with the wing gun ports covered.

The first production Mustangs that the USAAF actually received were repossessed from the batch of Mustang Mk IAs intended for Britain, and were simply designated P-51 with no suffix letter. They therefore had the same armament as the British Mustang Mk IA, namely two 20 mm cannons in each wing, with no nose guns. The A-36A dive-bomber had a completely revised armament, with the nose-mounted 0.5-in machine guns reinstated, but the wing gun layout was altered to two 0.5-in machine guns in each wing. Indeed, the whole wing structure was changed and strengthened, with provision for a pylon beneath each wing just outboard of the main undercarriage stressed for

the carriage of a 500 lb (227 kg) bomb (one under each wing). This version could also carry underwing jettisonable fuel tanks on these pylons (otherwise often called 'drop tanks').

The P-51A dispensed with the two synchronised machine guns in the lower nose of other Allison-Mustangs, and simply mounted two 0.5-in machine guns in each wing. It too had a pylon under each wing, which was usually used (if employed at all) for the carriage of a 'drop tank' (again, one under each wing). The 0.5-in wing machine guns in the P-51A and the A-36A were not installed upright within the wing, but were instead canted at an angle, actually tilted over towards the tip of the wing. This somewhat odd arrangement worked reasonably well for the Allison-engined Mustangs, but it was to have major repercussions later in the Mustang's story. Because the Allison-Mustangs operated predominantly at low to medium levels, and particularly the former, there was little hint of a coming problem when Mustangs started to operate at high altitude with the introduction from the P-51B/C onwards, of the higher-altitude capable Packard Merlin engine. When operations began with the Merlin engine at high altitude on bomber escort with the Eighth Army Air Force particularly from early 1944 onwards, gun jamming became a major issue. This was eventually traced in the main (though not entirely) to icing of the gun armament due to the unusual canted nature of the gun mounting arrangement with its associated equipment.

A notable feature of all the Allison-Mustangs regardless of their installed internal armament was the ease of access for the internally-mounted wing armament. Large access panels gave good accessibility to the weapons and their ammunition bays. This feature was further carried forward for all the marks of

Part of the cockpit interior of an RAF Mustang, probably a Mk I, showing right-hand side details. British Mustangs generally had the type of control column shown, with a circular handle at the top, and firing button for the guns, whilst US-operated P-51s featured a pistol grip-type control stick. The interior colour was a mixed shade similar but not identical to the interior grey-green often used for the insides of British-built fighters, and the gunsight is an early ST1A/N-2A-type. Under no circumstances was the interior the often referred to, but largely misunderstood 'Interior Green'. This was a US shade that was not introduced until 1943, by which time the production of Allison-Mustangs was ending
(Photo: NAA)

An illustration taken from a manufacturer's type manual/handbook showing the Allison engine installation, together with the fitment of the 0.5-in machine gun in the lower nose, probably of an A-36A Invader (Photo: NAA)

The port wing gun bay of an Allison-Mustang of either an A-36A, P-51A or Mustang Mk II type. These particular Allison-Mustangs were fitted with two 0.5-in machine guns in each wing. The guns were not mounted upright, but instead were canted over at an angle (Photo: NAA)

The starboard wing gun bay illustrated in a manufacturer's type manual/handbook containing two 0.5-in Browning machine guns of an A-36A dive-bomber. The ammunition feed to the guns is evident, as is the angle that these weapons were canted over, in the direction of the outer wing. The aircraft's dive brake can also be seen
(Photo: NAA)

Merlin-powered Mustang as well. In addition to these various weapons fits, unguided air-to-ground rockets were also tried out on Allison-Mustangs. In Britain some trials were performed with cumbersome rocket rails under each wing, which were never adopted. However, some combat use was made by the Americans of underwing three-tube 'bazooka' type rocket launchers. Each tube carried a single 4.5-in unguided rocket, and although many writers have claimed that these weapons were widely used and

highly effective, in reality they were unwieldy, drag-producing and inaccurate, they were additionally bad for the Mustang's centre of gravity and trimming. It was also impossible to effectively dog-fight with these cumbersome appliances installed. Much later in the Mustang production, and only applicable to Merlin-Mustangs, 'zero-length' rocket rails were made available by NAA for factory installation and they proved to be far more successful for the carrying and firing of rockets.

The A-36A and P-51A introduced underwing pylons to the Mustang line, from which a variety of stores could be hung. These included the metal 'drop tank' shown here. The introduction of underwing jettisonable fuel tanks, usually for these Allison-Mustangs of 75 US gallons, gave the potential to considerably add to the Mustang's already impressive range qualities. This had a very important impact in later years, when the carriage of 'drop tanks' beneath the wings of Merlin-engined Mustangs allowed the Mustang to have the range to escort heavy bombers all the way to distant targets and back again. The underwing pylon fitted to the A-36A and P-51A was different to that fitted to later, Merlin-engined Mustangs (Photo: USAAF)

Allison-Mustang Serial Numbers

Prototype

MODEL	NAA NO.	CIVIL REGISTRATION	QUANTITY
NA-73X	NA-73X	NX19998	1

With regard to Allison-Mustang production, it is surprising for such a well-known and well-documented aircraft, that there has been much confusion in the past over the Mustang's production numbers and in some cases the actual military serial numbers. This may well have been caused, in published sources at least, by typing errors and accidental duplication of batches. Some writers' arithmetic also appears to have gone astray, with batches of production aircraft being given an incorrect quantity without any attempt apparently being made to check how many serial numbers there are in a batch. The following is the most comprehensive and most recently-checked listing of Allison-Mustang serial numbers, although it is acknowledged that some of the serial number allocations within production batches remain contentious. The claim that has been made in a number of published sources that two, and not one, NA-73X aircraft existed, is complete nonsense.

Allison-Mustangs for Britain

MODEL	NAA NO.	SERIAL NUMBERS	QUANTITY
Mustang Mk I	NA-73	AG345 to AG664	320
Mustang Mk I	NA-83	AL958 to AM257 & AP164 to AP263	300
Mustang Mk IA	NA-91	FD418 to FD567	150
Mustang Mk II	NA-99	FR890 to FR939	50

It is important to stress that not all the above aircraft were delivered to Britain – some were retained for trials in the US; some were taken for use by the USAAF; a small number crashed on acceptance or testing before delivery; similarly several were lost at sea in transit. In addition to these actual production aircraft for Britain, a number of other Mustangs found their way into British service or were allocated British military serial numbers, sometimes for temporary service as required or for test/trials work. They include the following A-36A examples - EW998 (42-83685), 42-84016, 42-84019, and HK944 to HK947, and HK955 to HK956. Five Mustangs that were originally Allison-engined, were specifically employed by Rolls-Royce in Britain as test aircraft for the installation of the Merlin engine - AL963, AL975, AM121, AM203, and AM208; they have often been called Mustang Mk X aircraft. A further Allison Mustang, AG518, was evaluated during this programme but was not converted. AM121 was later passed to the Americans.

Allison-Mustang/Invader Production (US Contracts)

MODEL	NAA NO.	SERIAL NUMBERS	QUANTITY
XP-51-NA	NA-73	41-38 to -39	2
P-51-NA	NA-91	41-37320 to -37469	150
P-51A-1-NA	NA-99	43-6003 to -6102	100
P-51A-5-NA	NA-99	43-6103 to -6157	55
P-51A-10-NA	NA-99	43-6158 to -6312	155
XP-51B-NA	NA-101	41-37352, 41-37421	2
A-36A-1-NA	NA-97	42-83663 to -84162	500

'NA' was the 'code' for NAA's Inglewood (Mines Field – Los Angeles Municipal Airport), California factory production. Amongst these batches are some deliveries/intended deliveries to the RAF, therefore the totals referred to elsewhere in the text for deliveries to the USAAF do not necessarily tally with the overall total manufactured in specific batches as given here. These Allison-engined Mustangs were, of course, the precursors to the large number of Merlin-engined Mustangs that followed them for US and export service.

Fighter models of the Mustang in US service were designated P-51, with the P-51 being the original production version. Subsequently a suffix letter for the particular version (e.g. P-51A) was used, the 'P' standing for 'Pursuit' – the original US Army Air Corps title for a fighter. Following the creation of the independent US Air Force in 1947, outdated designations such as this were eventually changed. The old Pursuit title was altered in 1948 to 'F' for Fighter. Surviving Mustangs were thus redesignated, with the nomenclature F-51 being increasingly adopted. The A-36 Invader was designated in the 'A' for 'Attack' category.

US Reconnaissance Mustangs

Reconnaissance versions of the Mustang were designated F-6, where 'F' stood for 'Photographic' in the rather cumbersome and sometimes incomprehensible designation allocations of the inter-war US Army Air Corps. All photo-reconnaissance Mustangs were originally serial numbered in the blocks of fighter P-51s, and therefore their production quantities should not be added to the total number of fighter Mustangs that were built for US forces. They included up to 55 F-6As converted from Allison-engined P-51 airframes, and 35 F-6Bs converted from Allison-engined P-51A examples. They were followed by a large number of Merlin-engined conversions for reconnaissance employment.

RAF Allison-Mustangs

he initial user of the Mustang in combat was the RAF. This service successfully operated the type from 1942 until the end of World War Two, initially with Allison-engined Mustangs and then with Merlin-engined Mustangs – although, as pointed out elsewhere in this Book, Allison-engined examples persisted in service well into 1945. Initially, RAF Mustangs went into action a year before the first USAAF Mustangs saw combat. The type subsequently served with the RAF post-war until 1947, although the later service post-war was performed by Merlin Mustangs. In addition, Mustangs also served with a variety of Commonwealth squadrons which operated under the umbrella of the RAF during World War Two, and several squadrons that were manned principally by personnel from occupied countries also used Mustangs and served under the auspices of the RAF. The following is a listing of these squadrons and their officially-assigned squadron code letters where applicable (although these were not always applied) with, where possible, details of their time on the Allison Mustang – but it must as always be stressed that many units phased aircraft types in and out of service alongside their predecessors and successors, and so exact dates in that context are only a guide.

SQUADRON/CODE	APPROXIMATE ALLISON MUSTANG SERVICE DATES
2 (XV)	4/42 – 1/45
4 (TV)	4/42 – mid 44
16 (UG)	4/42 – 9/43
26 (RM, XC)	1/42 – 3/44, late 1944 – 6/45
63 (none)	6/42 – 5/44
168 (OE)	11/42 – 9/44
169 (VI?)	6/42 – 10/43
170 (BN)	6/42 – 1/44
171 (none)	9/42 – 12/42
225 (WU)	5/42 – 10/42 (also other types)
231 (none)	4/43 – 1/44

SQUADRON/CODE	APPROXIMATE ALLISON MUSTANG SERVICE DATES
239 (HB)	5/42 – 9/43
241 (RZ)	2/42 – 10/42
268 (NM)	4/42 – 8/45 (also Hawker Typhoons c.7/44 – late 1944)
285 (VG)	3/45 – 6/45
309 (AR) Polish	8/42 - 2/44
400 (SP) Canadian	7/42 – early 44
414 (RU) Canadian	6/42 – 8/44
430 (none) Canadian	1/43 – 12/44
516 (none)	4/43 – 2/44
613 (SY)	6/42 – 10/43
No.1437 Flight (none)	7/43 – 10/43

In addition to the above squadrons, various other organisations flew Mustangs with or in conjunction with the British and Commonwealth forces, notably the test establishments at Boscombe Down and Farnborough. These latter formations did not usually carry their own distinguishing markings or codes on the aircraft that were (sometimes briefly) assigned to them. Several RAF squadrons flew Mustangs 'borrowed' from US stocks additional to their main equipment, as dictated by operational circumstances, particularly in the Middle East and southern Europe. These included Nos.14 and 260 Squadrons, and also probably No.225 Squadron; No.225 had already operated Mustangs from England prior to deployment to the Mediterranean, whilst No.260 later became a (Merlin) Mustang squadron in its own right. Additionally, a number of Mustangs served with training units; records of these are sketchy, but one of these organisations appears to have been No.61 OTU. Further, several Allison-Mustangs were allocated to the Air Fighting Development Unit (AFDU), some of whose pilots flew them in combat over Northern France.

A badly damaged RAF Mustang AM104, 'L' of No. 268 Squadron RAF, seen on the ground at Odiham, Hampshire (UK), after returning from a sortie over the Rouen area in France.
Credit RAF Archives

Understanding the Subject

Appendix VI

North American Mustang Genesis
Drawings Copyright Chris Sandham-Bailey 2013

North American NA-73X

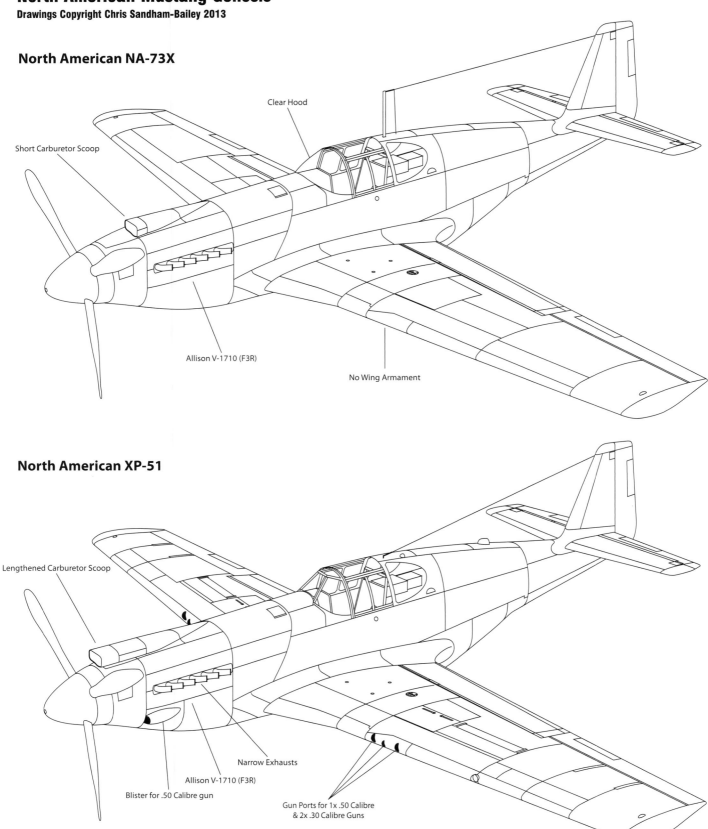

Clear Hood

Short Carburetor Scoop

Allison V-1710 (F3R)

No Wing Armament

North American XP-51

Lengthened Carburetor Scoop

Narrow Exhausts

Allison V-1710 (F3R)

Blister for .50 Calibre gun

Gun Ports for 1x .50 Calibre
& 2x .30 Calibre Guns

North American A-36 Apache (NA-97)

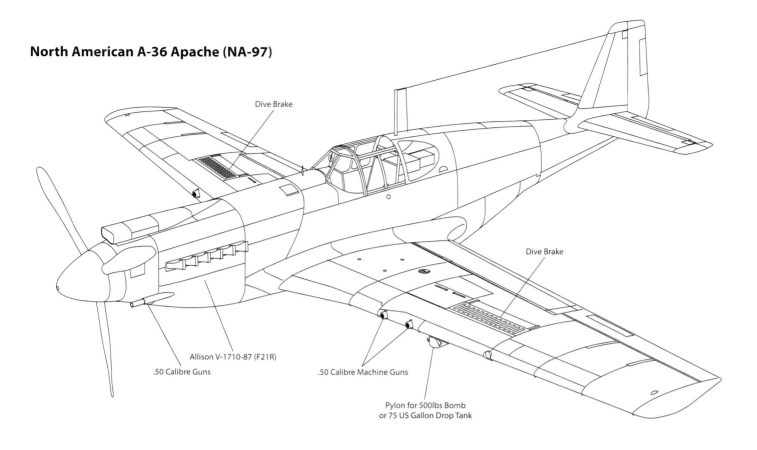

Dive Brake

Dive Brake

Allison V-1710-87 (F21R)

.50 Calibre Guns

.50 Calibre Machine Guns

Pylon for 500lbs Bomb
or 75 US Gallon Drop Tank

North American P-51(F-6A) Mustang

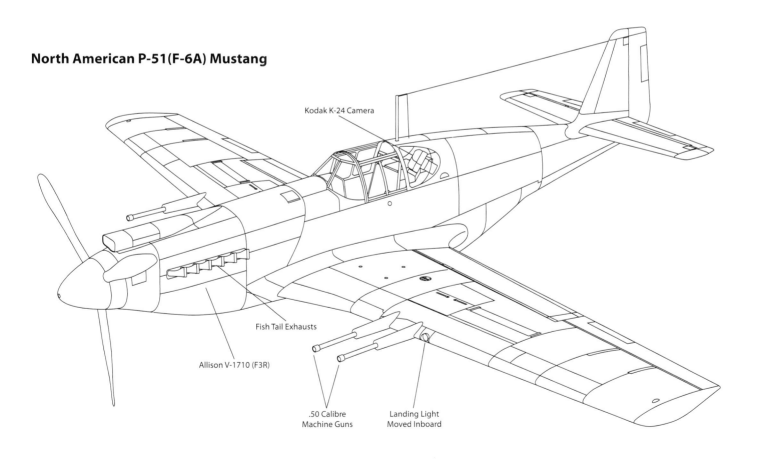

Kodak K-24 Camera

Fish Tail Exhausts

Allison V-1710 (F3R)

.50 Calibre
Machine Guns

Landing Light
Moved Inboard

North American P-51 (NA-83) Mustang I

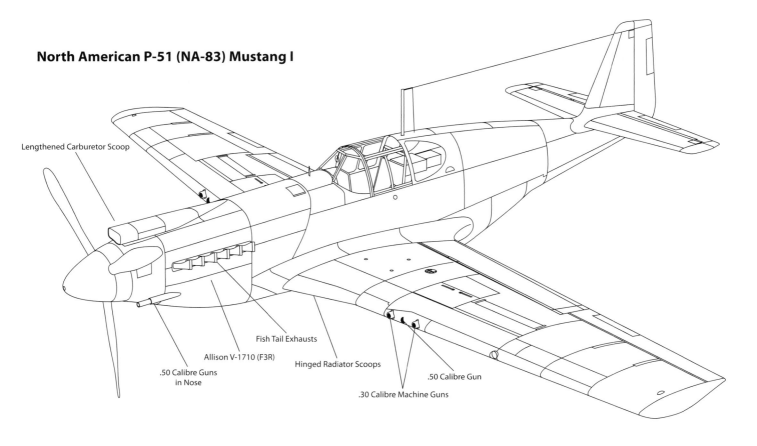

Lengthened Carburetor Scoop

Fish Tail Exhausts

Allison V-1710 (F3R)

Hinged Radiator Scoops

.50 Calibre Guns
in Nose

.50 Calibre Gun

.30 Calibre Machine Guns

North American P-51 Mustang IA

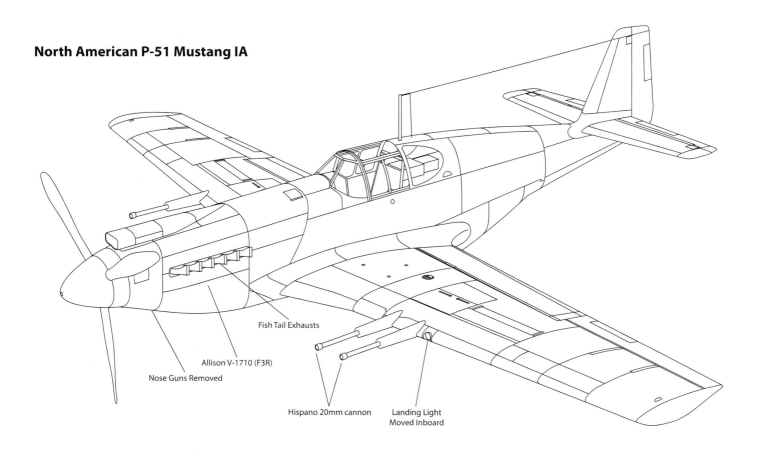

Fish Tail Exhausts

Allison V-1710 (F3R)

Nose Guns Removed

Hispano 20mm cannon

Landing Light
Moved Inboard

North American P-51A Mustang II

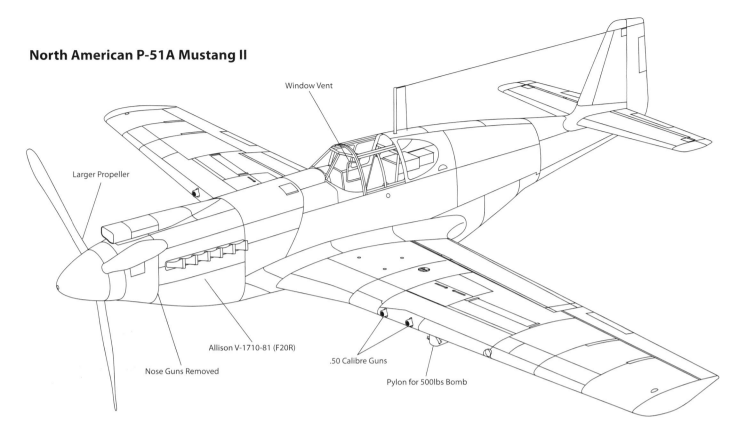

Window Vent

Larger Propeller

Allison V-1710-81 (F20R)

Nose Guns Removed

.50 Calibre Guns

Pylon for 500lbs Bomb

Dimensions, Performance And Armament

	MUSTANG MK.I	A-36	P-51A
Wingspan	37ft 0in (11.277m)	37ft 0in (11.277m)	37ft 0in (11.277m)
Wing area	233.0ft² (21.65m²)	233.0ft² (21.65m²)	233.0ft² (21.65m²)
Length	32ft 3.5in (9.83 m)	32ft 3.5in (9.83 m)	32ft 3.5in (9.83 m)
Height	12ft 2in (3.71m)	12ft 2in (3.71m)	12ft 2in (3.71m)
Empty weight	5,990lb (2,717kg)	7,240lb (3,284kg)	6,800lb (3,084kg)
Loaded weight	8,633lb (3,915kg)	10,000lb (4,535kg)	9,600lb (4,354kg)
Engine	Allison V-1710-39	Allison V-1710-87	Allison V-1710-81
Power	1,220hp (909 kW) at 10,000ft (3,048 m) (44.7" Hg, 3,000rpm)	1,325hp (988 kW) at 5,400ft (1,646 m) (47" Hg, 3,000rpm)	1,330hp (991 kW) at 11,000ft (3,353m) (War Emergency 57" Hg, 3,000rpm)
Max. Speed	382mph (615 km/h) at 13,700ft (4,176m)	368mph (592km/h) at 14,000ft (4,267m)	409mph (658km/h) at 10,000ft (3,048m)
Rate of Climb			2,660 ft/min (13.5 m/s) at 14,750 ft (4,496 m)
Wing Loading	37.0 lb/ft² (180.6 kg/m²)	42.9 lb/ft² (209.46 kg/m²)	41.2 lb/ft² (201.1 kg/m²)
Power/Mass	0.14 hp/lb (0.23 kW/kg)	0.13 hp/lb (0.21 kW/kg)	0.14 hp/lb (0.22 kW/kg)
Combat Range	480 miles (644km) on internal fuel	400 miles (644km) on internal fuel	400 miles (644km) internal fuel
	750 miles (1,207km), 2 × 75 US gal (284lt) drop tanks	750 miles (1,207km), 2 × 75 US gal (284lt) drop tanks	750 miles (1,207km), 2 × 75 US gal (284lt) drop tanks
Ferry Range	900 miles (1,448km) on internal fuel	900 miles (1,448km) on internal fuel	900 miles (1,448km) on internal fuel
	1,600 miles (2,575km), 2 × 75 US gal (284lt) drop tanks	1,600 miles (2,575km), 2 × 75 US gal (284lt) drop tanks	1,600 miles (2,575km), 2 × 75 US gal (284lt) drop tanks
	2,500 mi (4,023 km), 2 × 150 US gal (568 l) ferry tanks	2,500 mi (4,023 km), 2 × 150 US gal (568 l) ferry tanks	2,500 mi (4,023 km), 2 × 150 US gal (568 l) ferry tanks

Armament

Mustang Mk.I 4 × 0.303 in (7.7mm) Browning machine guns, two in each wing; 500 rpg, 4 × .50 (12.7 mm) M2 Browning, two in fuselage, one in each wing; 400 rpg wings and fuselage.

A-36 6 × .50 in (12.7mm) M2 Browning, two in fuselage, two in each wing; 350 rpg inboard guns, 280 rpg outboard, 400 rpg fuselage, 2 × 250 lb (113 kg) or 2 × 500 lb (227 kg) bombs

P-51A 4 × .50 in (12.7mm) M2 Browning, two in each wing; 350 rpg inboard guns, 280 rpg outboard, 2 × 250 lb (113 kg) or 2 × 500 lb (227 kg) bombs

Kitography

Kits

Condor CN7216	1:72	North American A-36 Apache
Special Hobby SH72041	1:72	North-American Mustang Mk.IA
Special Hobby SH72043	1:72	North-American P-51A F-6A Mustang
Condor CN7215	1:72	North-American P-51 Mustang 1A
Italeri IT0090	1:72	North-American P-51 Mustang I Razorback
Special Hobby ACM3410	1:48	North-American Mustang Mk.IA (RAF P-51A)
Italeri IT2729	1:48	North American A-36 Apache
Accurate Miniatures 480010	1:48	North American F-6B Tactical Recce
Accurate Miniatures 483410	1:48	North American RAF Mk IA
Accurate Miniatures 483400	1:48	North American P-51 Mustang
Accurate Miniatures 483401	1:48	North American A-36 Apache
Accurate Miniatures 483402	1:48	North American P-51A
Special Hobby SH32014	1:32	North American A-36 Apache
Special Hobby SH32005	1:32	North-American P-51 Mustang Mk.I
Special Hobby SH32012	1:32	North-American P-51 Mustang Mk.IA
HobbyCraft HC1710	1:32	North-American A-36A

Accessories

CMK/Czech Master Kits	1:72	North-American P-51A Interior
True Details	1:72	Diamond Tread Wheels for any P-51
Quickboost QB72061	1:72	North-American P-51A Mustang Engine
Quickboost QB72234	1:72	North-American F-6D Mustang Recce Conversion
Falcon FNCV5448	1:48	Canopies for NA-73X prototype North-American P-51A/North-American A-36A plus later types
Eduard ED48134	1:48	North-American A-36/North-American P-51A Mustang Detailing Set
True Details	1:48	North-American P-51A and North-American A-36 Mustang Cockpit Detail Set
Verlinden VL1789	1:48	North-American P-51A Mustang Cockpit and Moving Surfaces Set
Quickboost QB48551	1:48	North-American P-51A Mustang/Mk.IA Exhaust
Barracuda Studios BCR48050	1:48	North-American P-51 Mustang Tread Pattern Tyres
Barracuda Studios BCR48051	1:48	North-American P-51 Mustang Main wheel Hubs
Barracuda Studios BCR32032	1:32	North-American P-51 Mustang Tread Pattern Tyres
Barracuda Studios BCR32034	1:32	North-American P-51 Mustang Main wheel Hubs
Falcon FNCV3248	1:32	North-American P-51/North-American A-36 Mustang Canopy plus other makes

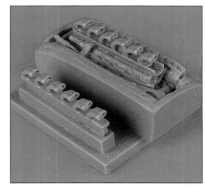

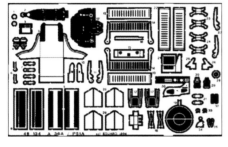

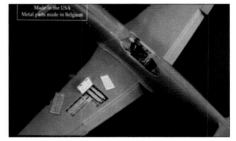

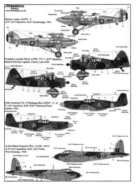

Decals

Model Alliance ML72112	1:72	On Target North American P-51 Mustangs, includes Mk.I AG522 SY-L 613 (City of Manchester) Sqn
Model Alliance ML72195	1:72	RAF and Commonwealth Aircraft over the Middle East and Mediterranean between 1940 and 1945. Includes North-American P-51 Mustang WU.B of 225 Squadron, Royal Air Force, Algeria, May 1943
MPM MPM72085	1:72	North-American P-51/F-6A Mustang Reconnaissance Aircraft
Xtradecal X72148	1:72	The History of 4 Squadron includes North American Mustang Mk.I AP247/A RAF Twinwood Farm 1942
Xtradecal X72150	1:72	The History of 4 Squadron includes North Mustang Mk.I AG633 XV-E RAF Sawbridgeworth 1942
Microscale MS48014	1:48	North-American P-51A/P-51B/P-51D Mustang National Insignia, Stencil Data, Anti-Glare Panels
Ventura VA4869	1:48	Supermarine Spitfire and XP-51 Mustang Prototypes
Zotz ZTZ32034	1:32	North American A-36A Apache Mustang
Ventura VA3272	1:32	Prototype North-American XP-51 Mustang 1039

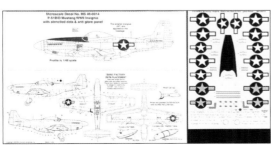

Index

Please note: this index does not reference appendices

86th Fighter Group A-36 Apache in North Africa *(Photo: USAF)*

A lovely plan view of the early mark of Mustang *(Photo USAF)*

Only one A-36A Invader actually reached the RAF in Britain, and this example EW998 was examined at Boscombe Down from March 1943 onwards. This images shows to advantage the wing air brakes unique to this mark of Mustang *(Photo: RAF)*

North American XP-51 1039 (41-039). This was probably the tenth Mustang to be completed and was the second example furnished to the USAAF for testing at Wright Field in 1942. *(Credit USAF)*